Creating a Business Plan

2nd Edition

T0349482

by Veechi Curtis, MBA

for dummies®
A Wiley Brand

Creating a Business Plan For Dummies®, 2nd Edition

Published by

John Wiley & Sons, Australia Ltd

Level 4, 600 Bourke Street

Melbourne, Vic 3000

www.dummies.com

Copyright © 2025 John Wiley & Sons Australia, Ltd

The moral rights of the author have been asserted.

ISBN: 978-1-394-23730-2

 A catalogue record for this book is available from the National Library of Australia

Cover image: © rh2010/Adobe Stock Photos

Typeset by Straive

Contents at a Glance

Table of Contents

Introduction

grew up in Scotland, where the winters can be wild, wet and cold. My father was a self-employed landscape gardener and, each year, as the days grew shorter, he would start hatching entrepreneurial plots to see the family through the scant earnings of the winter months. Handmade garden furniture, barrels from the local brewery scrubbed back and filled with violets, gold-leaf mirror restoration and beach-scavenged scallop shells were but a few of the ill-fated ventures that would transform our Victorian flat into a hive of industry for a few fleeting months of each year.

I started my first business at the age of 26 and have been in business ever since, oscillating in a manner not unlike my father's between the more stable income of business consulting and the somewhat precarious existence of writing and publishing.

Yet when working on this book, I realized something quite fundamental. While I've been steadily successful for more than 20 years, all too often the sensible-cardigan-wearing-accountant side of me wins out against the risk-taking-creative-why-don't-we-try-this side of me. Possibly due to the rather feast-and-famine finances of my childhood, I typically spend more time analyzing profit margins than I do thinking of creative new products; I focus more on managing risk than being a trendsetter. If you've been in business before, I'm sure you too have experienced this natural tension between your entrepreneurial side and the inner voice of 'reason'.

One challenge for me in writing this book has been to find ways to encourage dreams to flourish while simultaneously exploring the somewhat sobering process of writing a business plan. I'm writing this introduction having just finished the last chapter of this book and, happily, I think that the process has worked on me. I'm itching with impatience to begin my next business venture, and feel utterly optimistic about its prospects. (I remain my father's daughter, after all.)

I hope you have a similar experience with this book, and that I share enough inspiration for your inner entrepreneur to thrive while at the same time providing unshakeable feet-on-the-ground practicality.

About This Book

I like to think that this book is a bit different from other business planning books, not least because this book is part of the *For Dummies* series. Dummies books aren't about thinking that you're a 'dummy' — far from it. What the *For Dummies* series is all about is balancing heavyweight topics with a lightweight mindset, and sharing a 'can-do' attitude that encourages anyone — no matter how young or old, how inexperienced or how veteran — to give the subject at hand a go.

I like to think that the *Dummies* way of thinking has helped me to bring a fresh approach to the subject of business planning. I've tried not to get bogged down in the same old stodgy discussions of mission statements, values and organizational charts; instead, I've focused more on working with others, being creative and thinking of your business as something that's unique and separate from yourself.

You may be surprised by the fact that I devote seven whole chapters to the topic of finance (you'll only find one finance chapter in most business planning books). I'm a real advocate of the importance of financial planning and, in this book, I try to break the topic down into bite-sized chunks that anyone can understand, even if they haven't done any bookkeeping or accounting before.

I also understand that most people who've worked in business end up with knowledge that's patchy. You may know heaps about marketing but nothing about finance, or vice versa. The beauty of *Dummies* books is that you can just leap in, find the chunk of information that addresses your query, and start reading from there.

One more thing. Throughout this book you'll see sidebars — text that sits in a separate box with grey shading. Think of sidebars as the nut topping on your ice-cream: Nice to have, but not essential. Feel free to skip these bits.

Foolish Assumptions

When writing this book, I make no assumptions about your prior experience. Maybe you've been in business all your life or maybe you've never been in business before. It could be that you're a tech geek or it's possible that you hate computers. Maybe you love numbers or — much more likely — you may have a somewhat queasy feeling when it comes to math.

I also make no assumptions about the age of your business, and realize that for many people reading this book, your business is still a seedling waiting to be watered. (For this reason, I include practical advice such as how to budget for personal expenses while you're building your business, and why things such as your relationships and family situation are all part of the picture.)

Last, I don't try to guess where you live in the world. After all, the principles of business planning are universal, whether you're in the snowdrifts of Alaska, the stone country of Australia or the kilt-swaying highlands of Scotland.

Icons Used in This Book

REMEMBER

Tie a knot in that elephant's trunk, pin an egg timer to your shirt but, whatever you do, don't forget the pointers next to this icon.

TIP

This icon points to ways to give your business plan that extra spark.

TRUE STORY

Real-life stories from others who've been there and done that.

WARNING

A pitfall for the unwary. Read these warnings carefully.

Where to Go from Here

Creating a Business Plan For Dummies, 2nd edition, is no page-turning thriller (probably a good thing given the subject matter) and doesn't require you to start at the beginning and follow through to the end. Instead, feel free to jump in and start reading from whatever section is most relevant to you:

New to business and you've never created a business plan before? I suggest you read Chapters 1, 2 and 3 before doing much else. Chapter 1 provides a road map for creating your plan, and Chapters 2 and 3 help you to consolidate your business concept. From here, you're probably best to read the chapters in the order that I present them, because these chapters follow the same sequence as the topics within a business plan.

If business strategy is more your concern, Chapters 2 to 5, 11 and 14 are the place to be.

Are financial projections a source of woe? Chapters 7 to 13 are here to help.

For advice on creating a plan that can't fail to impress prospective lenders or investors, Chapter 15 explains how to pull your plan together, and Chapter 16 offers handy suggestions to make sure your plan is as good as can be. And, finally, Chapter 17 provides advice and encouragement if things aren't looking as good as you'd hoped.

1

Getting Started

Explore the whole idea of business planning, and take a moment to consider the psychology behind this process.

Establish what's different about you and your business.

IN THIS CHAPTER

» **Getting started without another moment's hesitation**

» **Applying a scorecard to your business idea**

» **Deciding what elements to include in your plan**

» **Revisiting and checking your plan**

» **Understanding why business planning is harder than it looks**

» **Tricking yourself into doing the deed**

Chapter **1**

Letting Your Plan Take Flight

A business plan is as much a way of thinking as it is a document. Some of the most important elements of a business plan can be done while talking with colleagues, walking along the beach or taking time out over a cup of coffee.

Key to a business planning mindset is a willingness to be objective about strategy, the ability to think of your business as something that's separate from you, and the discipline to analyze your financials (even if you're not naturally good with numbers).

Importantly, a business plan doesn't necessarily require days or weeks of your time. I often recommend to people they approach their plan in bite-sized chunks, whether this be redesigning pricing strategies, spending time researching competitors, or experimenting with different pricing models.

In this chapter, I talk about who a business plan is for, what goes into a plan, and how you might start thinking about your business model. I also explain why it can be hard to be objective and motivated about planning for your business, and share a few insights into how to keep yourself on track.

Getting Your Feet Wet

In *Creating a Business Plan For Dummies*, 2nd edition, I place less emphasis on the importance of creating a written plan and more on why planning is best viewed as a frame of mind. The neat thing about this way of thinking is that you can start with your plan at any time, even if you know you have only one hour free this week and you're flying overseas for a holiday the next.

Planning can even be fun once you get started. Some of my best business ideas have come to me while lying in the hammock on holidays, digging up weeds in the garden or having a quiet coffee.

Thinking about success and failure

I'm sure you've heard of the adage that if you spend time working *on* your business — rather than just working *in* your business — you have a better chance of realizing success. However, I was talking with some friends the other day about this book, and one of them asked me just how much difference a business plan makes to the success or failure of that venture. Later, because I couldn't help myself, I spent many hours going down the rabbit hole of studies people have done on this topic. After all those hours, all I could confirm was that a neat, definitive answer on this question does not exist.

One reason such an answer is elusive is that the very definition of success or failure is fraught. Relatively few business owners go bankrupt or lose their life savings when their business idea goes wrong. Similarly, few business owners achieve private-helicopter-mega-wealth success. Instead, most businesspeople land somewhere in the middle, working pretty hard to achieve a reasonable, but not exceptional, standard of living.

However, even if lottery-like luck isn't on your side, my observation is that the disciplined thinking a business plan engenders provides you with an edge over others. Maybe you won't join the ranks of the mega-rich just yet, but you'll likely make higher profits than those of your peers who are without a plan.

Choosing your dance partners

Unless you've run a business before, creating a business plan almost certainly needs a little help from outside. The good news is that all you have to do is ask. Consider the following sources:

TIP

- **Business planning courses:** In my opinion, a structured course spread over several weeks or even months is the very best possible way to accumulate basic planning skills. Not only do you have the discipline of working on your plan at least once a week, but you also usually receive expert mentoring from the teacher or teachers, as well as peer support from other people in a similar position to you.

- **Business advisory centers:** Depending on where you are in the world, business advisory centers have different names and structures. However, most state and federal governments fund some form of free advisory centers.

- **Business consultants:** While I warn against delegating the whole planning process to outsiders, expert consultants can be a great resource, especially if you retain control and ownership of your plan.

- **Your accountant:** I strongly recommend that you do your own financial projections, rather than delegating this task to a bookkeeper or accountant. (I explain just how in Chapters 7 through to 13.) However, after you have made your best attempt, consider asking your accountant to review your figures, and help you to identify anything that doesn't make sense or seems unrealistic.

- **Your lawyer:** In Chapter 14, I talk about managing risk, including protecting your name and your brand, and limiting liability through company structures. Your lawyer is an excellent source of advice for this part of the planning process.

- **Friends and family:** Not only is the advice of friends and family usually free, but these people also understand you like nobody else. Support and encouragement from friends and family is invaluable on those doubtful days when you think you (and your new business idea) may be crazy.

- **Your spouse/life partner:** Last but not least. Need I say more?

REMEMBER

Even if you don't have all of the skills required to create a plan, you won't find a better motivator for acquiring these skills than the feast-and-famine of your business venture. Experience is a generous teacher.

Deciding who this plan is for

The easy answer to the question of who your plan is for is you, of course. Your plan is an ongoing process, not a massive document that you create every year or so. When you create a business plan for your own use only, you can pick a structure, time and format that work well for you.

Of course in real life, the impetus for most business plans is to seek capital, either from an investor or via a bank loan. In Chapter 15, I explain how to frame your plan according to your audience: Investors are typically more interested in a high rate of return and the excitement of a clever business idea; banks are usually more interested in collateral, consistent trading results and your personal credit rating.

WARNING

Regardless of who is likely to read your plan, I strongly suggest that when it comes to the financials — sales targets, income projections, profit projections and so on — you be consistent. Don't have one version of financials for your own purposes, and another spruced-up version for the bank.

TRUE STORY

I remember my first job after graduating, working for a small but growing company. Money was always tight and we were forever presenting new plans and cashflow projections to prospective lenders. Part of my job was to 'massage' the figures to show that while cash was desperate in the coming six months or so (and hence a loan was required), things would soon turn the corner and, within a couple of years, we would be awash with funds. I discovered how easy it was to manipulate figures. By adding 10 per cent to sales, trimming expenses by the same amount, and maybe increasing the gross profit a little, I could transform dire predictions into something that looked amazing. The trouble was these figures were pure fiction. The manipulated scenarios inevitably created a false sense of security, and led to some pretty poor long-term decision-making.

The moral of the tale? Don't get hoodwinked into 'selling' your plan and exaggerating your likely success. Stay as realistic as possible. This tactic helps you gain respect from any likely investors and keeps you grounded as to what lies ahead.

Subscribing to a business planning app

In this book, I try to provide you with all the information you need to build your plan. You may be wondering how to use this book alongside the many business planning apps available.

Even with this book to hand, a business planning app undoubtedly makes the process easier. Apps such as Bizplan, Enloop, LivePlan and PlanGuru help you to structure each section of your plan, can offer suggested wording based on your industry, and are excellent for creating financial forecasts, particularly if numbers doesn't come naturally to you.

TIP

I suggest you weigh up the pros and cons for yourself by subscribing to a service such as www.liveplan.com for a month or so. The monthly fee is usually fairly modest, and represents a small financial commitment for what is potentially a significant saving of your time.

I've written this book so it can go hand in hand with any business planning app, aiming to provide guidance as to what's important, and what's not. For example, almost anyone can explain the concept of strategic advantage in a few sentences, and most planning apps simply provide a definition, followed by a template where you can write your own. However, in real life, I find that strategic advantage is super tricky to understand and it's for this reason that I devote two whole chapters to the subject (Chapters 2 and 3), highlighting how fundamental this concept is to business success.

ARE YOU READY?

I find that if someone really wants to start their own business, wild horses can't hold them back. The idea keeps coming around and around until that person finally takes the leap and says, 'I'm going to give it a go'.

So if you're champing at the bit to start your new business, I have just three questions to ask you first:

- Do you have experience in the kind of business you're planning to start? For example, if you're looking at buying a coffee van, have you actually spent a few weeks selling coffee in this way? Do you have barista or retail experience?

- Do you definitely have enough capital to get started? If you're not sure, do you think you may be better saving for a while before you launch your business? (See Chapter 7 for more on budgeting for start-up expenses.)

- Is your partner/spouse/family supportive of this venture?

If your answer to any of these questions is 'no', I suggest that you try to temper your enthusiasm just a little. And if you still can't wait, hey, I completely understand — but perhaps check out the nearby section 'Scoring Your Business out of 10' for a touch of reality.

Scoring Your Business out of 10

Are you still at the stage of thinking about your business idea and wondering if it's worth you even doing a plan? Maybe your business idea is still a glint in the eye but you're raring to go, or maybe you've been mooching along half-heartedly with a new business for a little while now and don't know where you're headed. Just for a bit of fun (this is Chapter 1, after all), why not take a few minutes and see how you and your business idea rate?

Use the scorecard in Table 1-1 if yours is a business that's been done before. By 'done before', I mean a business selling a service or product that many others already provide, such as a gardening business, general store, physiotherapist, or restaurant. Alternatively, if your business or business idea is a niche business or a new invention, use the scorecard in Table 1-2. For each question, a score of 1 is bad, and a score of 10 is good.

TABLE 1-1

Rating a Business that's Been Done Before

Ask yourself. . .	Score (1 to 10)
Can you think of something that will make your product or your service different from your competitors?	
Can you do something that will allow you to deliver a better product or service than your competitors?	
Have you got a skill, design or tool that enables you to be cheaper than your competitors?	
Do you love the day-to-day activity that this business demands?	
Do you know for sure that demand exists for your product or service?	
Do you (or someone in your team) have strong marketing skills?	
If your business is place-based, do you have a strong community network?	
Do you have enough start-up capital to give your business the best possible chance of success?	
Are you good with money, and able to understand budgets and stick to them?	
Is your vision for your business to build something that can ultimately run without your day-to-day attention?	
Does your family support you in this venture?	

TABLE 1-2

Rating a Niche Business or New Invention

Ask yourself. . .	Score (1 to 10)
How unique is your product?	
If your idea is unique, do you have some way of safeguarding this idea from a competitor who might steal it?	
Do you know for sure that demand exists for your product or service?	
Do you have a clear strategy for launching your product or service?	
Can you do something that will allow you to deliver a better product or service than your competitors?	
Do you have enough start-up capital to give your business the best possible chance of success?	
Do you (or someone in your team) have strong marketing skills?	
Are you comfortable in the online environment (social media, e-commerce platforms, and so on)?	
Is a window of opportunity emerging due to a change in the business environment, such as changing regulations, government grants, or new technology?	
Does your family support you in this venture?	

Wondering what a niche business is? A *niche business* is one that specializes in a small market segment. (I came across a quirky example of a niche business just today, where the company specializes in 'divorce gifts', each one designed with a generous serve of humor.)

What score are you looking for? Overall, you probably want to get a score of 35 or more, although don't be dismayed if you score less than this. Chapters 2 through to 5 provide lots of inspiration for developing your business ideas, Chapters 7 to 13 help you consolidate your financial skills, and Chapter 6 helps with the marketing side of things. You can return to this scorecard later in the planning process and see if your score improves.

Structuring Your Plan

The best business plan format for a company with a turnover of $100 million and 200 employees is going to be utterly different from the best format for a start-up business with no employees. For this reason, you can find as many possible formats for a business plan as recipes for Bolognese sauce.

What most formats have in common, however, is certain key elements, although the sequence of these elements varies:

>> **A cover page and table of contents.**

>> **An Executive Summary.** I explain how to write this in Chapter 15.

>> **Your point of difference and strategic advantage (usually but not always part of your Executive Summary**). For more on these topics, see Chapters 2 and 3.

>> **Your vision for the future.** Although I devote most of a chapter to this topic (see Chapter 3), the aim is to distil this vision into a sentence or two, either as part of your Executive Summary, or part of your pitch for funding.

>> **A PESTEL analysis (optional) and SWOT analysis (expected in most business plan formats).** I cover these topics in Chapter 5.

>> **A competitor analysis and marketing plan.** Chapter 3 talks about competitor analysis and competitive strategy, and Chapter 6 provides a complete summary of how to construct a marketing plan. I talk about the marketing cycle later in this chapter (see 'Responding quickly to the market').

>> **A people plan.** A business isn't anything without the people who run it, and your skills, entrepreneurialism, and natural abilities are as much a part of the mix as anything else, as are the skills of the people you choose to involve in your business. This part of your plan needs to outline the people element of your business: Who does what, and why they're the best choice for the job.

Even if you don't have any employees yet, you can still include details about any consultants, advisers, mentors, or professionals who you plan to involve in your business. These details help to establish credibility for anybody else reading your plan, and prompt you to think further outside the business than just yourself.

Chapter 2 touches on this topic, while Chapter 4 explores the people side of your plan in more depth. (People planning doesn't necessarily take a huge amount of time at first, but is something that can be a huge time-waster if you don't get it right.)

>> **A risk-management plan, if appropriate.** As I explain in Chapter 14, the more risk in your business, the more important it is to include a risk-management strategy in your plan.

>> **A summary of operations, if appropriate.** I talk about how to write this summary in Chapter 15.

>> **Financial reports.** For most new businesses, the financial part of your plan may be as simple as a Profit & Loss Projection for the next 12 months. Established businesses may include projections for 24 or 36 months ahead, as well as historical Profit & Loss reports and Balance Sheets for the previous year or years. Financials often also include break-even analysis, Cashflow Projections and budgets.

For more on creating a Profit & Loss Projection, see Chapters 8 through to 11, for break-even analysis see Chapter 12, and for cashflows and budgets, see Chapter 13.

TIP

For new or growing businesses that require a certain sales volume before the model becomes profitable, I suggest you extend your projections for at least a couple of years to demonstrate the long-term viability of your concept.

>> **The ask.** I talk more about asking for money in Chapter 15.

TIP

If you feel daunted by the preceding list, I suggest you start with the basics: Your point of difference, a SWOT analysis, a marketing plan and a Profit & Loss Projection for the next 12 months. With these elements in place, you can return to complete more details in your plan as soon as you have the stamina.

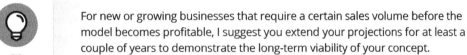

LOOKING INTO THE FUTURE

In this book, I emphasize the importance of including financial projections in your business plan, rather than reporting on actual financial results. I do this for two reasons.

First, many people reading this book are going to be working on their first business plan and won't have any results for previous months or years as yet.

Second, even if you've been trading for some time, you will always reap benefits from making financial projections and experimenting with different scenarios, such as what could happen if you increased profit margins by 10 per cent or decreased expenses by a similar amount.

This said, if you've been trading for a while, you do need to include historical figures (Profit & Loss and Balance Sheet) for the last year or two years in your business plan. These results provide a great reality check for you (or anybody else) when comparing future projections against past performance.

Planning for Continuous Change

For most businesses, the two elements within a business plan that require the most ongoing attention are your marketing plan and your financial plan. Each of these activities has its own planning cycle.

Responding quickly to the market

When you're in business, the process of marketing never stops. By marketing, I don't just mean advertising or sales strategies; rather, I mean everything from understanding competitors to analyzing customers, and from reviewing pricing to ensuring excellent customer service.

The pace of change in most business environments is so fast that you can't afford to let a whole year go by without reviewing your marketing plan, sales targets, pricing strategies, marketing strategies, competitors, and more.

Figure 1-1 shows a possible marketing cycle (I explain each step of this cycle in detail in Chapter 6). Can you see how the fifth step of the marketing cycle (review pricing, rates and sales projections) is exactly the same as the second step of the financial cycle (shown in Figure 1-2 in the next section of this chapter)? That's because setting sales targets is always the point at which the sales and marketing team and the bean counters connect.

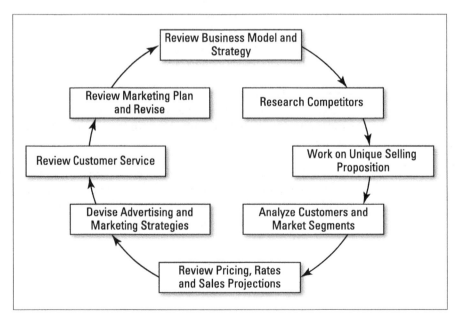

FIGURE 1-1:
The marketing planning cycle.

Reviewing your financial model

Figure 1-2 shows a typical financial planning cycle, with the review of your business model at the beginning and end of each process.

Here's how you can work through the financial planning cycle:

1. **Review business model and strategy.**

   I talk about business models and strategy in Chapters 2 to 6, including marketing plans in Chapter 6.

2. **Review your prices, rates and sales projections.**

   Setting prices and sales targets (a topic I cover in Chapter 8) is both a financial and a marketing activity, and sales projections usually form part of your marketing plan.

   TIP

   You may wonder how you can create a marketing plan without confirming pricing, and how you can confirm your business model without completing sales projections. After all, if you haven't set your prices, you can't do any meaningful financial forecasts. Without financial forecasts, you don't know if your business model has any chance at all. And without having your essential idea confirmed, what is the point of doing a marketing plan? All very chicken-and-egg in its nature, but essentially you just have to start somewhere.

3. **Confirm the direct costs of providing your service or making your products.**

   I talk about costing products and services in Chapter 9, and explain how to create a Gross Profit Projection for the next 12 months.

4. **Create a forecast for expenses.**

   If you're just getting started, I suggest you create a budget both for business and personal expenses (see Chapters 7 and 10). For simple cash-based businesses, this expense forecast becomes your budget for the months ahead. For established businesses, see Chapter 10 for managing expenses.

5. **Create a Profit & Loss Projection for the next 12 months.**

   In Chapter 11, I explain how to create a Profit & Loss Projection, and how to forecast your net profit over the next 12 months.

6. **Work out your break-even point.**

   You can calculate your break-even point in several different ways (and Chapter 12 explains just how). Understanding this information is a powerful weapon in your business artillery.

7. **If necessary, generate a Cashflow Projection.**

Even if you're making a profit, you may find yourself short of cash. In Chapter 13, I explain how to generate a Cashflow Projection so that you can anticipate any cash shortfalls. Note that not every business needs to go to the trouble of generating Cashflow Projections, but Chapter 13 explains when this report is advisable.

REMEMBER

8. **Set sales targets and expense budgets for the 12 months ahead.**

Committing to budgets is one of the most important elements of the financial planning cycle. In Chapter 10, I explain the subtle difference between projections and budgets.

9. **Continually review actual results against budgets, and tweak your pricing, strategy, and budgets accordingly.**

With finances, you can't 'set and forget'. Instead, the trick is to monitor your actual performance and compare this against your budgets every single month. For example, if sales fall short of targets, you need to sell more, change pricing or pull back on expenses. If sales go over targets, you probably want to look at your Cashflow Projection and check that you can finance this growth.

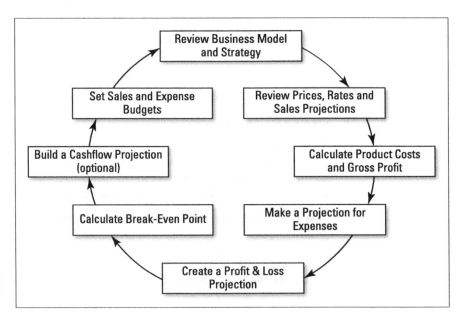

FIGURE 1-2:
The financial planning cycle.

REMEMBER

Can you see how it really doesn't work to create a 12-month Profit & Loss Projection as part of your business plan and then congratulate yourself on the process being finished for the year? I've yet to see a business where actual results are exactly the same as budgets. You will always get a difference, and you need to manage these differences on an ongoing basis.

Getting Beyond First Base

We humans often like to stick with what we know and what feels right — and business plans are no exception. In this section, I delve into the psychology of business plans, focusing on how human bias and subconscious behaviors can serve to undermine the objectivity so essential to good planning.

Guarding against your inner optimism

People often ascribe the high failure rates of venture capital to perceived levels of risk, and proof that the system is working as it should. However, I'd argue that these failure rates have more to do with the nature of what it means to be human. Specifically, we humans are an overly optimistic bunch, with subconscious instincts that often override rational decision-making.

The majority of humans are endowed with something known as *optimism bias* — the tendency to overestimate the likelihood of positive events, and underestimate the likelihood of negative events. And, as someone who has spent their life around entrepreneurs, I reckon the average business owner has optimism bias on steroids.

Of course, optimism is one thing, but wearing blinkers is another. How can you temper such optimism, along with other unconscious biases, to ensure your business plan is as good as can be? In this section, I consider how some innate and completely normal human behaviors might affect your ability to create a smart business plan.

Confirmation bias

Humans love *confirmation bias* — that inexorable pull that makes us look for evidence to validate what we already think, and disregard information supporting other points of view. (Next time you're making a decision or expressing an opinion about something, see if you can spot your own confirmation bias. Perhaps you like to you seek out stories that confirm your political viewpoint? Or you cling to one-off customer anecdotes that validate your new idea, and dismiss negative customer reviews that suggest otherwise?)

Confirmation bias is, of course, counter-productive to creating a business plan, particularly if you're seeking fresh ideas or wanting to assess the potential of a new business model.

REMEMBER

When creating your business plan, be wary of placing too much emphasis on information that reinforces your existing beliefs. Try to involve outside advisers during the information-gathering stage, perhaps even seeking out those who you know are likely to challenge or disagree with you. (Chapter 5 provides some good frameworks for this information-gathering process.)

The planning fallacy

As I write this paragraph, I'm feeling very sheepish! Despite this being Chapter 1, I'm actually at the end of updating this new edition of *Creating a Business Plan For Dummies*. I'm already 10 weeks past my deadline, and my publisher has given up asking me for a completion date.

I could, of course, email her and inform her that I am but human, and that like 95 per cent of the population, I've fallen foul of the *planning fallacy*. A concept developed by Daniel Kahneman and Amos Tversky in 1979, the planning fallacy is about the predisposition of humans to be overly optimistic about timelines or planning outcomes, even in the face of more general knowledge or past experience that would suggest otherwise.

The planning fallacy is most likely to arise when we trust our intuition and disregard past experience. Unfortunately, because planning is inherently about the future, we're inclined to look forward, rather than backwards, and we happily forget how often projects run over, things cost more than budgeted, or sales orders fall through. We're also likely to forget how our competitors behave — for example, getting excited about new opportunities while simultaneously disregarding the likelihood of our competitors doing exactly the same thing.

So, how do you avoid falling foul of the planning fallacy? Similar to avoiding confirmation bias, try to involve multiple perspectives and get input from experts or external advisors of the challenges or time required. In addition, you may be able to refer to past projects or industry benchmarks to guide your estimates, rather than relying solely on gut feeling. (For more about benchmarks, see Chapter 10, and for more about budgets, see Chapter 13.)

The Dunning-Kruger effect

Humans also tend to be optimistic in their struggle to make sense of the future and its mix of certainty and uncertainty. Or, put another way, because we don't yet know what we do not know, we tend to overestimate ourselves. This overestimation of competence, along with the inability to critically analyze our own abilities, is known as the *Dunning–Kruger effect*.

I've observed the Dunning–Kruger effect in action more times than I care to mention and, indeed, can see how often I've overestimated my own abilities. I've been influenced by life experiences that have been ultimately quite misleading, and sometimes my intuition and business decisions have been quite unhinged from reality.

WARNING

If you're new to business, or to a particular industry, beware of the risk that you could overrate yourself and underrate others who are more experienced. While self-confidence is essential, knowledge and rational decision-making processes are key to tethering your dreams. Instead, try to surround yourself with people who know a lot about the subject, particularly if the financial or legal stakes are high. Also, if you can, try to expand your knowledge by any means you can, be this through online courses, specialist training or business coaching.

Accepting uncertainty and complexity

Unconscious biases that affect our business judgment don't only relate to over-optimism. Consider some other patterns of behavior, and how these might affect the way you approach your business plan:

» **Action-oriented bias:** An *action-oriented bias* is the tendency for people to move to action-oriented discussions too soon during the strategic planning process. I find this bias often comes from time pressures, or simply a lack of systematic thinking skills.

  If you're making a significant decision, one trick to avoid action-orientated bias is to spend almost as much time justifying what you're *not* going to do as you spend justifying what you are going to do. For example, if you were to decide to purchase a factory, you might spend just as much time exploring what it would mean to lease instead, or even to outsource production.

» **Anchor bias and the primacy effect:** An *anchor bias* is about depending too much on initial information (the anchor) to make subsequent judgments, and not taking time to evaluate other strategic alternatives objectively. Similar is the *primacy effect,* which is the tendency to consider the first information you encounter more than later information.

One of the main ways to guard against anchor bias and the primacy effect is to slow down. Doing business plans can be hard work, and you may be tempted to hurry through certain stages. Pause regularly and ask yourself whether you've genuinely taken enough time to consider all your options. Sometimes, just an hour or two of objectively considering all your alternatives can prevent you spending months or even years pursuing a subpar business model.

>> **Framing effect:** The *framing effect* is about we respond to the way information is framed. For example, if a business proposal is framed as cutting costs to prevent losses, this may seem more attractive than investing in growth despite risks.

To avoid the framing effect, always be aware about how strategic alternatives are framed. Try to reframe positive suggestions in a negative light, and vice versa, to see how that makes you feel. Alternatively, seek out external expert advice to evaluate alternatives, and ask for fresh opinions.

Hoodwinking Yourself into Actually Creating a Plan

I'd love to know how many people reading this chapter will actually go on to complete a business plan. Far be it from me to express doubt about you, dear reader, or indeed about my own abilities to write a coherent tome on this topic, but my experience is that for every ten people who intend to create a proper business plan, only one or two do.

I reckon that this reluctance is less about businesspeople lacking tenacity to see the process through, and more about the predisposition of humans to avoid thinking too far into the future, and to favor present not-so-big gains over long-term greater gains. Termed *present bias* by psychologists, an estimated 97 per cent of people experience this bias in day-to-day life.

Present bias explains why so many people intend to create a business plan but why so few people actually do — or, indeed, why so many people think, *I'll start working on my business plan tonight*, and end up binge-watching a Nordic noir series on Netflix instead.

Present bias not only hinders the desire to spend time planning, but can also get in the way of you making good business decisions. Prioritizing immediate financial gains over longer-term returns, drawing money out of your business for personal spending rather than reinvesting profits, and setting prices low to attract immediate business are all examples of present bias in action.

If you think you too may find it hard to complete the whole business plan shindig, here are a few life hacks to help:

>> **Don't rely on your own willpower.** Instead, make planning into a habit, allocating a specific half-day per month, or a specific hour per week. Block out this time on your calendar.

>> **Subscribe to a business-planning app.** I talk about apps earlier in this chapter (refer to 'Subscribing to a business planning app'). Most apps make the planning process a little easier to navigate and more fun. And for some, that monthly debit for the app subscription may prove motivation in itself.

>> **Break the planning process into small steps.** Set small, actionable goals for each part of the business plan process — for example, completing a marketing plan one week, a pricing strategy review the next, and setting up financial templates the next.

>> **Trick yourself into making the plan feel urgent.** Perhaps set a deadline to meet with an investor, nominate your business for an award, or schedule planning meetings with staff for which you need to prepare materials.

>> **Find an accountability buddy.** Like finding a gym partner, find a friend or colleague who also needs to create a plan for their business, and agree to keep each other on track.

>> **Spend time actively visualizing the future for your business (and you).** By making the future seem more real, you can sometimes motivate yourself into acting now.

You may be wondering why I spend so much time in the very first chapter of this book talking about how the psychology of the average human is not ideal for business planning. After all, might it not be better if I was a bit more encouraging? My hope is if you do end up finding the process a little daunting, you can take comfort from knowing that the problem isn't personal. And, with a little understanding about the psychology of the process, you can embark on your business plan with a greater chance of success.

Good luck, dear reader!

WHEN A SIDE HUSTLE SHOULD REMAIN JUST THAT

When is a successful side hustle an indicator of the perfect business idea, and when should a side hustle remain just that?

I suggest you ask yourself two questions. Firstly, will you have enough demand for your product or service if you expand what you're doing five- or ten-fold? For example, perhaps you have a side hustle selling products at local markets. If you seek to expand your business, you probably need to look for new channels to sell your product, and the cost of reaching additional customers (for example, renting a retail space or selling products through a distributor) may skew your business model and make it less profitable.

Secondly, do you properly cost the value of your own labor? Perhaps, for example, you make homemade jams and pickles and you find time to do the manufacture around your day-to-day life, perhaps making batches of produce in the evenings or on weekends. If you turn this side hustle into your main hustle and you need to value your time (or indeed, the time of others) at a decent hourly rate, can your pricing model sustain this adjustment?

IN THIS CHAPTER

» **Determining the edge you have over others**

» **Working out the relationship between risk and potential gain**

» **Figuring out why you can succeed when others fail**

» **Articulating your strategic advantage statement**

» **Getting technology to fine-tune your business idea**

Chapter **2**

Figuring Out What's So Special about You (And Your Business)

What is it that makes you, or your business, so special?

Even if you have a business that's similar to thousands of others — maybe you mow lawns, have a hair salon or tutor high-school students — if you wish to make above-average profits, you still need to come up with an idea that makes your business different from others, or that provides you with a competitive edge.

Similarly, if your business caters for a very specific niche — maybe you sell gluten-free cookies or baby clothes made from organic cottons — to make above-average profits, you need to identify how you can service this niche in a way that others can't, or what it is about your skills or circumstances that enables you to service this niche better than others.

If your business centers on an idea that you reckon nobody has tried before, the million-dollar question is why nobody else has bothered to try this idea until now. Not only that, but in the event that you're successful, a key question is what prevents others from copying your idea straightaway.

The essence of what makes your business special, or more likely to succeed than others, is called your *competitive* or *strategic advantage*. I believe that this advantage is the single most important ingredient for ongoing business success, and is elemental to how you frame your business plan.

In this chapter, I outline how to determine your edge, and how to include your strategic advantage in your business plan.

Gaining the Edge

In the introduction for this chapter, I mention the terms *competitive advantage* and *strategic advantage*. Like many people, I tend to use these terms synonymously but, to be really precise, you could argue they relate to slightly different aspects of your business.

A *competitive advantage* is something that's different, better than, or not offered by your competitors. For example, if a town has two hair salons and one offers a mobile service but the other doesn't, the first salon has a competitive advantage because they're providing something their competitors aren't.

A *strategic advantage* is something that stems from capabilities within your business that are hard for others to copy. These capabilities tend to be a unique blend of assets, know-how, networks, skills or technology. For example, imagine the owner of the salon with the mobile haircutting service has a background in nursing, and so has a natural understanding of the needs of her many elderly, housebound clients. Imagine also that the owner's husband is a mechanic, which means the vehicle used for providing the salon's mobile service is kept on the road at minimal cost. This unique blend of skills and cost efficiency forms a key part of this salon's strategic advantage.

Having said all this, competitive and strategic advantages tend to overlap so much that I avoid arguing about the distinction. I use the term strategic advantage in this chapter (because, after all, a true strategic advantage should ultimately result in a competitive advantage) but if you'd rather use the term competitive advantage in your business plan, that's just fine.

Looking at examples of strategic advantage

How can your business beat the competition, and what benefits can you provide that the competition can't? Here are some ways that your business may be able to secure a strategic advantage against others in the same industry:

TIP

>> **Added value:** Can you offer added value in comparison to your competitors? Think 24-hour delivery, ethically sourced product, a mobile service, or a quality of product or service that's beyond industry norms.

>> **Exclusive distribution rights:** Do you have exclusive distribution rights to a sought-after product or service?

>> **First cab off the rank:** Do you have a new idea that nobody else has tried before? Or a new way of doing something that makes the product or service better, quicker or cheaper?

>> **Intellectual property:** Do you have unique intellectual property (IP) that customers want and that's hard to copy? IP includes copyright, patents and trademarks. If you're just getting started with your business, your IP could be as simple as a clever business name, an eye-catching logo or a well-chosen domain name (that is, a web address).

>> **Logical location:** If you have a retail shopfront, do you have a great location in a central shopping area? (Location is always *the* prime strategic advantage for retailers.) Or are you the only business providing a service in a particular suburb or region? Are the demographics of your location ideally matched to your business, or are you located in a central spot for freight and transport?

>> **Lower costs:** Do you have an innovative way of doing things that reduces costs, creates economies of scale or significantly improves business processes?

>> **Obsession and drive:** Do you have exceptional vision or drive? Is this drive connected with a particular obsession? (For example, think of Coco Chanel with her ambitious vision and flair for design.)

>> **Perfectly matched team:** If you're in a business partnership of some kind, do you have a unique combination of skills and do you work well together as a team? (The synergy created by two or more people who have complementary skills and who work well together can be a force to be reckoned with, and something that's hard for competition to copy.)

>> **Specialist skills:** Are you a specialist who has an insight into a particular industry that nobody else is likely to have? Maybe you can see a gap in the industry that nobody else is catering for, or maybe you can see a way to do something better.

Think of a business that has been really successful (maybe a local business or a friend's business, or even a big name such as IKEA, Patagonia or Microsoft). Go through the strategic advantages listed here, and think about which of these advantages could apply to these businesses.

Applying these examples to real life

Try to deepen your understanding of strategic advantage (refer to the preceding section) by applying the concept to a few real-life situations that are easy to imagine. Picture yourself sitting in a room with four people and each of these people sharing their idea for a new business:

>> Lloyd plans to start a business mowing lawns in his local neighborhood.

>> Tess has recently qualified as an acupuncturist and plans to start up a practice specializing in children's health.

>> Dave plans to provide a home-safety service for parents, installing devices such as gates, cupboard latches and electrical safety switches to make homes toddler-proof. Dave is a qualified electrician and excellent handyperson; his business partner, Alex, is in real estate and has great marketing skills.

>> Leila, who is a musician and gifted songwriter, has partnered with Sam, who has excellent marketing and design skills. Their plan is to create a personalized songwriting service that will use a combination of AI, smart automations and their exceptional creative skills. Their savvy use of technology will enable a bespoke service that is both competitive on price and swift.

Referring to the strategic advantages listed in the preceding section, have a think about which of these advantages could be relevant. You can see how I've rated the strategic advantage potential for each of the four businesses in Table 2-1.

Of course, me writing 'yes' against a strategic advantage doesn't mean that this advantage necessarily exists. Rather, what I'm saying is that potential exists. For example, I've written 'yes' against 'intellectual property' for the songwriting platform, even though Leila and Sam haven't started developing their idea yet.

Have a look at Table 2-1 and see if you agree with my assessment of potential advantages. For example, can you think of ways that someone with a lawn mowing business could get an edge over competition, perhaps using added value services, ideal locations or lower costs?

TABLE 2-1 **Rating Businesses According to Potential Strategic Advantage**

	Lawn Mowing	Acupuncturist	Toddler Safety	Personalized Songwriting
Added value	Maybe		Yes	
Exclusive distribution				
First cab off the rank				Maybe
Intellectual property				Yes
Excellent location	Maybe	Maybe	Maybe	
Lower costs	Maybe			Maybe
Obsession and drive				Yes
Perfectly matched team		Maybe	Maybe	Maybe
Specialist skills		Yes	Yes	Yes

Understanding Risk, Gain and Pain

In most situations, the business with the highest potential strategic advantage is going to be the business that requires the most capital or involves the most risk of failure. For example, in Table 2-1, the business with the highest number of yeses in the strategic column is the personalized songwriting platform. However, the idea itself is full of risk. Leila and Sam will have high development costs, an unknown and untested market, and a product that may not even work that well when complete.

On the flip side, lawn mowing has few potential strategic advantages but probably the lowest risk of all, where even the costs of setting up a lawnmowing business might be less than a few hundred dollars or so. The challenge in finding strategic advantages for Lloyd's business is that a lawn is only ever a lawn, and Lloyd may find it tricky to differentiate his service from that of his competitors. However, I've still written 'maybe' against three possible strategic advantages for Lloyd's lawnmowing business:

>> **Added value:** Maybe Lloyd has some specialist horticultural knowledge that could set him apart from his competitors.

>> **Location:** Maybe Lloyd would be providing the only lawnmowing service in his neighborhood, or maybe he lives in a very exclusive suburb with lots of high-income earners.

>> **Lower costs:** Perhaps Lloyd uses electric tools, including an electric vehicle, and the solar panels on his home generate excess energy. This could result in lower costs than those competitors who are reliant upon petrol for their mowers and transport.

REMEMBER

Identifying potential strategic advantages for a business or service that lots of other people provide, and where it's difficult to differentiate between your service and those of your competitors, can be tricky. The upside of this kind of business is that the risks are usually lower; the downside is that it's always going to be tricky to charge premium rates or make above-average profits.

Can you think of a company operating in your industry that started small, but has since turned the whole way of doing business on its head? A business such as Airbnb, Netflix, Tesla or Uber? Such businesses are known as *disrupters* and typically catch their competitors unawares with their unique approach.

Justifying Why You Can Succeed

In the preceding sections in this chapter, I explore the concept of strategic advantage in relation to a range of possible businesses. I like to work with examples in this way because the different business scenarios help to highlight how much this concept changes depending on the context.

In this section, I help you to apply the concept of strategic advantage to your business. I help you go digging to identify what it is that makes you different.

REMEMBER

If you're struggling to come up with anything that's special about your business — maybe you haven't stumbled on that winning idea quite yet — please do persist. If you wish for your business to thrive, and hopefully generate above-average profits, the process of identifying your strategic advantage is important for all businesses, no matter how large or small.

Uncovering your inner mojo

If you're already in business, one good way to identify your strategic advantage is to look at your existing customers and their buying patterns. (Or, if you haven't started your business yet, imagine what these answers might be.) Ask yourself these questions:

>> When customers come to me, why is that?

>> When potential customers go to my competitors instead, why is that?

>> When potential customers make an enquiry but end up not purchasing my goods or services, why is that?

>> Are the benefits I offer (or intend to offer) to my customers unique?

The thing that I like about asking these questions is that getting the answers usually means you have to engage in some market research. This naturally crosses over with competitor analysis (which just happens to be the subject of Chapter 3).

TIP

Honest, ongoing market research that compares the benefits your business provides to customers against the benefits your competitors provide is essential to identifying and maintaining your strategic advantage.

Asking three key questions

For a strategic advantage to be really worth something — in terms of the goodwill of your business or your likely financial success — this advantage has to be something that you can sustain over the long term.

A strong strategic advantage should have three attributes:

>> **The advantage can't be easily copied by others.** The ideal strategic advantage is one that's really tricky for your competition to copy. Examples are a winning recipe or flavor (think Coca-Cola), a unique synergy of skills within your organization, or expert knowledge that few others have.

>> **The advantage is important to customers.** Think of the farmers who switched to growing organic produce in the early 1990s, before organics became more mainstream. Many of these farmers did really well because organics were so important to particular customers. (And although the advantage was relatively easy to copy, many authorities required a seven-year lead time with no chemicals before a farm could be officially certified.)

>> **The advantage can be constantly improved.** If you can identify the thing that gives you an edge and constantly work this advantage, you have a strategic advantage that is potentially sustainable in the long term.

TRUE STORY

When Steve Jobs and Steve Wozniak started Apple, one key strategic advantage was that they were a perfectly matched team, and were passionate about design. The synergy of their skills was hard for others to copy, the beautiful design was something that customers really wanted, and Apple were in a position to continually improve and develop this advantage.

Don't fall into the trap of thinking that because you're cheaper than everyone else, this is a strategic advantage. Being cheaper than everyone else usually means one of two things: Either your business isn't as profitable as it should be, or your competitors can grab your strategic advantage at any moment just by dropping their prices too. Usually, being cheaper than others is only a strategic advantage if you have some special skills, technology or volume of production that enables you to be cheaper.

Finding purpose and authenticity for what you do

Being true to your ideals doesn't automatically result in business success. However, when coupled with judicious business decision-making, a business that is authentic and values-driven is more likely to succeed than one which isn't.

Patagonia, one of the world's leading retailers of outdoor equipment and clothing, is an example of how authenticity and purpose-driven actions can, over time, create a strong brand and clear strategic advantage. Since 1985, Patagonia has donated 1 per cent of annual sales to fight climate change, been openly self-critical in debating the contradiction between sustainability and revenue growth, and ultimately making the radical move to give the company away to a trust, with all future profits going towards climate crisis initiatives. Despite the seemingly uncommercial nature of these actions, Patagonia's consistent authenticity has been a major element in driving customer loyalty, ultimately creating a strategic advantage that's hard for others to copy.

Of course, only you will know what authenticity means for your business. However, look around and you'll quickly find inspiration: Perhaps a lawyer offering pro bono services for victims of domestic violence, a personal trainer blogging candidly of successes and failures, or a tourist operator campaigning for environmental protection of the region from which their business operates. What can you do to reflect your values in the way you run your business?

Developing Your Strategic Advantage Statement

In this book, I'm realistic about the written part of business plans. I know how few people actually write a 20- or 30-page business plan, despite their best intentions (which is why I also cover creating pitch decks and one-page business plans in Chapter 15).

However, even if you put nothing else in writing, I do recommend you write a statement of strategic advantage. In this statement, your purpose is to articulate exactly what gives your business an edge over others.

TIP

Your strategic advantage statement is usually similar but slightly different from your 'elevator speech' (something I talk about in Chapter 3). The difference is that a strategic advantage statement may include information about your business that you wouldn't necessarily share if 'giving the sell' about your business to a prospective customer.

Note that if you are writing a full business plan, your strategic advantage statement forms part of your Executive Summary. (For more about Executive Summaries, see Chapter 15.)

Focusing on where you have the edge

Your strategic advantage statement needs only be a paragraph or two, but should include the following:

>> Your company name

>> How your product or service benefits your customers

>> What makes your business different to your competitors, seen from the perspective of your customers

>> Your strategic advantage or advantages: What knowledge, skills, synergy, team, technology or processes your business has that enables you to deliver these additional benefits to your customers

I like to put this statement right at the beginning of any business plan because this insight into how you're different, and how you can succeed where others may fail or flounder, is so foundational to success.

Figure 2-1 shows an example of an extract from Dave's business plan (making homes toddler-proof).

In Figure 2-1, Dave and his business partner, Alex, stress how the synergy of their skills and current occupations form their main strategic advantage. Some of these skills are also selling points for their business (for example, Dave's experience with risk assessment), but some are not (knowing when people are buying new homes so you can sell your product to them may be a strategic advantage, but it's definitely not a selling point).

FIGURE 2-1:
An example statement of strategic advantage.

Honing your difference over time

Sometimes your strategic advantage isn't something that's blindingly clear from the moment you set out in business, but instead grows over time. Your skills grow as you develop in business, and your understanding of how you're different from the competition consolidates as well.

From time to time, you can review your strategic advantage by asking yourself these questions:

>> What am I naturally good at? (Or what is my team good at?) Where do I feel I have been particularly successful in my business?

>> What do I offer to my customers that's either cheaper than my competitors, better value or unique in some way?

>> Does a point exist where what I'm naturally good at connects with what I do better than my competitors? If so, how can I build and develop this?

TRUE STORY

When our local osteopath first started out in business, he didn't really have anything that separated him from the competition. The only thing that was really different about him was that he was an elite rock climber in his spare time. However, as his business grew, he became expert at treating other climbers for their injuries. His business developed, and now he treats not only climbers who live locally, but also climbers from interstate. He even does some international consultations. (And, yes, if you're wondering, some parts of an osteopathic consultation can be conducted online!) This combination of skills — being an elite climber and a highly trained osteopath — is hard to beat, and a true strategic advantage.

Applying a critical eye

A strategic advantage only holds water if customers really want what you're offering. One of most common mistakes made by entrepreneurs is to be over-optimistic about the demand for their products or services. A sunhat with a solar-powered fan on top may *seem* a good idea, but is anyone going to be seen dead wearing such a thing?

TRUE STORY

A friend of mine had an idea to start a business selling handmade timber beds. He reckoned he had a strategic advantage with the unique combination of his carpentry skills, eye for design and ready supply of quality timber (his parents had a large acreage close by). However, he soon found that people were reluctant to pay the extra dollars for his products, with people comparing his prices against the mass-manufactured timber beds made from poor-quality pine and available from large discount furniture chains. In short, customer demand wasn't sufficient to exploit this particular strategic advantage in a way that made business sense.

Using AI to Generate More Ideas

Whether you're still tossing around ideas for a new business or you've been running a business for years, keep an open mind about new ways of doing business. I find that an AI app such as ChatGPT can be useful for this purpose.

The trick with AI is phrasing your question in the right way. When using AI to explore different ways of doing business, be as specific as possible and try asking the same question in a few different ways:

>> **Ask AI to generate a list of successful companies in your industry**. While you may know which businesses are most successful in the country where you live, have you checked out other businesses overseas? What might you learn by visiting the websites of those companies? For example, if you're thinking of starting an e-bike business, you might ask AI to 'list the most successful e-bike businesses in France', or 'list the best e-bike retailers in Singapore'.

>> **Ask AI how you can make money from a particular business idea.** I was genuinely impressed with ChatGPT's response to the question, 'How do I make money from a business mowing lawns?' (Although I did chuckle at the absurd suggestion that I 'consider offering mobile services to mow lawns off-site'.) What comes up for you if you type into AI 'How do I make money from a business [insert your business idea here]?'

>> **Ask AI how you might create a strategic advantage in a particular industry.** The question, 'How do I create a strategic advantage for a hair salon?' yielded some interesting results, as did, 'I'm a designer creating websites for medical professionals. How can I create a strategic advantage?'

>> **Ask AI for suggestions about businesses doing things completely differently.** Writing questions that include both your industry or business model as well as the word 'disruptor' can lead to some interesting ideas.

TIP

When trying to generate ideas for how to gain strategic advantage, don't limit your research to the state or even the country in which you live. Go global with your online research, visiting websites of similar businesses all around the world. Consider how you might emulate good marketing strategy ideas, innovative pricing models, smart online services, or other clever approaches.

REMEMBER

Be prepared to revisit your ideas repeatedly and keep reshaping the concept that you have for your business until you can come up with a strong strategic advantage.

2

Looking to the World Outside

Analyze your competitors, land your competitive strategy, and develop a killer elevator speech.

Explore different ways of doing business, and picture where your future lies.

Use a structured approach to consider industry trends, unearth business opportunities, and evaluate whether you have the skills needed to succeed.

IN THIS CHAPTER

» Getting motivated about understanding your competition

» Looking at who your competitors really are

» Going undercover with Sherlock Holmes

» Doing (yet another) reality check

» Preparing the big sell

Chapter **3**

Sizing up the Competition

'm still surprised at how often I come across people planning to start a new business, or who are in the first couple of years of business, who have yet to research who their competitors are.

Detailed competitive analysis helps clarify what it is that your business is going to do better than others. As part of this analysis, organizing your competitors into groups is worthwhile, differentiating between 'head-on-head' competitors, and competitors who only take away business from you on an occasional basis. You also need to think about future competitors — competitors who aren't a big deal yet, but could become so if circumstances change.

In this chapter, I talk about doing a thorough profile for key competitors, picking apart the differences between them and your own business. I also return to the question: Given what the competition are doing and how they are faring, how does this reflect on the likelihood that your business will perform similarly?

Once you've clarified where your strengths lie compared to the competition, you're ready for the 'big sell'. At the end of this chapter, I provide some tips on how best to sell your idea in a short amount of time — otherwise known as an 'elevator speech'.

Understanding Why Competitor Analysis is Important

Business planning can be a dry topic at the best of times, and you may already feel that you have a handle on who your competitors are. However, thinking about your competitors in detail is important for three key reasons: First, as a reality check; second, for spotting opportunities; third, as a way to figure out how you're going to stand out from the pack.

Avoiding blind faith

Part of the excitement of starting a new business is the buzz you get when coming up with new ideas. However, the trick is to know when confidence crosses the line to become blind faith.

Checking out potential competitors thoroughly is one way of getting a reality check. For example, in a town near me, a whole strip of cafés come and go with every change in season. If I were thinking about starting a café in this town, a competitor analysis may well reveal that the rents in this strip are high, the land-lords difficult, and nobody is making enough profits to survive, let alone thrive.

Similarly, without competitor analysis, you can't be sure of your financial model-ling. If you have direct competitors, you want to be right across the services these businesses provide, and the prices they charge. Unless a massive undersupply exists or you're offering a valuable difference, charging significantly more for your product or your service than your competitors may prove to be a highly risky business model; similarly, undercutting competitors on price is unlikely to be viable.

Spotting potential opportunities

Your competition isn't just the marker of who you have to 'beat'. Your competition can also be a source of inspiration or the benchmark that enables you to establish realistic expectations for your business, and provide insight into where you can gain a possible edge.

Buying goods or services from your competitors (as opposed to just researching them online) can be a great way to reveal potential opportunities. Indeed, the seed of many a winning business idea is sown by someone receiving poor service or a disappointing product. Whenever you think, *I can do better than that*, the potential for a new business idea or marketing strategy is born.

Of course, you may well find that your competitors have some pretty good ideas you could potentially adapt for your business. Pricing specials, weekend packages, discount offers, online services, creative advertising or clever sales techniques are just some of the things you may decide to explore. After all, imitation is the greatest form of flattery (although your competitors may not see it that way!).

Clarifying your difference

Always look for differences other than price when comparing yourself against competitors. Keep asking yourself what makes *you* special and how you intend to convey this difference clearly in your marketing materials. Unless you know exactly what your competitors provide, you won't know how to sell your differences.

Figuring Out Who Your Competitors Really Are

You can't create a battle plan without knowing the enemy. In the following sections, I explore how to figure out who the enemy really is (otherwise known as your competitors, of course) and how to create a battle plan for each act of combat.

TIP

When doing your competitor analysis, don't hesitate to compare your business against big-time competitors such as supermarket chains or large franchises. While you may find it hard to imagine how your fledgling business could ever compete, the mass-market nature of these competitors often leaves niches that are underserviced, providing opportunities for smaller players.

Organizing competitors into groups

I like to organize competitors into three broad groups, and I suggest you try to do so too, as follows:

>> **Head-to-head competitors** provide exactly the same service or exactly the same product as you do.

>> **'Sometimes' competitors** provide a slightly different service or product, or are in a different location.

>> **Left-field competitors** don't normally compete with you but, if circumstances were to change, could possibly do so.

Imagine you're a digital marketing agency specializing in brand development. Your head-to-head competitors are likely other digital agencies with this same focus working in your region or state; your 'sometimes' competitors could include freelance copywriters operating from anywhere in the world; your left-field competition might include an AI tool designed to generate creative copy.

In the same way, if you're an osteopath specializing in back pain, your head-to-head competitors would include other osteopaths providing exactly the same service in the same area; your 'sometimes' competitors could include allied health practitioners such as physiotherapists; left-field competition could include prescription pain killers.

WARNING

Although figuring out current competitors may sound relatively easy, future competitors are not always be so easy to spot. For example, a watchmaker repairing and selling watches 40 years ago would have probably thought that the main competition was other watchmakers. The idea that the mobile phone could almost completely annihilate this industry would have seemed a long shot.

REMEMBER

When you're thinking about the competition for your proposed business, don't be too literal — think about where both your business and its industry are headed.

Homing in on head-to-head competitors

For most businesses, the priority is to spend time analyzing head-to-head competitors. After all, these are the competitors that your customers are most often going to come across when they seek to purchase your goods or services.

One of the purposes of identifying head-to-head competitors is so you can develop a competitive strategy to deal with each one (refer to the section 'Understanding Why Competitor Analysis is Important', earlier in this chapter, for more reasons). However, when you create a list of head-to-head competitors, this can sometimes be a long list.

For example, if you're starting up a business installing solar panels, you may find 50 other companies working in your local area offering similar services. You don't want to have to come up with 50 different competitive strategies, so your best tactic is to try to group these competitors in some way.

Try this process:

1. **List your competitors in a small number of groups based on similarities.**

For example, a solar panel company may split its list of 50 similar companies according to the size of each business, and focus (maybe some focus on battery storage, others on off-grid, others on new buildings), or by locality or suburb.

2. **Think about how you've organized these groups. Will a customer looking for your kind of business use these same criteria?**

For example, if a customer is searching online for a solar panel company, are they going to search by suburb, by specialty, or by services provided?

3. **Have a think about where you belong in the scheme of things.**

The solar panel company may decide to focus on solar systems but within a two-hour travel radius only.

4. **Think to the future. Do you want to be in this same group in five years' time?**

For example, maybe the solar panel company has a vision that ultimately they want to offer not just solar installations, but home-energy consultations also, and they want to expand to offer this service nationwide.

TIP

By organizing your competitors into groups, you can build a clearer idea about how to develop different competitive strategies, depending on what kind of competitor you're dealing with.

WHY YOU CAN SOMETIMES BEAT THE BIG GUYS

When you're checking out competitors, you may come across lots of factors that make it tough for you to compete with the big guys in town, such as high capital costs, expensive IT systems or huge distribution networks. These factors are called *entry barriers*.

The flipside of entry barriers can be *exit barriers*. Sometimes competitors have invested so much in expensive rentals or specialized equipment, or sometimes competitors can be so management top-heavy, that they can't easily get out of the less profitable parts of their business, and also can't act quickly when opportunities arise.

For smaller businesses, these exit barriers sometimes point to opportunities. Maybe you can distribute product much more cheaply online, while the competition is wedded to expensive retail rents. Similarly, maybe you can act quickly in response to new trends, creating and promoting products in a fraction of the time a big company takes to do the same thing.

Thinking about future competitors

In Chapter 5, I talk about your vision for the future, and how important it is to keep your eyes open to trends in the economy, the environment, and in your industry. This macro way of thinking is also useful at the early planning stages of your business, particularly if you spend a while thinking about not just who your competitors are right now, but also who your competitors could be in one, two or five years' time.

Ask yourself questions relating to the following areas:

>> **Automation potential:** Could any existing competitors automate their processes using advanced technology and, therefore, become more of a threat than they already are?

>> **Big chains coming to town:** Could a franchise chain or large company move into your village, suburb or town and take lots of your customers? (In my neighborhood, the longstanding boutique wine store was greatly impacted when two big liquor chains moved into the same neighborhood.)

>> **Buyout of minor competitors by a larger competitor with more capital and muscle:** Could one of your existing competitors be bought out by someone with more capital and better distribution and, in the process, become a very formidable competitor? (Think about how some producers of gourmet food products have been purchased by supermarket chains and the products suddenly appear in every store.)

>> **Changes in technology:** Could changes in technology mean your product or service becomes obsolete? (Think of the long-lost corner video store, the TV repairer or the 24-hour photo lab.)

>> **Cheaper imports:** Could the goods you provide be substituted by imported goods if the exchange rate changes?

>> **Customers doing it themselves:** Could your main customer or customers decide creating your product or providing your service in-house makes more sense? (Think of the supermarket chains that now manufacture their own generic food lines.)

>> **Life cycle of business idea:** Is the life cycle of your business reaching maturity or beyond, meaning numerous competitors and fewer profits to go around? (Think of the mobile coffee vans that were once a clever niche business but are now a dime a dozen.)

>> **Offshoring of labor:** Could the services you provide be performed offshore instead? (Almost anything that's mostly labor and can be done online is vulnerable to offshoring.)

>> **Service offered online:** Could the service you provide be sold online and, therefore, open to international competition? (Even some things that I would never have imagined could go online have done so. I don't go to my local yoga class any more, but instead log onto a yoga website that offers hundreds of pre-recorded classes to fit any duration, level or style of yoga.)

Engaging in Cloak-and-Dagger Tactics

The time has come for you to don your dark sunglasses, felt hat and fake moustache. Adopt a strong accent and pose as an undercover agent.

Doing a competitor profile

Earlier in this chapter, I cover making a list of your key competitors (refer to the section 'Figuring Out Who Your Competitors Really Are' for more). The bad news is just writing down the names of your competitors isn't enough. Your next step is to do a full-on assessment of each one. (This detailed assessment probably won't end up being part of your final business plan, but does form the basis for your marketing strategies.)

Predicting exactly what you need to include in your competitor dossier is a tad hard for me, because it depends so much on the type of industry you're in and also how practical it is to find out certain information.

Your best starting point for all of this information is probably online (visiting your competitor's website or e-commerce store), but other methods include checking out online reviews for this competitor, purchasing products or services from this competitor, looking at your competitor's marketing materials, or chatting to this competitor's customers, suppliers or distributors.

TIP

You can also ask AI to analyze your competitor's online performance (including their followers, online engagement and content shares). Search 'social media analytic tools for competitors' to find companies offering this service.

In Figure 3-1, I list a few questions you can use as your starting point with your research.

```
Competitor Analysis

Competitor Name: _____ Date: _____

What customers does this competitor target in particular? ...............................

What are their service rates, or price per unit? .........................................

Do they offer any special pricing, discounts or pricing packages? ........................

What image is this competitor trying to convey? .........................................
..........................................................................................

Do they have a specialty or particular niche? ...........................................
..........................................................................................

How does their range of services compare? ..............................................
..........................................................................................

Does this competitor seem to be doing well? ............................................

How long has this competitor been around? .............................................

How many employees do they have? .....................................................

How tech-savvy is this competitor? ....................................................

How does this competitor's social media presence compare in terms of content,
engagement and followers? .............................................................

What distribution networks does this competitor have? ..................................
..........................................................................................

What are the likely competitive advantages that this competitor has? ....................
..........................................................................................
..........................................................................................
```

FIGURE 3-1:
Building a dossier for each key competitor.

Mirror, mirror on the wall . . .

Who's the fairest of them all?

One thing to remember when you compare yourself against others is that you don't need to be perfect, offer rock-bottom pricing or provide unbelievable service and availability. Instead, all you need to be is that little bit better than your competitor.

For example, imagine a physiotherapist starting up in a new town has decided they want to offer an after-hours service. They discover that the only competitor offering an after-hours service is still only available until 6.30 pm on weekdays.

In order to be competitive for an after-hours service, this physiotherapist doesn't need to be available 24/7 — staying open until 8 pm will do just fine, and will meet the needs for those customers hunting around for someone after hours.

Of course, opening hours aren't the only variable that you need to consider, and Table 3-1 shows a detailed competitive analysis of how this physiotherapist compares with others in the local area, rating competitors according to what they do better (or worse).

TABLE 3-1   **Rating Head-to-Head Competitors**

Does this competitor . . .	Move Plus	Physio Now	Injury+	JPS
Have cheaper pricing than me?	Yes	No	No	No
Offer longer opening hours or availability?	No	No	Yes	Yes
Offer specific services that I don't?	No	Yes	No	Yes
Have better distribution or service a wider region?	No	No	No	Yes
Offer a larger variety of pricing packages?	No	No	Yes	Yes
Have more expertise/higher level of skill/higher qualifications?	No	No	No	Yes
Service all the niches that I service?	No	No	No	No
Have respect and trust in the community?	Yes	No	No	Yes
Have an active social media presence?	No	No	Yes	Yes
Have a good online marketing strategy?	No	No	Yes	Yes
Have more capital and power to expand?	No.	No	Yes	Yes

When you do this competitive analysis for your own business, you may want to insert additional criteria against which to compare yourself, or include more than four competitors in your analysis. The important thing is that you list your comparison criteria in the first column, and the names of the competitors that you're comparing yourself along the top. Below each competitor, write yes if they're better and no if you're better (or not applicable if this isn't relevant to you).

Choosing your competitive strategy

After you complete the rating process for each competitor (refer to the preceding section), grab a highlighter pen (or use the Fill function in Excel) and highlight any rows that have 'no' in every column. For example, in Table 3-1, the physiotherapist has 'no' against all competitors for the question of whether the competitors service all the niches that they service.

The fact that this physiotherapy business is servicing a specific niche that others aren't servicing (in this case, an online service for housebound clients) highlights a clear opportunity. Selling specific skills and qualifications is also potentially an opportunity for this business, given that their combined team has higher qualifications than three out of four of their competitors.

So what next? To put it simply, the physiotherapist has three possible competitive strategies. They can try to lead on price, they can attempt to differentiate their services in some way or other, or they can focus on a specific niche.

In fact, any business, including yours, is faced with these three possible competitive strategies, which are usually described as *cost leadership*, *differentiation* or *niche*. You may choose only one of the strategies, you could choose two, or you may choose a combination of all three:

>> **You can choose to be the cheapest (cost leadership strategy).** With this strategy, you're not necessarily the cheapest across all products you offer or the cheapest for every service but, in general, you're aiming to compete on price. Price leadership can be a tempting strategy — after all, customers are always looking for a bargain — but is risky over the long term. Unless you have a strategic advantage that enables you to deliver your product or service more cheaply than your competitors, competing on price can mean weak profitability, and a business model that is doomed to underperform from the get-go.

>> **You can set out to create a point of difference (differentiation strategy).** With this strategy, you set out to differentiate yourself from similar competitors. For example, an electrician could seek to make response time and punctuality a point of difference ('We'll arrive within 30 minutes of the agreed time or the first hour is free'), or could make availability a point of difference ('24-hour call-out service, 7 days a week').

REMEMBER

Ideally, if you choose differentiation as your competitive strategy, you want to find a synergy between this differentiation and your strategic advantage (for more about strategic advantage, refer to Chapter 2). To illustrate this, let's return to the physiotherapist example. Maybe a strategic advantage for this physiotherapist is that they are also an elite athlete, and have several strong partnerships with sports coaches. By selecting a differentiation strategy and focusing on expertise treating sports injuries, they combine their strategic advantage with their competitive strategy.

>> **You can find a particular focus or niche (niche strategy):** With this strategy, your aim is to serve a specific market segment rather than dealing with the whole market. You can combine this niche strategy with a cost strategy, of course (by focusing on one specific niche, you may end up being the cheapest), and you can certainly combine a niche strategy with a differentiation strategy (because the differentiation itself becomes a niche). In a market where niche products or services are increasingly discoverable online and people are seeking bespoke choices more than ever, this competitive strategy is increasingly viable for many businesses.

REMEMBER

You can choose cost leadership or differentiation as competitive strategies in their own right. However, if you choose a niche strategy, implicit in that is that you're also choosing a differentiation strategy. (In other words, you can choose differentiation as your competitive strategy without having a niche, but by its very nature choosing a niche as your competitive strategy means that you're also choosing to differentiate.)

THE TRICKY ISSUE OF DISTRIBUTION

If your business idea is based around a product that you manufacture yourself, one issue you'll need to address when comparing your product offering against that of competitors is distribution. After all, distribution is generally a business in its own right. Do you plan to do all the selling, packing and shipping as well as the manufacturing?

If your answer is yes, you may find that the problem is the number of products you offer. Distributors generally deal with a large number of products, and they gain efficiencies by doing so (in terms of aspects such as sales representation, IT systems, freight costs and warehousing). If you only manufacture one or two products, you won't have any of these efficiencies. Not only will you almost certainly find that distribution is very expensive, but you may also find that some retailers don't want to deal with you because they don't want to bother opening a new account for just one or two products.

One solution may be to find another business that's prepared to do the distribution for you. For example, a local grower may be able to find a wholesaler to distribute their produce, or a small publisher may find a larger publisher to distribute books on their behalf. Using a distributor usually makes good sense in terms of reaching more customers, but can of course make significant inroads into your margins.

Matching your competitive strategy to your strategic advantage

In Chapter 2, I talk about strategic advantage and explain that a true strategic advantage is something that your business has that offers real value to customers but is hard for your competitors to copy.

If you managed to identify a strategic advantage, you may well find that this translates into a particular opportunity when you do your competitor comparison (as per Table 3-1, earlier in this chapter).

With these factors in mind, what you want to do is pick a competitive strategy (focusing on cost, differentiation or a particular niche) that complements both your strategic advantage and any opportunities you've identified in the competitive landscape.

REMEMBER

Always try to pursue a clear strategy. If you choose to muddle along not doing anything that's clearly different to others, you will find it difficult both to compete and to establish a clear strategic advantage in the market.

Summarizing Your Competitive Strategy

If you've been reading this book straight through, you may be feeling a little muddled by the way the concepts of strategic advantage, competitor analysis and competitive strategy all interrelate.

But interrelate they do, with each concept triggering off one another. In the following sections, you can see how these concepts relate and how you get to measure up the likely success of your business model.

Joining the dots

The thing about being in business is that your competitive environment is constantly changing. Maybe you have a particular advantage over competitors but then something changes that takes away that edge. Or maybe you've positioned yourself in a very specific way against a particular competitor but that competitor suddenly changes their business model entirely.

Figure 3-2 shows how the concepts of strategic advantage, competitor analysis and competitive advantage interrelate. You can see that the process of identifying your strategic advantage, comparing yourself against competitors and choosing a competitive strategy is a continuous cycle of using your analysis to assess your own business idea.

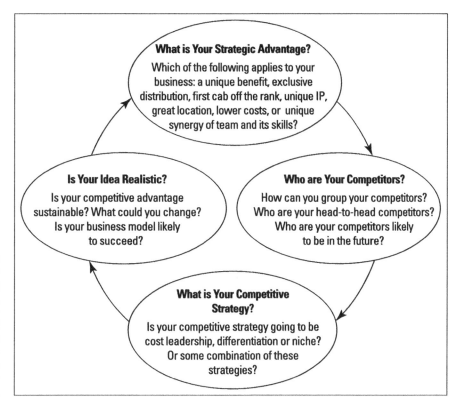

FIGURE 3-2: Using your strategic advantage, competitor analysis and competitive strategy to continually improve your business idea.

REMEMBER

The question of what your business can do better or differently than others goes to the heart of your business plan, and usually forms the essence of your likely business success. The first part of your business plan needs to include a summary of your strategic advantage (a topic I explain in Chapter 2), which then flows into an analysis of your competitors and a summary of your competitive strategy (which is what this chapter is all about). You may also choose to expand on your competitor analysis as part of the marketing section of your business plan. (Chapter 6 explores marketing plans in detail.)

Measuring up the risks

I mentor a start-up business group from time to time. One of the things we work on at each session is identifying what it is that a business is going to do better than others, and what the competitive strategy is going to be.

I sometimes find that when people do an honest appraisal of their business idea and the competition, the resulting business proposal is quite weak. Usually this is because the person starting up in business has limited skills or minimal capital, or because so many big guys are out there dominating the market that getting a foot in the door seems impossible.

I think a business plan that results in someone saying, 'This idea is a dud' or 'The idea is okay, but I'm not the right person to do it' is actually a very successful business plan. The plan, which has probably taken up many days or weeks of research but cost very little, has probably saved that person thousands of dollars (if not more), not to mention months or even years of time.

More often, however, a plan that's built around a weak business idea (maybe the business model has no clear strategic advantage or competitive strategy) provides no definitive answer as to whether that person should continue. In this situation, what becomes relevant is measuring up the risks. If starting (or continuing with) this business means little capital outlay and a few lost weekends and holidays, you could argue the person doesn't have much to lose. On the other hand, if this business involves someone's retirement savings and/or the threat of a failed relationship if things go wrong, the risk may be unjustifiable.

REMEMBER

However much you want to believe in your business idea, if a high level of risk is involved (either personally or financially), do weigh this risk against the likely strength of your business model.

Preparing an Elevator Speech

The last section of this chapter focuses on creating an *elevator speech*, shorthand for a 30-second verbal pitch selling your business. While not essential for a written business plan, an elevator speech forces you to articulate your business model succinctly, which in turn is super helpful when writing the introduction to your business plan.

Imagine you're in an elevator going up to the 25th floor and this guy who you've seen around a couple of times before gets in. You catch his eye and he says to you, 'Hi, I'm Lorenzo. I've seen you here before. Remind me, what's your business all about again?'

You look at the orange numbers flickering on the elevator control panel. You're on the fifth floor, with 20 floors yet to go. You reckon you have about 30 seconds to convey what your business concept is, what you do, and what makes you so damned special. So, what do you reply?

Your answer, of course, depends on the context and the situation, but whatever wording you use, you should always start by thinking of your competitive strategy — what it is that makes you special in the eyes of your customers, and what makes you different from the competition.

Saying what you do in 30 seconds or less

Are you ready to take the challenge? Don't think about what you're going to say. Instead, click the Record button on a note-taking app on your smartphone and answer this question in 30 seconds or less:

> 'What's your business all about?'

How did you go? Listen back and rate yourself out of 10.

Now have a go at doing your speech again but this time, make sure you include the following elements:

>> Your name (and probably your business name too)

>> The way that you help others

>> What makes your business different from others

Sounds simple, but trust me, this 30-second snapshot is surprisingly demanding.

What to avoid with your elevator speech

When honing your elevator speech, stick to simple, everyday terms. If you tell someone that your business aim is 'to achieve a user-centric portal framework' they're likely to die of boredom on the spot. They won't ever arrive at the 25th floor and you'll be stuck dealing with a string of paramedics.

TIP

Here are some more tips for an elevator speech that works:

>> **Avoid clichés and jargon.** Some words I reckon the English language could do without include client base, commitment, core, customer-orientated, empower, enhance, facilitate, implement, input, issue, integrated, maximize, outcome, outside the box, prioritize, scenario and synergy. To name but a few!

>> **Don't start your speech with the words 'I am'.** Remember that this person wants to hear what *your business* can do for them, and this isn't the time to be talking about yourself.

WARNING

>> **Don't have a memorized speech that you stick to, word for word.** A good elevator speech changes with the context and the audience. What you say to a fellow parent in the queue at parent-teacher night is going to be different to what you say when sitting next to somebody at a conference function.

>> **Don't fail to mention what sets you apart.** This is your point of difference, the thing that makes you interesting and memorable. Even if you have a relatively everyday business — maybe you're an electrician or you tutor kids after school — you should be able to find something that sets you apart.

REMEMBER

If an average 12-year-old kid can't understand what it is that you do after listening to your elevator speech, you need to start again.

Practice makes perfect (and a little AI helps too)

When I run business-mentoring courses, I talk about elevator speeches in the very first session. I explain how you don't necessarily have to be in an elevator; you can find yourself in lots of situations, such as conferences, business meetings, online chats or social groups, where someone asks you conversationally what it is that you do.

I go around the room and ask everybody to have a go at their elevator speech. Generally, only one or two people even come close to a decent speech in that first session. But then every single week thereafter I start the session by going around the room and getting everyone to do their 30-second spiel.

I find it fascinating how these speeches change as the weeks go by, and people get clearer and better at selling what it is they're doing. Doing an elevator speech puts you on the spot.

So in this first stage of getting your business off the ground, keep in mind that practice makes perfect. Say your speech aloud when you get in the shower, start your car, or make yourself a cup of tea. Your family may think you're a little bit mad, but that's a small price to pay.

TIP

If you're feeling completely stumped, use an AI tool such as ChatGPT to get started by asking to 'write an elevator speech for a business doing [insert your business here]'. Add some information about yourself, your region or your planned niche, and check out the response. Even if you chuck out 90 per cent of what's offered, you may get a useful idea or two!

IN THIS CHAPTER

» **Working out where you're headed: Home-based business or multimillion dollar enterprise?**

» **Playing with the different roles needed to make a business work**

» **Creating a business that's independent from you**

» **Understanding that some businesses are harder to grow than others**

» **Building the people part of your business plan**

Chapter **4**

Separating Yourself from Your Business

Many years ago, I did some consulting work for a guy who'd started his own industrial welding business. The reporting systems for this business were a complete nightmare. As I trawled through the accounts, trying to make sense of it all, my client looked across the room at me and announced, in a somewhat apologetic tone, 'You know something? I'm a really good welder.'

For me, this brief interchange summarizes the dilemma many business owners face. People start out in their business doing what they're good at, and what they love to do (whether this is welding, performing music or face-painting at kids' parties). But before long, they find they spend more and more time doing stuff they're not naturally good at, such as bookkeeping, looking through contracts, hiring employees or managing websites. Sometimes this extra work becomes such a burden that the joy of being in business is lost. Or sometimes the business owner rises to the challenge, thriving on these extra demands and enjoying the reprieve from day-to-day tasks.

In this chapter, I explore the questions that get to the heart of what *you* want to achieve with your business. Do you plan to take on employees and grow your business? Do you have a unique concept that means you could potentially sell your business for a substantial profit in five or ten years' time? Or are you happy tinkering away in your home office, earning a modest income with little stress and few demands?

No answer is right, no answer is wrong. However, the process of creating a business plan provides an ideal opportunity for you to decide the direction in which you wish to head.

Deciding What Path You Want to Take

Generally, business-planning books assume that you want to grow your business, take on employees, maybe even develop a franchise or expand internationally. (After all, the very expression 'business planning' implies an intention to expand and develop.)

However, in the first part of this chapter, I want to spend a bit of time exploring whether you feel this desire for expansion. Maybe you're quite content pursuing a small home-based part-time business, or maybe you don't want the stress of taking on employees.

Taking a step back and thinking of all the businesspeople I know or have worked with, I can see that most people follow one of three paths (or occasionally all three paths, but one after the other):

>> A simple owner-operated business with no employees.

>> A business where the owner focuses on providing the service but employs others to help run administrative functions of the business.

>> A business founded by the owner that then has a life of its own, where employees deliver services or manufacture products and the owner is in a management role as a company director. Ultimately, the business expands to operate independently of its original founder.

Which path do you want to take? Even though most business books imply that if you're serious about being in business, the third path is the only way forward, this isn't necessarily true. Small owner-operated businesses may have less opportunity for profit, but profit is only one of the many motivators for being in business.

Doing the thing you love to do

Most people start a business doing the thing that they have experience doing, or possibly the thing that they've just completed studying. So the person who was working as a high-school teacher starts a business tutoring high-school students, the physiotherapist who was working at her local hospital opens her own practice, or the qualified chef opens a restaurant.

The upside of running a business in this way is that you get to do what you love to do, and usually what you're good at. You also have the perks of self-employment (choosing your own hours, possibly charging more for your services and being your own boss).

REMEMBER

The downside of being a solo owner-operator is often long hours, with no income when you're on holidays or if you're sick. The experience of being cleaner, shop assistant, bookkeeper, marketing manager and finance manager all within the course of a single day can be relentless, and you may end up feeling that you're a jack-of-all-trades but a master of none. Your business is utterly dependent on you; if you don't turn up, you don't get paid. In addition, the amount of money you can make from your business is always limited by the number of hours you're able to work.

Some people would argue that the kind of work involved with an owner-operator business, where it's just you and you do your own thing, defeats the purpose of going into business. They would argue that unless you want to conceive of a business that has a life of its own beyond yourself, you're better just to keep working for someone else. Otherwise, you're not really creating a business; rather, you're creating a job with a pile of overheads.

I disagree. Although I acknowledge that this small-scale kind of operation has its drawbacks, I've lived in a regional area and been self-employed for too long to be that naïve. Sometimes no jobs are available and the only option is to be self-employed. Sometimes you may have such substantial family commitments that your business becomes a relatively peripheral part of your life, and the income it generates is just a bonus, not the core. Sometimes the way you generate income is so personal, so idiosyncratic (maybe you're an artist, a faith healer or an inventor) that you can't conceive of a way that this business can be grown beyond yourself. All of these reasons are perfectly valid reasons for being in business, yet staying small.

So, having explored the pros and cons, what is my advice for people who are currently self-employed with no employees (or planning to start a new business with this structure)? If you have valid reasons for staying as an owner-operator, and don't want to expand, then that's okay. However, if you haven't yet spent time thinking of ways to grow your business so that it's not entirely dependent on your labor, I recommend you take the time to do so.

Conceiving a way to run your business so that it can operate without you can be challenging, but is the only way forward if you want to generate profits that aren't directly dependent on the hours that you work — which, incidentally, is what the rest of this chapter is all about.

Getting help and delegating what you can

If you're not content to be an owner-operator doing everything yourself, the first and most natural stage of expansion is usually to employ some assistance. Maybe you hire a bookkeeper, employ a casual laborer or contractor, or get assistance with marketing or website design.

Many experts and professionals end up with this kind of model. For example, our local orthodontist hires several employees (two receptionists, a dental hygienist and an office manager) but she is the only person delivering the specialist service on which the business depends. Sure, she could probably hire another orthodontist to work for her, but she has a great deal invested in her reputation and, for whatever reason, feels she can't trust another person to provide the same quality of service.

In a way, the part of my business income that I generate writing books is similar. I employ a bookkeeper and office admin person, and occasionally get help researching topics, but at the end of day (and I confess that it's truly the end of the day as I write this), the only ones left standing are me and my little silver laptop.

This way of working is what many people choose. You get to do the thing you love and you can choose your own hours, be your own boss and usually make a decent living. And, unlike single owner-operators who do everything themselves, you can hire others to help with day-to-day business operations, so that you can focus on doing the thing that you're good at.

The downside, of course, is that you're still 'it' as far as the business is concerned. You are your business, and your business is you. Your income is always limited by the number of hours you're able to work, and if you're on holiday or sick, the business doesn't generate income.

If your business has this kind of structure, you may find it hard to imagine how you can expand your business so that employees could provide the same services as you currently do. However, nobody is indispensable, and no matter how smart or talented you are, chances are someone's out there who can do all the things you do.

TIP

One of the tricks to making the leap to hiring others to provide the services you currently provide is to imagine a little person is sitting on your shoulder, watching everything you do and documenting your activities in a 'how-to' manual. This is the first step towards separating yourself from your business, so that you can describe to others the attitudes, skills and standards that you expect. (For more on this topic, see the section 'Creating systems to build a business that survives on its own', later in this chapter.)

Building a business that's separate from you

The third path that you can take (refer to the preceding sections for an outline of the other two paths) is to create a business where employees are the ones providing your service or manufacturing your products. To work in this way, you need to find a business model where the service or product sold is not reliant on your continuous input.

If you look around you, most medium-sized businesses fall into this category. For example:

>> A digital media agency employs a team of specialists to deliver their services; the two company directors who set up the agency now focus primarily on staffing and customer acquisition.

>> A music school has several tutors teaching different instruments, with studios in several locations. The founders of the school focus on branding, systems and expansion, and rarely deliver one-on-one music lessons to students.

>> A sourdough bakery that started as a home-based project during the pandemic now has outlets all around the state. These days, the two friends who started this business focus on staffing, quality control, distribution and supply chain management; neither misses the pre-dawn starts involved in baking bread themselves.

>> A supplier of customizable sleeping bags for babies, which started as a home-based business, now has offshore production, a sales distributor, and a team of administration and marketing staff.

Can you see that for each of these examples, the business owners have made a leap in how they think of their businesses? The digital media consultant is now the manager of a digital agency; the music tutors started their own music school; the baker opened a chain of bakeries; the craftsperson runs a manufacturing company. In all of these examples, the owner no longer writes copy, teaches violin, bakes bread or stitches fabric. In return, the potential for each of these businesses is that the owners can have more freedom and earn more money than they otherwise would have done.

For me, this transition from owner to entrepreneur is really exciting. Freedom from the shackles of the daily grind provides an opportunity to do the other things in life that have only been dreams up until now.

If you haven't made this transition, and your business is still dependent on you for pretty much every cent of income, my question to you is this: Have you ever consciously made the decision *not* to be entrepreneurial? Or have you never really let yourself imagine how you could do things differently?

If not, do try to give the visionary in you some room to breathe. Spend time thinking about how you can grow your business and create something that has a life of its own.

TIP

In Chapter 13, I make a distinction between budgets and Profit & Loss Projection reports, explaining that a budget sets sales goals and spending limits that you must try to stick to, whereas a Profit & Loss Projection answers the 'what if?' questions, and enables you to model different scenarios. Even if you're just starting out in business, I suggest you spend some time experimenting with what your Profit & Loss Projection might look like in a few years' time if you were to have a team of employees and possibly multiple locations or a much-increased product range.

Creating a new way of doing business

The queen diva of all business models is, of course, the franchise. A *franchise* is where you figure out such a neat and unique way of doing business that this concept itself becomes something you can sell. A franchise embodies the whole way you do business, including buying policies, logos, marketing techniques, pricing and uniforms. Table 4-1 outlines various business models, and how specific owner-operator businesses could move into the franchise or international model.

Note: I'm not talking about you purchasing a franchise here; rather, I'm talking about you building such a successful way of doing business that you create your own franchise.

TABLE 4-1   **Moving from a Small Business to a Big Business**

Owner-Operator	Business with Employees	Franchise/International Model
Yoga teacher	Yoga school	Patented method of teaching and streaming online yoga classes
Personal trainer	A gym with three employees	National franchise of fitness outlets
Online bookstore with national distribution	Online store selling books, electronics and music with international distribution	An international e-commerce business spanning multiple industries, including logistics and delivery
A farmer selling home-made chili sauce and pickles	A chili sauce company with a recognized brand and national distribution	A method of manufacturing and distributing sauces/pickles that can be replicated worldwide
A corner cafe in the local town	A couple of cafes with several employees	A franchise restaurant chain
A fashion blogger selling clothes online	An online clothing store with 50 brands and national distribution	An innovative system (including software) for selling clothes online that can be replicated in other countries
Your business	_____ (fill in the blanks)	_____ (fill in the blanks)

Creating your own franchise takes the requirement that you separate yourself from your business to a whole new level. To use the example of the digital media company I refer to in the preceding section: When the company founders delegated consulting work to employees, they entrusted others to provide the core service of the business on their behalf and, to do this, they had to provide a certain level of supervision and training.

However, how could the owners take their business to the next level, and create a franchise that could operate in other countries or other industries? At this point, the founders would need to analyze what it is that makes their business different. They would need to quantify these differences and create systems so that others can copy these differences.

The upside of expanding to become a franchise is the opportunity to make very healthy profits. In many ways, a franchise is the ultimate realization of the entrepreneur's dream.

Wearing Different Hats

Have you heard of *The E-Myth* or *The E-Myth Revisited* (written by Michael Gerber and published by HarperBusiness)? This book, while a little dated now, sold over 3 million copies, and the terminology that Gerber used to describe the roles owners play in their businesses has become almost standard in some circles.

Gerber likes to describe the roles of a business owner as being technician, manager or entrepreneur. I may not describe these roles here exactly as Gerber might, but here's the general idea:

>> **Technician:** These are people who work in their business, not on their business — the plumber who unblocks drains, the café owner who serves coffee, or the freelance consultant who goes out to meet clients.

>> **Manager:** A manager is someone who organizes the day-to-day running of a business, ordering stock, looking at profit margins, paying the bills and replying to customers.

>> **Entrepreneur:** An entrepreneur is the visionary, the person who's thinking of the business as a thing that's separate to the service it provides or the product it sells, and who is looking for ways to build the business and expand.

I really like this way of thinking of the roles in a business, because it goes a long way to explaining that feeling I've felt so often as a business owner, of having all these balls in the air that I have to juggle. The idea is that if it's just you in your business (which it is for most people when they start out), you need to balance out these roles. The idea sounds simple, but is tricky to do.

These roles correspond to some degree with what I talk about earlier in this chapter. Someone who is happiest being a 'technician' often ends up not expanding their business, and instead typically provides services or makes products themselves (refer to 'Doing the thing you love to do' earlier in this chapter). A person whose 'manager' side wins out typically ends up organizing others. This person is content to get employees to assist in running the business and is good at monitoring costs and ensuring efficient operations (refer to 'Getting help and delegating what you can'). The 'entrepreneur' personality is the one who's always looking for the winning idea, and is keenest to create a business with a life of its own (refer to 'Building a business that's separate from you' or 'Creating a new way of doing business').

WARNING

If your business is still pretty small, letting any one of the three roles of technician, manager or entrepreneur dominate at the expense of the others can be a problem. The technician will probably fail to grow the business, the manager may well fail to look to the future and plan for change, and the entrepreneur, if left to their own devices, may burn through a whole load of money very fast pursuing one idea after another.

What I think is so clever about the way Gerber identifies these roles is that you can apply this thinking to yourself and your own business. For example:

>> Most people find that the technician role (doing the thing that they're good at, such as fixing pipes, teaching music or making a mean espresso coffee) feels comfortable and safe.

>> The role of manager fits well with some people but not with others. (Many businesspeople hate having to think about money, tax, legals, schedules and so on, but others are relatively okay with this role.)

>> The role of entrepreneur is the role that comes hardest to most people. If you're inherently a bit conservative (as I confess to being myself), whenever the entrepreneur voice pipes up with a good idea, your inner conservative manager voice likely calls out, 'Oh no, that's way too scary'. The entrepreneur and manager are so busy tussling away that the only person left to do anything is the technician, who continues to get on with the job. And then nothing changes.

The way to move on from this situation, and give all three roles a part to play, is to build a business that has a life of its own — which just happens to be the next topic in this chapter . . .

Building a Business with a Life of its Own

In the preceding sections in this chapter, I talk about why creating a business with a life of its own is generally the best way to gain more freedom and flexibility, and hopefully more profits to boot. I also talk about the different roles or 'hats' people typically wear in business, and how important it is to balance these roles, especially when you're just getting started and you have only you in the business.

However, the transition to creating a business with its own identity, separate from you, isn't always easy. In the following sections, I provide some guidelines as to how you may be able to make this happen.

Defining your difference

The first step in giving your business some of its own life force is to be clear about what it is that makes you different. I spend a heap of time deliberating on this very topic back in Chapter 2, so I won't repeat myself here. Suffice to say that you must identify what makes your business different, and this difference must relate to the identity of your business, and not you personally.

Some examples may help to set this in context:

>> A solar panel installer provides energy audits and a carbon footprint calculator as part of their service.

>> An online clothes store offers multiple views and videos of each item of clothing, and provides recommendations as to the body types each garment is best suited for.

>> A car repair shop offers a free home drop-off and pick-up service, and routinely details all vehicles as part of any service or repair work.

None of the preceding ideas is particularly revolutionary but, if executed well and combined with a cohesive marketing strategy and company commitment, they have the potential to make these businesses stand apart from others.

I find that business owners can be very vague regarding what it is that makes their business successful, especially with smaller businesses where the owner is still very much hands-on. To use the car repair shop example from the preceding list, this auto mechanic may offer free home drop-offs and detailing, but is this really the reason for the success of this business? Or is it that the head mechanic is such a lovely guy that customers instantly warm to him? Or that this is the only auto repair service within a 30-minute radius?

Without an understanding of what makes this business successful, the owner is vulnerable. If the drawcard is the head mechanic, what might happen to the business if he leaves? If the lack of competition in a 30-minute radius is the reason for steady business, what might happen if another auto mechanic opens up shop nearby?

You can try to deduce the reasons for your success using a few techniques:

>> If your business operates in more than one location, experiment by trialing specific services or marketing techniques in one location but not the other, and see what happens.

>> Return to the competitive analysis you did in Chapter 3 (or if you haven't already done it, do it now). This objective comparative process is a good way to get a sense of why your customers come to you.

>> Ask your customers why they love you! You can ask customers face to face, run surveys, put up quick questions on social media, or do whatever fits your customer base best.

>> Try opening a new location and trying to replicate your success from the first location. If the new location performs differently, try to get to the bottom of why.

>> If you think that part of your success is due to something relatively simple (I think of my local butcher who, after each interaction, looks at me with a smile and says, 'Can I get you anything else today?' — even if a queue of people is waiting behind me), then try measuring sales when you employ this technique or strategy for a week, and compare sales to another week where you don't do this.

TIP

If you can figure out why you're successful, and measure how much difference this strategy, product or technique makes to your business, you're well on the way to being able to replicate your success and grow your business.

Creating systems to build a business that survives on its own

One of the things that a franchise offers, in contrast to other businesses of a similar type, is consistency. As a friend of mine likes to say in a satisfied voice regarding the coffee he buys from a certain fast-food chain, 'This bunch make the best worst coffee in the world'. In other words, he knows the coffee is going to be average, he knows it won't be that hot, but still it hits the spot and it's the same every time, wherever he is in the country.

This consistency is one of the secrets to expanding a business beyond one location, building a recognizable brand, or even preparing your business to become a franchise in its own right. Take the example of my aunt, who ran a guesthouse in the wilds of northern Scotland for 30 years or more. She was a wonderful hostess, but occasionally she'd be away for the weekend or even for a week or two. How could she guarantee that her guests would get exactly the same quality of experience when she was away as when she was there?

REMEMBER

A happy customer may share the love with one or two people, but unhappy customers share their disgruntlement with ten. If you can get rid of the hit-and-miss element that plagues so many businesses, positive word-of-mouth recommendations may be almost all the marketing you need.

So how do you guarantee consistency, particularly as your business grows and you're not around to serve each customer or supervise each employee? The answer lies in procedures and documentation. First, you figure out what it is that your business does well (which I cover in the preceding section); next, you articulate this difference in a way that employees can follow.

Here are some examples of how to provide a consistent experience for customers:

>> **Automations:** For any customer interactions that happen regularly (such as a customer signing up to a newsletter, purchasing a product or making an enquiry), implement automations in your CRM (customer relationship management) software. Automations are simple sequences of emails or text messages that help you to provide a swift response, ensure quality customer service and secure customer engagement.

>> **Checklists:** For any complex activities, where employees need to fulfil several tasks in a specific sequence, create a checklist. For example, if your business is such that a customer order can be quite complex (maybe you need to check aspects such as quantities, availability, delivery dates and payment methods), a checklist ensures nothing gets forgotten.

>> **Complaints procedures:** Do you know that one of the ways to make customers happiest is to do everything you can to fix something when they complain? However, the gentle art of responding well to a grumpy customer isn't something that comes naturally to most people, and so procedures for dealing with complaints are essential.

>> **Customer service procedures and processes:** Ideally, you need a procedure for any customer interaction that happens on a regular basis, whether this is a customer enquiry, order or sale.

>> **Manufacturing procedures:** If you're a manufacturer, even if you're operating on a relatively small scale making things to sell locally or at markets, the quality of your product needs to be the same each time. Sounds simple, but imagine you're making homemade jams, and the quality of produce available varies according to the time of year. In this scenario, you may need to limit production to certain times of year in order to guarantee consistency.

Similarly, if you've been manufacturing products yourself and you're now ready to delegate this process, you need to document exactly what you do, using precise quantities, times, production methods and so on.

>> **Phone scripts and email templates:** I can feel you wincing a little here, as you wonder if you're really so dictatorial that you can bear writing out scripts for employees to follow when they answer the phone, or templates for when they reply to emails. Remember two things, however: First, what you're trying to achieve is consistency for the customer; second, if you have spent time figuring out the ingredients that have made your business successful and you know that how you answer the phone or reply to emails is part of this success, then, of course, you want to be able to repeat this formula, time and time again.

>> **Presentation:** As someone who hates uniform in almost any shape or form, I squirm a little as I write this. But businesses love uniforms for the reason that they provide consistency for the customer and reinforce the company's

image. Even something as simple as a polo shirt with your company logo monogrammed on the front can make a difference to how customers perceive you.

>> **Rates and pricing:** Standardized rates and pricing are a must. So if you tend to quote on a somewhat intuitive basis for jobs, you need to spend time figuring out a method for pricing and stick to that instead.

TIP

If you're still small and you're thinking about how to expand your business, one great source of inspiration (if available) is to look at franchises that offer a similar service or product to your own. For example, if you're starting a lawnmowing business, take a look at how the lawnmowing franchises approach their branding, marketing and customer service. If you're starting a bookkeeping business, look at the bookkeeping franchises and how they organize their pricing and services. I'm not suggesting you steal intellectual property here or that you try to copy the systems of a franchise without paying to belong — more that you take a look at the general approach of this franchise and use this as inspiration. (Or, of course, you may even consider becoming a franchisee.)

Setting goals for you and your business

In my work as a business consultant, I've noticed a certain quality in the successful businesspeople I encounter. Each of these people has had a very specific goal in mind, and they've been possessed by an inner drive to meet this goal.

Interestingly enough, these goals have been ultimately personal, rather than business-orientated, such as the desire to be able to retire by the age of 50 on a guaranteed income for life, or the dream to be able to buy a house for each one of the children, or to be able to work only 20 hours a week and still be financially secure.

If you're trying to create a business that grows and is ultimately independent of you, ask yourself what you want to achieve from this growth. Do you have a specific financial goal or a certain time frame? If not, spend some time thinking what this goal might be, and then building your business plan around this goal.

WARNING

While setting goals is an important part of business success, just wanting to be a millionaire isn't enough. You need to ensure that your business has some kind of competitive edge or winning strategy (refer to Chapters 2 and 3 for more on this topic) and then build on this strategy with good systems. Unless you have these elements in place, ambitious plans to open a new shop every six months or become an internationally recognized brand are just pie in the sky.

Planning for a graceful exit

One of the best ways to get yourself into the mindset of thinking of your business as independent from you is to imagine selling it.

Always try to have an exit plan simmering away, even if you don't plan to sell any time in the immediate future. Ask yourself the following questions: If I were to sell this business today, what could I get for it? Can this business run independently of me? What assets or business systems do I have to sell? How can I maximize the price I can get for this business?

Appreciating the Limitations of Your Business

In the preceding sections in this chapter, I talk about the idea of creating a business that has a life of its own, separate from you. I also mention early in this chapter that not everyone wants to go down this path, and I talk about the pros and cons of operating your business in different ways.

When thinking on these topics, you also have to keep in mind that some businesses are much harder than others to expand. Here are some of the kinds of businesses that can be hard to grow, along with why:

>> **Businesses limited by physical constraints or high start-up costs that require substantial capital:** Farmers are an obvious example here, limited by the amount of land they have, and lacking capital to expand. Other examples could be a professional truck driver limited by the high capital cost of additional trucks, or the capacity of a guesthouse owner to expand due to the high cost of purchasing real estate.

>> **Businesses based on the artistic skills of the owner:** Examples include a classical pianist performing around the country, a stand-up comedian or a theatre producer. Sure, you could team up with other artists in a similar field, but the actual core of what you do (such as playing virtuosic piano) is almost impossible to delegate.

>> **Businesses making products that require very specific skills, particularly those of an artistic nature:** For example, glass blowing, fine-art painting and pottery. Custom manufacturing of one-off goods also falls into this category, where the craftsperson (such as a cabinetmaker) builds a reputation that is very much linked to that person as an individual, rather than to the business.

>> **Businesses with expert services where the service provided is very much associated with the individual providing the service:** Think specialist medical professionals (acupuncturist, pediatrician, orthodontist) or specialist consultants (business mentors, human resources consultants).

>> **Businesses servicing a rural location where the owner provides the services and expansion involves too much travel:** Our local horse dentist (yes, such a thing as a horse dentist exists!) springs to mind.

If you have more of an entrepreneurial personality, you may be reading the preceding list thinking I'm lacking imagination, and that the businesses in the list could be expanded in plenty of ways. The artist could commercialize her images as cushions, postcards or wallpaper; the cabinetmaker could spend oodles on high-end marketing and build up an international reputation; the horse dentist could set up an online consultancy. In my defense, I'm not saying that these businesses are impossible to grow — I'm just saying they're harder to grow than others. (And, besides, the artist may not want to design wallpaper, and online horse dentistry may prove massively impractical.)

TIP

If your business falls into one of the categories outlined in the preceding list and you're having problems imagining how you separate yourself from your business, hop online and search worldwide for the product you sell or the service you provide. Look for examples of others similar to you and how they have grown their business to be something bigger.

REMEMBER

Although businesses with expert services can be hard to expand, for those who manage to do so and build a network of professionals who provide a high consistency of service, the rewards can be substantial.

Planning for People

If you're creating a written business plan (and given the title of this book I guess you likely are) and have read the earlier sections in this chapter, you may be wondering how this chapter relates to what you include in your plan.

In truth, what I've written in this chapter up until this point is more about creating a mindset for your business, setting goals for what you want to achieve, and planning for how you will employ others to help you realize these goals. In terms of your plan, the main information you need to include is how you plan to structure your business, who you have (or plan to have) on your team, the skills that your team has, and who is going to do what.

Building an inclusive and innovative team

What kind of team do you want to create? As your business grows, your employees will likely become a kind of second family to you and (unlike the family you were born with) this time you have a strong say in how this family operates in the world. Hiring any new employee provides an ideal opportunity to reflect on your core values, and how you intend to permeate your team with these values. How can you create a positive workplace from the very beginning?

Open communication, celebrating successes, collaboration, workplace diversity, positive leadership and a clear vision are all vital ingredients of a positive workplace. I don't have enough scope in this book to explore creating a positive workplace in detail, but what I can say is that if you don't have experience being a manager and creating excellent teams, you probably want to seek some mentoring in this area as your business grows.

Figuring what others can do

Even if you don't have any employees yet, take some time to think about the skills involved in running your business and the different roles involved. Reflect on your areas of weakness, and where it may be best to seek help (this help may be from a casual employee, a part-timer, a consultant or an outside professional).

Key roles integral to most businesses include:

>> **Accountancy, taxation and legals:** If you don't already have a trusted accountant and a lawyer, I recommend you start looking.

>> **Bookkeeping:** When you first start in business, you can probably get away without hiring a bookkeeper, especially if you use accounting software to automate data entry. However, hiring a bookkeeper on a contract or casual basis makes sense once your business starts to grow.

>> **Human resources:** A dedicated employee for managing human resources (HR) is a luxury most small businesses can't afford, yet managing people, pay and workplace culture is critical. An HR consultant who is available on a contract basis can be a great investment.

>> **Marketing and social media:** Unless marketing forms the guts of your business (perhaps you're a copywriter, influencer or digital media consultant), then getting help with this role is a must. Whether this role is best as a casual, part-time or contract position depends on your business.

>> **Office administration:** Delegating day-to-day office tasks such as phone calls, billing, customer enquiries or order processing is an easy thing to delegate if it works for your business.

In terms of your business plan, I suggest that you include a descriptive section about the people involved in the business and who's responsible for doing what. For each key person, write a short description of that person's role, including relevant work experience and qualifications.

REMEMBER

If your plan is going to be read by outsiders (that is, the plan isn't just for your own use) don't hesitate to blow your own trumpet (or your employees' trumpets for that matter) to emphasize the skills and qualifications that you have.

TIP

The ability to seek out the best possible people and 'glue' them on to a business is a common attribute I've observed in successful businesspeople. Don't worry if you can't hire someone as an employee; a day a week or a day a month consulting may be all that you require. For example, if you need help with your bookkeeping, going hunting for a bookkeeper with excellent qualifications and a great reputation is infinitely better than employing your sister's daughter or your best friend's aunty (unless that person also comes with excellent qualifications and a great reputation, of course).

Deciding whether to make someone an employee, or not

One of the practical considerations when getting help is whether to use contractors or professionals, casual employees or permanent employees. Here are some things to bear in mind:

>> **Cheaper rates:** An employee is generally cheaper on an hourly basis than a contractor. However, when comparing rates, ensure that you include all relevant employee on-costs (see the following section to find out more).

>> **Flexibility during quiet times:** If your business is seasonal or experiences highs and lows in demand, permanent employees can prove expensive because you have to pay them all year round, regardless of requirements. In this scenario, casual employees or contractors are a better bet.

>> **Reliability and commitment:** If you find someone who has just the skills you're looking for and you feel that this person would be a real asset for your business, locking this person in by offering a permanent job, if you can afford to do so, is going to be preferable to hiring this person as a contractor.

TIP

>> **Securing skills for your business:** If your business requires very specific skills and these skills are in high demand, putting a skilled person on the payroll (rather than hiring a contractor) means that this person cannot also work for your competition.

Calculating the costs of labor

Employee wages are likely to make up a large percentage of your ongoing expenses. Yet one thing that I've found, from years of working with clients, is that most business owners don't take the time to calculate the true cost of labor expenses.

Some of the direct costs (depending on where you are in the world) include health insurance, workers accident insurance and superannuation or retirement/pension payments.

Indirect costs include things such as uniforms or providing tools, computers, mobile phones and vehicles. Other hidden costs for part-time or full-time employees include holiday leave, sick/personal leave and public holidays.

To do your own calculations, ChatGPT or a similar AI interface can be useful. Ask a question such as, 'How do I convert an hourly rate for a permanent employee into an equivalent rate for a contractor?' followed by the country in which you live and the industry in which you operate.

WARNING

An important part of the business planning process is for you to be right across the minimum pay and the statutory obligations of being an employer. See Chapter 14 for more about managing risk and complying with regulations.

WARNING

KEEP HOLD OF THOSE REINS

One of the things that you may experience when you hire your first employee is a feeling of relief so strong that you declare, 'Here you are. I trust you. Please feel free to organize me, my business and my life.'

Don't kid yourself that this letting go is you being a hands-off manager or a good delegator. Handing over the reins to someone else in this way is bound to end in tears: If an employee takes over and does everything well, you'll be left with a huge hole when that employee leaves (with no documented systems in place) and your business will suffer; if the employee fails to perform, you've just given that employee the chance to do a great deal of damage.

Instead, your responsibility is to delegate, but delegate using clear instructions and good systems. (I talk about creating systems in 'Building a Business with a Life of its Own', earlier in this chapter.) You never want an employee to become indispensable because, at that point, you have built a business that may not be dependent on you, but sure as anything is dependent on someone else.

Chapter **5**

Exploiting Opportunities and Avoiding Threats

I n this chapter, I talk about preparing your business for change. I reflect on all kinds of change — everything from new competitors to the latest influx of government regulation, and from the impact of a booming economy to the demands of new technology.

I also talk about how change can take the form of both opportunities and threats, and how important it is that you evaluate your own strengths and weaknesses in light of these. Are you in a position to capitalize on opportunities, or to shield yourself against threats?

If you're just getting started in business, this might be the chapter in the book where you find it hardest to sustain interest. After all, if you're planning something relatively small (maybe beautician services, bookkeeping, jam-making or landscape gardening), it may feel irrelevant to be thinking about the rise and fall of the economy or the impact of changing technology.

However, almost every industry around the world is currently experiencing change, and the pace of this change is only increasing. Look at the way the retail industry has transformed in the face of online distribution, or how artificial intelligence is transforming education.

Even a simple business such as bookkeeping could be affected by new government regulations, and a small owner-operator such as a landscape gardener could be impacted by climate change. Anticipating change so you don't miss out on new opportunities is vital for business success, in the same way as safeguarding yourself against threats or industry decline is essential for survival.

Two frameworks for organizing these insights are a PESTEL analysis and a SWOT analysis, and most investors or bank lenders would expect to see at least one out of these two frameworks in your business plan.

Taking an Eagle-Eye View

To be strategic in business, you need an understanding of how the industry in which you're operating is faring, and what outside factors may affect this industry in the near future.

Imagine you were the owner of a video and DVD rental business 20 years or so ago when this industry was thriving. Maybe your business was very profitable (you had great taste in movies, your shop was in a central location and you had no competitors). Despite all these advantages, you would have ceased trading long ago. Why? Because the movie-rental industry transformed, replaced by streaming services and other forms of online entertainment.

Looking at what's happening in your industry

If you've been working in an industry for a while already, you probably have a feeling for general industry trends on an intuitive level. However, I recommend you take time to think more analytically about all outside factors that influence your business, such as the economy, the demographics of your target market, and the average profitability and trends of your industry.

This analysis is known as a *PESTEL analysis*, standing for political, economic, social, technological, environmental and legal. The primary purpose of analyzing the overall environment in this way is to identify the drivers of change affecting future industry growth.

Here's what you should focus on:

>> **Political:** What political forces could affect your industry? For example, think about how solar rebate policies have affected solar panel retailers, or how federal legislation has affected financial planning businesses.

>> **Economic:** How do recessions, interest rates and exchange rates affect this industry? Exporters and importers, for example, are particularly vulnerable to exchange rate fluctuations.

>> **Social:** Consider the interaction between the industry and demographic trends. For example, businesses in the aged care industry are benefiting from the aging population.

>> **Technological:** How is this industry affected by technological change? Think of how online portals have created enormous challenges for many kinds of retailers, including bookshops, music stores and travel agencies.

>> **Environmental:** Increasing environmental awareness may present opportunities for an industry — for example, organic foods — or challenges — for example, chemical garden fertilizers.

>> **Legal:** Increasing government regulations can often serve to polarize an industry, especially if compliance is very expensive, making an industry more profitable for the larger players but tougher for the small fry.

Table 5-1 provides a very summarized analysis for three different kinds of business, and the many forces which can shape future success.

TIP

As part of researching these outside influences, I recommend you hunt for 'state of the industry' reports wherever possible, and also interrogate ChatGPT or a similar AI app for information.

Responding to industry trends

The idea behind doing an industry analysis is to get a sense of what's happening overall in your industry. Of course, an industry that's in decline is going to be a whole load tougher (if not impossible) to succeed in than an industry that's growing very fast.

TABLE 5-1   **Industry Analysis Example**

	Craft beer brewery	Fashion retailer (shop front)	Solar panel installations
Political	Increasing government taxes impact price, lowering demands from customers affected by cost-of-living increases.	Changing textile tariffs impact cost of imported products. Government regulations also affect labor costs.	Government subsidies and R&D tax concessions continue to offer a major boost to the industry.
Economic	Fierce competition is making the product more price-sensitive, especially for microbrewers distributing state- or nationwide.	The average price per item of clothing sold has declined by 10% in the last two years due to competitive pressures. This trend is probably unsustainable.	The cost of solar panels has declined by 22% due to improved technology but the cost of labor has increased by 15%.
Social	Contemporary brews are popular with a younger demographic keen to be seen as discerning.	Bricks-and-mortar retailers, depending on location, can respond to a social need that online retailers don't meet.	Many customers driven to purchase solar because of personal values.
Technological	With AI, the customization of alcohol content, flavor, color, aroma, and product development is much more viable and faster.	Virtual try-on technology is likely to improve the shopping experience for online customers and further increase pressure on bricks-and-mortar retailers.	Any technological progress that makes solar panels more affordable or efficient will translate to significant growth.
Environmental	Water and energy consumption are all high, likely leading to increased costs as environmental impacts are increasingly accounted for.	The fast-fashion industry is responsible for approximately 10% of global carbon emissions and 20% of waste water. Only 15% is recycled or donated. Customers may start moving away from these sorts of items.	Solar panels are vital to meeting greenhouse gas emission targets. Concerns still exist regarding disposal/recycling of solar batteries, particularly long-term.
Legal	Value of intellectual property jeopardized by AI replacing the skilled development process.	Increased trends for customers to be litigious, although the risks in this industry are very low.	Working at heights and with electricity carries significant health and safety risks for installers.
Overall trends	Overall trends for the industry are negative, with increased competition, cost-of-living pressures, increased taxes and increased costs creating the perfect storm.	According to IBISWorld analysis, the clothing retail industry is in decline, with an average decline of 0.9% per year over the last 5 years.	Rising costs in non-renewable energy sources will result in lower demand overall for power, but demand for solar energy is likely to continue to grow at current rates.

HA, HA. YOU CAN'T CATCH ME!

One of the points you may want to consider as part of your industry analysis is *barriers to entry*. Barriers to entry are very high setup costs that make it hard for other competitors to enter the fray.

Obvious examples are new airlines, car manufacturers or supermarket chains. (Although I guess it's unlikely that anyone reading this book would really be planning to start a new airline.) At a more everyday level, barriers to entry can be expensive tools or specialist equipment, many years of study, big infrastructure costs such as software systems or warehousing, complex distribution networks or expensive real estate.

If you plan to start a new business within an industry where significant barriers to entry exist, you may find growth is impossible because you don't have enough capital to invest. If this is the case, you need to be open to the idea of changing your business model.

On the other hand, changes in technology have caused entry barriers in many industries to crumble, opening up a gamut of opportunities. For example, owners of small businesses who formerly couldn't compete because they didn't have enough capital to fit out an expensive retail outlet can now sell direct to the consumer using online channels; authors who couldn't secure distribution without going through a publisher can now self-publish their own ebooks; animation studios using AI require significantly less labor to create competitive products.

If you are a small player, see if you can identify any new technologies that present opportunities in markets where, up until now, the big players have dominated the field. Not only are barriers to entry crumbling at an ever-increasing pace, but large companies can also be slow to change.

I mention the decline of video and DVD rental stores earlier in this chapter and, when doing so, I was thinking of the video store that used to be in my village. The business was a solid one, and the store (as one of the only places open after 6 pm) was always social and lively. When this business first started to decline, I remember thinking to myself that the owners should have downsized and halved the rent, or explored a niche market in foreign films, or perhaps developed an online presence. Pish tosh. For this particular business, there was no hope. The best thing they could have done (which for whatever reason they didn't) is close their business while they were still ahead.

WARNING

If your industry is in severe decline, your best bet is probably to try to sell your business now, close your business if it's already unprofitable or, if you're still at the planning stage, walk away from the idea of starting a new business. Closing a business can be particularly scary, because you may have significant funds invested that you'll never recoup. However, if you're already trading at a loss, selling your business in the context of a declining industry may be impossible. The longer you trade unprofitably, the more you stand to lose financially.

Aside from an industry in decline, what about other scenarios such as enormous industry growth? Generally, industry growth is a great thing for anyone involved, and if you're in the right place at the right time, you can make handsome profits. The flipside is that any industry experiencing rapid change carries higher risks because the direction of change and new technology can be hard to predict.

Part of the secret to mitigating this risk lies in matching the internal strengths of your business against the potential opportunities of the industry. And guess what? That's what the next section of this chapter is all about . . .

Rating Your Capabilities

I'm sure you don't have to pause for very long to think of someone who always seems to seek challenges in their life. Maybe you have a friend who's dyslexic but has chosen to be a linguist as a career, or you know someone in a wheelchair who loves to travel the world.

Chasing one's dreams and persisting in the face of adversity is often deeply rewarding. However, in the world of business, you will find that it usually pays to be more strategic about where you channel your energies. What you want to do is identify possible business opportunities and see if you can match these opportunities against your natural skills and abilities.

Putting yourself through the griller

As part of objectively assessing your strengths and weaknesses, it's good to think about business skills, and assess both your own capabilities against each of these skills, as well as the importance of this skill to your business. Table 5-2 provides a simple checklist against which you can rate yourself and business importance on a scale of 1 to 5, with 5 being the highest rating.

TABLE 5-2   **Rating Your Capabilities**

Business Skill	How You Rate Yourself (1 to 5)	Importance to Your Business (1 to 5)
Ability to learn new skills and adapt quickly		
Bookkeeping and financial systems		
Branding, packaging and presentation		
Budgeting, cost analysis and reporting		
Business strategy		
Cashflow management		
Company management and compliance		
Customer service culture		
IT and business systems		
Legal systems and protection		
Marketing and promotions		
Product design and development		
Professional expertise specific to your industry		
Sales and customer relations		
Social media and marketing		
Staff management		

REMEMBER

When you complete the ratings in Table 5-2, respond from the perspective of your business, rather than from you as an individual. Think of the collective skills that you, your employees, any family members, business mentors or outside consultants bring to the party. Also, keep your competition in mind when you rate your business on things such as customer service or marketing. (For example, you may be aware of areas where you can improve your customer service but if you know that you beat all of your competition hands down, you can probably award yourself a pretty strong rating.)

WARNING

When rating how important each function is for your business, I suggest you rate all aspects of financial management as 4 or 5 (the highest rating). Even if your business chugs along just fine, poor financial management is almost always a limiter to business success and growth.

Prioritizing where you need to do better

If I'm a psychologist running a counselling business, chances are that cold calling or IT skills aren't going to be key to business success. On the other hand, if I'm selling a new product that few people have ever heard of, business strategy, branding and product design become essential.

WARNING

Returning to Table 5-2, see if you can spot any business skills where you've rated yourself poorly, but where you've assessed the importance of this skill to your business as being high. These are areas of weaknesses in your business to which you need to pay attention, either by upskilling yourself or by employing staff, contractors or advisers who can help fill the gap.

Identifying Opportunities and Threats

Industry trends aren't the only things that can greatly affect your business but over which you have little control. What about changes in the economy, or the arrival of new competitors on the scene? For you to stay one step ahead, the name of the game is to try to anticipate the impact these outside factors may have on your business.

TIP

For each of the following categories, ask yourself what opportunities and what threats lie in store. Remember that any change can be an opportunity or a threat (or even both) depending on where you stand in the scheme of things. Organize these opportunities and threats in two columns, similar to Table 5-3. (Although bear in mind that Table 5-3 is a somewhat simplified example — your list will almost certainly have a bit more detail.)

Consider the following:

>> **New competition:** How likely is it that new competitors could affect your business? Do you have special skills or a strategic advantage that safeguards you from competition? (I talk more about strategic advantage in Chapter 2.) Or is the thing that makes your business so successful easy to copy? What if the competitor has more capital, a better location or superior marketing abilities?

>> **Emerging technologies:** How is technological change affecting your industry? Could new technology end up putting you out of business? Or are you skilled in the direction that new technology is heading, and could this be an opportunity?

>> **Changes in demographics:** Demographic change is a long-term thing, but so (hopefully) is your business. If your business serves a local population (as opposed to having national distribution or being online), it pays to watch the trends in population patterns for your area.

>> **Changes in government regulations:** If your business is dependent in some way on government regulations (maybe you're a taxi driver, you work in health, or your business relies heavily on government policy in some form or other), you're particularly vulnerable to changes in the political landscape. Ask yourself what impact changing regulations or changes in government could have on your business, and how you could respond.

>> **Changes in the economy:** Is your business very dependent on the ebb and flow of the economy? Some businesses (for example, those selling staple food products) are relatively stable regardless of what's happening in the economy; other businesses (such as those selling high-end luxury goods) tend to move in tandem with the economy.

TABLE 5-3   ## Summarizing Opportunities and Threats

Opportunities	Threats
Analysis for Elgin Craft Brewery	
New tourist trail being developed by local municipality — potential to join this	Growth in number of competitors
Use of AI for swift product development	Rising costs of supplies, energy, taxes and interest rates
Demand from customers seeking something different from mainstream suppliers	Takeovers of small breweries by large conglomerates, thereby devaluing the craft beer experience
Opportunity to create short-term brands and product offerings responsive to trends and events	Cost of finance increasing
Analysis for solar panel installation company	
Customers more discerning about types of panels and nature of installation	Some serious new competitors with major muscle
Government subsidies in certain regional locations for installs	Exclusive distribution license ends in two years
Demand for batteries as well as panels is growing rapidly	Rapid growth requires high borrowings and puts pressure on cashflow
	If new government elected, all subsidies could finish

AN OPPORTUNITY OR A THREAT?

One overriding long-term global trend that's unlikely to change any time soon is the demand for ecological products and services. Couple this with global zero emission targets, and you end up with a perfect example of something that is both a business opportunity and a business threat.

For those in the 'green' industry (ecological products, renewable energy, environmental consulting and so on) this long-term trend presents an opportunity. For those in industries with high energy demands, particularly those dependent on fossil fuels, this trend is a threat.

When you're thinking about opportunities and threats for your business, also refer to the industry analysis process outlined earlier in this chapter (refer to 'Taking an Eagle-Eye View'). However, keep in mind that opportunities and threats in this context have a different scope than just one particular industry. For example, a global recession or a change in government isn't industry-specific. Or at the other end of the scale, the arrival of a new competitor may be a reflection of a growing population in one geographic region rather than an indication of general industry trends.

TIP

Keep your mind open to the fact that some things don't fit neatly into boxes as an opportunity or as a threat. Be willing to get creative. Although your analysis of threats and opportunities usually reflects your current position, stay open to new possibilities.

Doing a SWOT Analysis

If you've read any other business books or worked in larger organizations, you've probably already heard of a SWOT analysis (**S**trengths, **W**eaknesses, **O**pportunities and **T**hreats). As a model, the SWOT analysis sticks around while other business concepts come and go, simply because this way of looking at things is both easy to understand and surprisingly powerful.

Putting theory into practice

The idea of a SWOT analysis is simple:

>> Aim to build on your strengths but minimize your weaknesses.

>> Endeavor to seize opportunities and counteract threats.

Are you ready to try your own SWOT analysis? Then here goes:

1. **Make a list of the strengths and weaknesses of your business.**

   By strengths and weaknesses, I'm talking about the things that you and your staff are good at (or not-so-good at). I explain how to assess your strengths and weaknesses earlier in this chapter in 'Putting yourself through the griller'.

   When you think about strengths and weaknesses, this is an internal examination just of you and your business.

REMEMBER

2. **Make a list of possible opportunities and threats.**

   Identifying opportunities and threats is an external analysis that looks outwards beyond your business, to consider your industry, the economy, the environment and other factors. Refer to 'Looking at what's happening in your industry' and 'Identifying Opportunities and Threats' to find out how to make this list.

3. **Draw a grid similar to Figure 5-1.**

4. **Divide your strengths into two categories: Strengths that can help you take advantage of opportunities, and strengths that can help you deal with threats.**

5. **Write down these strengths in the first row of your SWOT grid, along with the related opportunities or threats.**

   Strengths that help realize opportunities go in the top-left of the grid; strengths that could help counteract threats go in the top-right.

6. **In the same manner, divide your weaknesses into two categories: weakness that may hinder you taking advantage of opportunities, and weaknesses that may make threats even more of a threat.**

7. **Write down these weaknesses, as well as the threats, in the second row of your SWOT grid.**

   Weaknesses that hinder opportunities go in the bottom-left of the grid; weaknesses that exacerbate threats go in the bottom-right.

Business SWOT Analysis		
	OPPORTUNITIES	**THREATS**
STRENGTHS	*Write strengths that assist with opportunities here, along with a description of the opportunity*	*Write strengths that help counteract threats here, along with a description of the threat*
WEAKNESSES	*Write weaknesses that may hinder you from exploiting opportunities here, along with a description of the opportunity*	*Write weaknesses that may compound threats here, along with a description of the threat*

FIGURE 5-1:
The principles of a SWOT analysis.

Translating your SWOT analysis into action

After you've completed your SWOT analysis (refer to preceding section), what next? Put simply, this grid encapsulates four different business strategies:

>> Aim to exploit any areas where your business is strong and is a good fit for an opportunity.

>> Keep a watchful eye on any areas where your business is strong, but a threat may be looming.

>> Try to improve on any areas where your business is weak but opportunities exist. (For example, you could consider getting extra training, hiring employees with different skills, or employing consultants.)

>> Take pre-emptive action and attempt to get rid of any areas in which your business is weak and a threat is looming.

Figure 5-2 shows a SWOT grid in action, matching strengths and weaknesses of the craft brewing company used as an example earlier in this chapter with the identified opportunities and threats.

>> **Top-left corner (where a strength meets an opportunity):** Strong marketing skills are a good fit for growth in customer demand; the company can quickly leverage new brands. The business should aim to exploit these strengths.

>> **Top-right corner (where a strength meets a threat):** Strong marketing skills also serve to mitigate the threat of rapidly increasing competition. The business needs to keep a watchful eye on both its marketing strategy and new competitors.

>> **Bottom-left corner (where a weakness meets an opportunity):** A significant weakness is technological expertise, with a reliance on old methods of brewing rather than use of technology and AI to develop new flavors. The business should aim to develop skills swiftly, possibly by hiring employees with these skills.

>> **Bottom-right corner (where a weakness meets a threat):** The weaknesses in financial management may create problems in the face of rising costs and increased interest rates. This combination of weakness and threat create an unhappy synergy, indicating an area in which the business needs to take action.

Business SWOT Analysis		
	OPPORTUNITIES	**THREATS**
STRENGTHS	*Strong marketing skills are a good fit for growth in customer demand; company can quickly leverage new brands*	*Strong marketing skills will assist in meeting the challenges of many new competitors*
WEAKNESSES	*Weakness in technological expertise, with a reliance on old methods of brewing rather than use of technology and AI to develop new flavors*	*Weaknesses in financial management skills indicates vulnerability in the face of rising costs and increased interest rates*

FIGURE 5-2:
Plotting business strategy using a SWOT analysis.

Creating a Plan for Change

In some ways, creating a business plan can be very 'bitty'. You have missions and visions and financials and marketing plans, then industry analysis and more. Each area feels like a separate topic in its own right, and may even require that you use a different mindset or different skills as you address each one. However, as you delve deeper and deeper into the process, you hopefully find that everything starts connecting.

At the beginning of this book, in Chapters 2 and 3, I talk about identifying your strategic advantage and analyzing how your business compares to the competition. In many ways, the industry analysis and SWOT analysis in this chapter follow a similar process, but provide another layer of clarity regarding what areas in your business to exploit, as well as the weaknesses to guard against.

In your business plan, try to include the following:

>> The issues or problems you face

>> The opportunities that lie ahead

>> A plan of action that outlines how you intend to mitigate your problems and exploit these opportunities

When drawing up a plan of action, try to express this plan in clear goals that are very specific and which have a timeframe. For example, 'A weakness in our business is our financial management skills. We intend to hire an external accountant as a business advisor who we will meet with monthly'. Or another example: 'A clear weakness in my business is my poor marketing skills. As well as doing a small business course in the coming months, I intend to employ a contractor to manage my social media and PR campaigns'.

REMEMBER

Are you a person who sees the glass half-full or half-empty? Sure, threats may be on the horizon, but do opportunities lie within these threats? As Winston Churchill is widely (although incorrectly) attributed to have said, 'A pessimist sees the difficulty in every opportunity; an optimist sees the opportunity in every difficulty'.

3

Laying the Groundwork

IN THIS CHAPTER

» **Structuring a marketing plan**

» **Crafting your point of difference and positioning statement**

» **Articulating who you want your customers to be**

» **Fine-tuning sales goals and objectives**

» **Developing a broad range of marketing strategies**

» **Pulling the pieces together**

Chapter **6**

Developing a Smart Marketing Plan

B y its very nature, marketing is a creative process, with the risk that marketing activities are driven more by impulse and instinct than by strategies and data. For this reason, I find creating a structured marketing plan is every bit as important as creating a detailed financial plan.

In this chapter, I talk about the elements that make up a marketing plan, and look at the important groundwork required to develop a distinctive brand and marketing strategy. What is it you're really selling and who do you want to sell this to? How do you set realistic sales targets and put strategies in place to make sure these targets are met? This chapter helps you answer such questions.

The format of your marketing plan depends on whether you're creating a stand-alone document or whether your marketing plan is part of a larger business plan document, and I talk about what information you might include in your plan at the end of this chapter.

Laying Down the Elements of Your Plan

Spend an hour or two browsing through different business resources and you're likely to find a dozen different formats for marketing plans. No right or wrong way exists to creating a plan, and indeed just articulating *something* in a structured fashion is 90 per cent of the battle. Having said this, here are some of the elements of a marketing plan I suggest you include:

>> **Introduction:** An introduction provides background on who you are, what you're selling, the brand you're trying to build, any market research you've completed, and how you compare against competitors. (I talk about these topics in the following section.)

>> **Competitor analysis:** In this part of your marketing plan, you describe who your competitors are, and how you compare to them. Chapter 3 focuses on competitor analysis, but in this chapter (skip ahead to 'Positioning yourself against competitors') I talk about condensing this information and developing a positioning statement.

>> **Target market:** Who are your customers, and what are the demographics and psychographics of the customers you most want to reach? Later in this chapter, 'Defining Your Target Market' explains how to develop descriptions of your customers, and what channels you might use to reach them.

>> **Sales targets:** How much are you going to sell, who are you going to sell to, and what is your pricing strategy? See 'Setting Sales Targets', later in this chapter, for details.

>> **Marketing strategies:** What marketing strategies do you intend to put in place? Later in this chapter, 'Deciding on Your Marketing Strategies' outlines possible tactics, the importance of developing a marketing budget, and the importance of planning for customer service.

>> **Connecting the different elements:** The last section of this chapter, 'Connecting the Dots', explains how to bring all these different elements together to create a coherent marketing plan.

Providing the Background

How much background information you include in the introduction of your marketing plan depends upon whether your marketing plan is a standalone document, or whether it forms part of a larger business plan.

In the next few sections, I err on the side of caution and talk about the information you'd include if this marketing plan were to be read in isolation. Of course, if your marketing plan is part of a larger business document and you've already covered some of these elements, you don't need to repeat them.

Selling the hole (and not the drill)

In Chapter 2, I suggest that you start your business plan with a strategic advantage statement that explains how your product or service benefits your customers, and what differentiates your business from its competitors. As I explain in Chapter 2, this strategic advantage could be many things, including having lower costs, a brilliant new idea, specialist skills, or a right to use certain intellectual property.

Your marketing plan needs to do the following:

>> Reiterate this strategic advantage.

>> Consider how this advantage gives you an edge on competitors.

>> Express this edge succinctly in a way that interests and attracts customers.

When you're selling this difference to customers, your aim is to encapsulate this message in just a few words. This becomes what is known as your *USP* — your unique selling proposition.

TIP

If you're struggling to express your unique selling proposition, go online and search for businesses similar to your own. For example, maybe you offer a piano-tuning service. Search for similar businesses all around the world and check out their marketing slogans: 'Technicians with 20 years' experience', 'Advanced technology for unbeatable accuracy', 'Event and concert specialists'. I'm not suggesting you pinch someone else's selling proposition; rather, you can lean on these ideas for inspiration.

In Table 6-1, I list some examples and demonstrate how a unique selling proposition is both clearly related to, but very different from, a strategic advantage.

TIP

The beauty of developing your own USP is that you can hone in on the thing that makes you different from your competitors, which is an infinitely better approach than trying to be all things to all people. Have a think about what you want your USP to be (or what it already is) and how you can best exploit this in your overall marketing.

TABLE 6-1   **Strategic Advantage versus Unique Selling Proposition**

Type of Business	Strategic Advantage	USP
Bookseller	Owner was formerly a respected publisher and is super well connected with authors around the country	'Exclusive access to author interviews and signed editions'
Carpenter	Specialist training in CAD software as well as a partner trained in interior design	'Help us to visualize and construct the interiors of your dreams'
Copywriting service	Strong working relationship with offshore subcontractor in different time zone	'24-hour service and swift turnarounds'
Games developer	Educational specialist with unique game mechanics	'Specializing in game development for middle-grade'
Musician	Phenomenal ability to memorize songs and lyrics	'Live performances of playlists of your choice'
Naturopath	Qualifications in both counselling and naturopathy	'A holistic service for body and mind'
Your business . . .	*Your strategic advantage . . .*	*Your USP . . .*
(fill in the blanks)	(fill in the blanks)	(fill in the blanks)

Pitching your brand

I imagine you have a pretty clear image of yourself and how you want the outside world to perceive you. You may see yourself as anything from an urban hipster to a double-income-no-kids executive, or from a savvy entrepreneur to a person working the land.

Your business needs to have an image in just the same way that you do. With a certain amount of forethought and awareness, you can build up this image. Businesses tend to have two types of image:

>> The image of the business (sometimes also called *corporate branding*)

>> The image of the things you sell (sometimes called *product branding*)

Think of your business as having its own identity, personality and image. This image is made up of lots of things, but includes the name and logo of your business, the quality of your products or services, and the values that your business projects. The appearance of your staff, the way in which you market your products, your color schemes and even the feelings that customers experience when they think of your business, are all part of your brand.

TRUE STORY

A fast-food takeaway opened in our village a few years ago in a location where many other businesses and restaurants had struggled. The owners had worked in a corporate environment before starting this business, and knew from the get-go about creating a distinct brand. Smart signage, quality produce, distinctive shop fittings and a sense of playfulness marked this venture as clearly different from its competition. Gone were the shriveled fries served lukewarm from a bain-marie. Not surprisingly, this business has flourished.

TIP

Franchises are typically very good at delivering a clear image and a strong brand. If you know of a franchise group that operates in the same kind of business as yourself, have a close look at what they do, and see what you can take on board.

If you're preparing a business plan as part of a pitch to investors or lenders, your brand should shine through in your presentation. For example, if your brand uses specific colors or fonts, apply these to the text and other visual elements in your plan; if playfulness is part of your brand, take time to word your plan in a way that sounds fun; if high-end design is key to your brand, ensure your plan goes to a graphic designer before being shared with others.

Presenting market research

If your business is very new or hasn't even started yet, I suggest you include some market research in your marketing plan. Market research sounds like such a technical term, but can be very simple in practice.

Here are some examples:

>> You may have conducted research evaluating trends, and spotted an opportunity. Perhaps you can refer to industry trends using an authoritative source such as IBISWorld or Statista, or demographic trends using government census data.

>> Perhaps you have done some research off your own bat, such as running a focus group or survey with existing customers.

>> Depending on the context, you may have been able to gather information from online research, examining the trends impacting different industries or types of businesses, looking at trading results for public companies, or using social media to analyze consumer interest.

>> Perhaps you've already tested your idea on a small scale, and can provide data about the response to your idea, and feedback received from test customers about the product or service, its pricing and its delivery.

AI tools such as ChatGPT can provide interesting data when it comes to researching business ideas. As with any AI interrogation, the quality of response will depend greatly on the phrasing of your question. Focus on really specific questions, such as 'What are the trends in using e-learning for email marketing?', or 'What are the trends in demand for solar battery storage solutions?'

Positioning yourself against competitors

I focus on competitors in Chapter 3, and recommend analyzing your competition early in your planning — without a good understanding of your competitors and their strategies, you can't decide how you'll differentiate yourself, and how much to charge for your products and services. And, if you don't know what you intend to charge, you can't do any meaningful financial forecasts. Without financial forecasts, you don't know if your business model has any chance at all. And without having your essential idea confirmed, what on earth is the point of doing a marketing plan? (Phew!)

So, in Chapter 3, I explain how to perform a competitive analysis and devise a competitive strategy (scoot back to Chapter 3 for more info). In your marketing plan, you need to include this analysis and confirm whether your competitive strategy will be one of cost leadership, differentiation or niche marketing.

TIP

With this information to hand, the final piece of the puzzle for this section of the marketing plan is to create a *competitor positioning statement*, a succinct description of how you want your brand to be perceived when compared to that of your competitors. This statement usually follows the format 'Target audience . . . category/market . . . key differentiator . . . primary competitor . . . point of difference'.

So for example, if you're starting an eco-tourism guiding business, your statement might be something like, 'For environmentally conscious adventurers, Eco Guides offers small-sized sustainable and ethical tours with a focus on connecting with nature. We differ from traditional tour operators, which often have large group sizes, low prices and a significant carbon footprint.'

REMEMBER

Your marketing plan must articulate what it is that you do better or differently than your competitors, and position your business against these competitors in a way that it is clear you can succeed.

MAKING SURE PEOPLE CAN FIND YOU

If you're still defining and building your brand, pause for a minute to consider how people will look for your product or services. If people are likely to look for you online, you want a company name (and brand) that includes words that say something about what you offer.

Imagine you have a holiday house on the west coast called 'Beach Daze'. Sure, you could register www.beachdaze.com as the domain name. However, how often do people search on the term *beach daze*? Never. (Well, surely close to never.) You're much better having a domain name such as www.westcoastbeachhouse.com, or www.westcoast holidays.com.

Another example may help. Imagine your name is Rick Dark and you're a dentist in Auckland. Do you think www.rickdark.co.nz would be a good domain name? No. Instead, look for domain names such as www.auckland-dentist.co.nz, or www.dentist.co.nz.

Researching domain name availability is straightforward: Simply go to the website of a company that offers domain name registrations to see if the name you want is available.

Defining Your Target Market

Traditionally, the second part of a standalone marketing plan (the Introduction covering background information being the first part — refer to the section 'Providing the Background', earlier in this chapter) is about defining your target market. For established businesses, defining your target market is largely about analyzing who your current customers are; for businesses just getting started, defining your target market is about describing who you hope your customers are going to be.

Sometimes you may find that your customers end up being a different kind of customer than what you originally anticipated. You may be fine with this, or you may decide that you want to change your mix of customers. In this situation, you need to implement specific sales targets and strategies to effect this change.

Playing with customer persona

The more niche and specific your marketing tactics, the more likely you are to succeed. One excellent way to ensure your marketing is targeted in the right way is to create three to five different customer *persona* — by persona, I mean archetypal representations of existing or target customers.

For example, imagine I'm trying to market a writers festival in a regional town. I know from previous years the kind of audience members who buy tickets, and I have a sense of how I might group them. My next step is to organize my thinking into archetypes of three ideal customers.

My first customer persona is Alex, a 67-year-old retired social worker who lives nearby, loves to read books, is well off and is highly politically aware. My second persona is Emma, a 40-year-old aspiring writer who works as an editor but is keen to publish her memoir. Emma lives two hours' drive away, but likes to go for weekends away with her friends. Then I have Ishara, a working parent with three kids. Ishara lives nearby, is always looking for things for her kids to do on weekends, and is interested in parenting, neurodiversity and the environment.

I then make up little stories about each customer, describing their education, values, and relationships, and maybe adding photos and other personal touches. I consider aspects such as age, gender, interests and lifestyle, as well as the challenges or problems this person is facing.

Next, I think about the marketing strategies for each persona. Alex lives locally, and I decide to reach him via posters, ads in the local paper, and postcards at the bookshop. Emma is trickier, but my marketing strategies include personalized emails, targeted Facebook and Instagram posts, and targeted ads on book-related sites. With Ishara, articles in parenting blogs, posters at the preschools and Instagram posts are my strategies.

The number of personas you should have depends on the size of your business, but three to five personas is ample to begin with. Remember that the idea is to create a tailored marketing strategy for each persona, and so the work required escalates with each persona you add.

TIP

If you're analyzing your existing customer base, keep in mind that each persona represents not just an existing market segment, but rather an ideal market segment. Don't spend time developing personas built on the kind of customers who are more trouble than they are worth. The idea of visualizing personas is to spend time thinking about what your ideal customer looks like, and then target marketing resources to reach that group.

Thinking creatively about channels

In the next part of your marketing plan, devote some space to *channel analysis*. Sounds technical, but channel analysis is simply a description of each channel that you plan to sell through. Here are a few examples of channel analysis:

>> Nina has a retail store in the suburbs. However, she also sells some clothes online. Her shop is one channel; online sales are another.

>> A manufacturer making gourmet jams sells through three different channels: Direct to stores, in bulk to distributors, and direct to consumers at farmers' markets.

>> Anita makes jewelry. She sells some at the markets herself, some to a local gift store, and some through a party plan. Each of these outlets is a channel.

>> An importer sells furniture via four different channels: Large department stores, independent stores, online via a distributor's website, and direct to customers from the warehouse shopfront.

Do you sell to more than one channel? (And if not, maybe you should!) Then devote some of your marketing plan to describing each channel. Analyze what proportion of your sales goes to each channel, and whether this channel is growing or declining.

Setting Sales Targets

Setting sales targets can be challenging even if you've been trading for many years, but is particularly difficult if you're starting a new venture.

Nevertheless, a marketing plan without sales targets is no kind of plan at all. In this section of this chapter, I talk about how to build on the work you've done so far to set sales targets that are both realistic and hopefully achievable.

Slicing goals into bite-sized chunks

If I could only offer one piece of advice about sales targets, it would be this: Avoid plucking random figures out of the air. Don't just aim to reach a certain value of sales without breaking this target into bite-sized chunks, and applying a reality check to each one.

For example, a hair stylist might set targets as to the number of cuts and colors each week, a wholesaler might set targets for each geographic region, and an independent theatre could set targets for the number of tickets sold per show.

For more on this topic, and for templates to help with this process, skip ahead to Chapter 8.

Creating goals that aren't just about money

I sometimes like to set sales goals that aren't just expressed in dollars or units sold, but in other attributes as well. (This strategy makes sense when you think about it: Customers don't rate your service or product simply on price; they look at lots of other traits of your business as well.)

In Table 6-2, I list a few examples of sales goals that aren't measured in dollars. In the first column, I list long-term goals; in the second column, I list short-term goals; and in the third column, I list the strategies the business intends to employ in order to support these goals.

TABLE 6-2   **Different Kinds of Goals and How to Reach 'Em**

Long-Term Goal	Short-Term Goal	Strategies to Support the Goal
Create a business that's inclusive and welcoming	To attract new types of customers, including those with disability and access requirements	Install ramp at retail outlet; provide concession discounts; create targeted socials campaign
Develop new business in eastern suburbs	One new customer a week in this locality	Create geo-targeted social media
Improve booking rates from email queries	Make 10 bookings for every 25 queries	Set up auto-responders, conversion funnels and email automations
Increase repeat business	Repeat business to be 25% of total sales	Set up loyalty/discount code system; create follow-up campaigns
Increase quality of service	Increase to an average 8.5 rating (out of 10)	Provide customer-service training for staff; commit to swift action for negative reviews
Improve on quote accuracy	Aim to ensure actual costs and time are within 10% of original quote	Issue weekly variance reports to review variances

Getting SMART: Five essential ingredients for any goal

One of the acronyms consultants often employ when referring to goal setting is the SMART approach: A goal needs to be **S**pecific, **M**easurable, **A**chievable, **R**ealistic and **T**ime-bound.

I love the SMART approach and find it works really well. Here's the lowdown on what each word means in practice:

>> **Specific:** When talking about sales goals, are you being really precise about what you are hoping to achieve?

>> **Measurable:** You need to able to measure every goal. (Dollars sold, units sold, new customers gained, email enquiries received, hits on the website and so on.)

>> **Achievable:** Setting goals is pointless unless you can reasonably achieve them.

>> **Realistic:** Even if a goal is potentially achievable, is it realistic? Do you definitely have enough time and enough funds to ensure the goal can be met?

>> **Time-bound:** Always specify the time frame for meeting this goal.

The sales goals outlined in Table 6-2 (earlier in this chapter) are pretty good in that they all seem to meet the SMART objectives. (Although, of course, it's hard for me to judge whether the goals in this example are definitely achievable and realistic.)

Just for fun, the following list includes some of the kinds of sales goals I really hate. They all sound cool at first glance, but scratch the surface and these goals are horrendously vague.

Try to avoid these kinds of goals:

>> 'I aim to increase online sales by 20 per cent.' (This goal fails the 'Time' test — by when will sales increase by this amount?)

>> 'We plan to open a new store every six months for the next five years.' (This goal almost certainly fails the 'Realistic' test.)

>> 'My main goal is to improve customer satisfaction by 100 per cent.' (Unless you add a whole heap of detail, this goal fails the 'Measurable' test.)

>> 'Our aim is to expand corporate sales and increase market share to 25 per cent.' (This goal fails the 'Specific' test in that it doesn't say how much corporate sales are going to expand by, and fails the 'Time' test in that it doesn't specify a time.)

How do your sales goals compare?

Deciding on Your Marketing Strategies

When it comes to marketing strategies, many people get stuck in their comfort zone. After all, few people enjoy cold calling, business networking meetings can be very hard on the introverts among us, and most PR activities require a high level of communication skills.

Only you can decide what marketing strategies are best for your business, but in this next part of the chapter, I encourage you to explore strategies you may not have considered. In this way, you're way more likely to end up with a marketing plan that is both well rounded and effective.

Brainstorming different strategies

Consider how you might apply each one of the following marketing strategies to your business:

>> **Advertising:** Traditional print media, online advertising such as Facebook or Google Ads, and radio advertising.

>> **Community engagement:** Partnering with other local businesses, hosting events, volunteering, and sponsoring community programs.

>> **Content marketing:** Advice, information or news that could be interesting to your customers delivered via blogs, newsletters, social media, podcasts, video channels, and your website.

>> **In-store promotions:** Seasonal sales, bundle deals, point systems, birthday rewards, samples, free trials, contests, giveaways, limited-time offers, and events.

>> **Loyalty programs:** Reward cards, membership benefits, special pricing, exclusive content, and point systems.

>> **Partnerships and networking:** Collaborations, cross-promotions, sponsorships, and networking functions.

>> **Public relations:** Press releases, media kits, and feature articles.

>> **Social media:** Facebook, Instagram, TikTok, YouTube, and X.

TIP

If you're struggling to think of how to apply any one of the preceding strategies to your business, try using an AI tool such as ChatGPT. Use the question 'How could I use a marketing strategy of [insert strategy here] for my [insert type of business here]?' to generate some fresh ideas you may not have considered up until now. For example, 'How could I use a loyalty program for my bookstore business?'

Choosing a marketing strategy mix

Steering clear of personal preferences and prioritizing sales strategies objectively can be very tricky. With this in mind, here's my suggested plan of action:

1. **Read through the list of marketing strategies in this chapter.**

   Refer to the section 'Brainstorming different strategies'.

2. **Get together with your business partners, staff, colleagues or advisers and arrange a marketing meeting.**

   If the business is just you, find somebody you trust to bounce ideas off.

3. **Brainstorm different marketing ideas.**

   Remember the rules of brainstorming — even if someone comes up with an idea that's hopeless, or something that seems ridiculous pops into your head, you can't judge. Simply write down the idea and keep going.

4. **When the brainstorming process starts winding down, stop generating new ideas and instead highlight the 15 or so best ideas.**

   REMEMBER

   Ensure you have ideas that relate to at least three of the marketing strategies listed in the section 'Brainstorming different strategies'. For example, don't restrict your marketing to social media or to advertising, but go beyond your comfort zone to include other strategies such as content marketing or community engagement.

5. **Next to the 15 best ideas, write approximate costs and the amount of time required. Score through any ideas that are plainly unaffordable or unachievable.**

   Don't forget to think about your target market at this point (refer to 'Defining Your Target Market', earlier in this chapter). You may need to generate different marketing strategies for the different kinds of customers you want to reach.

6. **Rank these ideas in order of most impact.**

   Don't worry about how much these ideas cost or how long they may take at this point.

7. **Select the combination of ideas that you feel will give you most bang for your buck and cross out any ideas that you know will be unaffordable.**

   Make sure you continue to have a combination of ideas across the range of strategies listed in 'Brainstorming different strategies'.

8. **With the amount of time you have available in mind, number your remaining ideas, starting with the number 1.**

   So idea 'number 1' will be within your marketing budget, achievable in a reasonable amount of time, and guaranteed or very likely to generate sales. (If you still have more than 10 ideas on your list at this point, score through any ideas numbered 11 or higher.)

You now have a list of marketing strategies, numbered in order of priority. The next step is to cost these strategies and determine whether you can afford them. Read on. . .

Developing a marketing budget

Once you've set your sales targets (refer to 'Setting Sales Targets', earlier in this chapter) and created a list of possible marketing strategies (refer to the preceding section), the next step is to figure out how much these strategies will cost to deliver, and whether this is affordable.

WARNING

Determining the right amount for your marketing budget is tricky, not least if you're at a start-up phase and your budget is tight. Even if finances are tight, however, try to avoid the pitfall of spending too little on marketing, especially in the early stages of building a business. In the ideal world, research what percentage of revenue other businesses similar to your own are spending on marketing, and try to allocate this amount at least. (For small businesses, this is often between 5 and 10 per cent of revenue, but you will probably need to allocate additional funds in the first couple of years of trading, particularly if you want to build brand awareness.)

Your marketing budget should list all planned marketing activities and their associated expenses, and include a timeline that spreads your budget across the year ahead. Start by costing each one of your proposed marketing strategies and then assess what you can realistically achieve. It may be that you need to focus on one target market at a time, or that you spread your activities over a year or more, testing each strategy as you go to evaluate its return on investment.

TIP

If you're spending money on online advertising, particularly if you have an e-commerce business, endeavor to set up some form of conversion tracking so that you track the cost of acquiring a customer or making a sale. For example, if you spend $500 on Facebook advertising and this leads to the acquisition of 20 new customers, that's $25 per customer. Calculating conversion costs in this way is a great way of trialing different marketing channels and comparing their performance.

Keeping customers front of mind

Ask successful businesspeople what they think their secret is, and chances are they say something about their customers. In fact, the majority of established businesses list customer service right at the top of attributes vital to their success.

Doing the right thing by your customers is the best possible form of marketing. The way you treat your customers influences their decision to come back to you. Customers are also getting more and more vocal about the value they place on being treated properly, so listening to your customers reaps rewards. If something matters to customers, it has to matter to you, too.

Customer service *does* mean different things to different people. I've heard excellent service described as 'being at your best with every customer' or 'figuring out new ways to help people'. Regardless of the description, the principle remains the same for all businesses — excellent service means always doing the right things, in the ways customers want them done. Applying this principle in practice depends entirely on your business.

As part of your marketing plan, I suggest you include a few paragraphs summarizing your customer service plan. In particular, you may want to include:

» Customer service goals (for example, your target response time for enquiries or order turnaround time)

» How you plan to seek feedback from customers

» How your customer service standards compare with the competition

» How you intend to guarantee the consistency and quality of your products and/or services

Similar to your sales targets, your customer service goals should ideally be SMART (specific, measurable, achievable, realistic and time-bound — refer to the section 'Getting SMART: Five essential ingredients for any goal', earlier in this chapter, for more).

Connecting the Dots

Pulling the together the many strands of a marketing plan is tricky, not least because of the whole chicken-and-egg nature of the beast. For example, you may start by defining your target market but then, once you progress to considering your preferred marketing strategies, this changes the way you're thinking about your target market.

However, here's a summary of what I've covered in this chapter, as well as how to link the different elements together:

1. **Articulate your unique selling proposition.**

   Refer to 'Selling the hole (and not the drill)', earlier in this chapter.

2. **Describe how you will position yourself against competitors.**

   Refer to 'Positioning yourself against competitors', earlier in this chapter.

3. **Define your target market, possibly using a handful of customer persona to bring clarity.**

   Refer to 'Defining Your Target Market', earlier in this chapter. The level of detail you provide here may depend on whether you're writing a standalone marketing plan, or whether your marketing plan forms part of an overall business plan.

4. **Set sales targets for the year ahead, providing as much detail as possible.**

   I talk about this in 'Setting Sales Targets', earlier in this chapter. Of course, if your business plan spans a longer period than the next 12 months, these sales targets will need to span a longer period also.

5. **Brainstorm different marketing strategies, keeping an open mind about all the possibilities.**

   Your final marketing plan or business plan will simply articulate the strategies you land on, but at this stage it pays to consider as many possibilities as you can.

6. **With target markets, customer persona and marketing strategies in mind, itemize how much you intend to spend on each marketing activity.**

   At this point, you may find you need a few iterations of your plan. With the budget you have available, can you afford to deliver on the marketing strategies you've selected? Do you have sufficient funds to reach all of your desired target markets? With this in mind, are your sales targets possible?

   In your final marketing plan or business plan, a simple summary of intended marketing expenditure is probably sufficient.

7. **Settle on a timeline for the next 12 months at least that lists marketing activities and how much each one will cost to deliver.**

   Ideally, this list of activities relates strongly to your favored marketing strategies, your desired target markets and, of course, your budget. Again, the level of detail you include here depends on whether this is a standalone marketing plan or part of a bigger document.

8. **Describe how you're going to review and evaluate your marketing plan.**

   Although sometimes more of an art than a science, the calculation of return on investment (ROI) of each marketing activity is crucial. Google Analytics, conversion tracking, budgets versus actual reporting, and referral source reporting are all examples of ways you can track the effectiveness of your marketing initiatives.

IN THIS CHAPTER

» Making a list of everything you need, and how much it's likely to cost

» Differentiating between start-up expenses and ongoing business expenses

» Calculating how much finance your business requires to get off the ground

» Taking out loans, looking for investors and more

» Understanding interest, repayments and what you can afford

Chapter **7**

Budgeting for Start-Up Expenses

I f you're planning to start a new business or expand your existing business in some way, chances are you're going to need a bit of capital behind you. The question is, of course, how much?

When starting a business, you need to budget not only for capital items such as new equipment, vehicles and merchandise, but also the variety of additional expenses you're bound to encounter in the first few months of trading. You may also need additional finance for living expenses until your business becomes profitable. This detail is essential to the budget you include in your business plan, and calculating how much finance, if any, you need to secure.

In this chapter, I talk about how to calculate how much start-up capital you're going to need. I also talk about the pros and cons of business loans, credit cards, equity partners, outside investors, leases, and last (but not least) borrowing funds from benevolent friends and family.

Creating a Start-Up Budget

Creating a budget for start-up expenses is a good idea, no matter how large or small your proposed business. Unless you know how much capital you're going to need to get started, you won't have any idea about how much finance is required, nor will you have a sense of the risk involved.

TIP

If you're still at the conception stage for your business — maybe you're testing your product at local markets or trialing the service that you offer — you're probably still working from home or manufacturing on a small scale. As part of the planning process and testing the long-term viability of your business idea, I suggest you create a start-up budget for how much money you would require if you were to manufacture your product on a large scale or if you were to set up a proper office servicing a wide range of clients.

Estimating your start-up expenses

In Table 7-1, I show a possible format for a start-up budget. I suggest you create this list using a spreadsheet option such as Excel or Google Sheets or, if you're using business planning software, look to see if you can find a suitable template. (This way, if you change your forecasted figures, all the totals recalculate automatically.)

Here are some pointers to help along the way:

>> The start-up expenses listed in Table 7-1 are generic, and you may well wish to add additional types of expenses specific to your own business.

>> Before adding items not listed in Table 7-1, remember that you're only budgeting for start-up expenses here, not operating expenses. (If you're not sure what counts as a start-up expense, skip ahead to the section 'Separating Start-up Expenses from Operating Expenses', later in this chapter.)

>> Have you already paid for some start-up expenses using your own funds? See the following section for more details regarding whether to include these transactions in your start-up budget.

REMEMBER

>> If consumer tax applies in the country or state in which you're operating (for example, sales tax in the United States, VAT in Canada or the United Kingdom, or GST in Australia and New Zealand), and you know that you will be able to claim a refund for any tax you pay, show your start-up expenses excluding, rather than including, tax.

TABLE 7-1   **Start-up Expenses Budget**

Description of Start-up Expense	$
New Equipment or Tools	
Computers systems and accessories	
Motor vehicles, including special fit-out, if required	
Office furnishings	
Retail equipment (scanners, point-of-sale software)	
Tools and equipment	
Other (describe here) _____	
Premises Fit-out	
Local government fees, if necessary	
Fit-out of new premises	
Lease agreement fees	
Rental bond and rent in advance	
Other (describe here) _____	
Other Start-up Expenses	
Accounting fees (advice for new start-up)	
Branding and logo design	
Consultant fees	
Contingency reserve (approx. 10 per cent of start-up expenses)	
Incorporation of company	
Insurance (public liability/business indemnity/property insurance)	
IT infrastructure (servers, networks, cloud storage)	
Legal fees (incorporation, trademarks)	
License fees and permits	
Marketing launch expenses (including online advertising)	
Product development or content production	
Professional membership fees	
Registration of business name and domain name(s)	
Security bonds for electricity, gas and telecommunications	

(continued)

TABLE 7-1 *(continued)*

Description of Start-up Expense	$
Signage	
Stock for resale	
Training and recruitment of staff	
Website design	
Other (describe here) _____	
TOTAL	**$__.__**

I often get asked how much is reasonable for a start-up budget. My answer is that I've seen business start-ups that require not one brass razoo, and others that require several million dollars. If you're not sure about the accuracy (or completeness) of your start-up budget, I suggest you bounce the figures off your accountant, business adviser or a colleague working in the industry.

One thing I have noticed is that people planning a new retail business often seem to underestimate start-up expenses. Items such as shop fit-out and opening stock are invariably more expensive than expected. Make sure you're budgeting enough to cover all likely expenses.

Including expenses paid for out of personal funds

Have you already purchased an asset in your own name that you're intending to use for business purposes (likely examples are a computer or vehicle)? If so, should you show this item in your budget for start-up expenses? The answer depends, as follows:

>> If you're setting up as a sole trader or a partnership, your start-up budget doesn't need to include assets that you've already purchased (although at tax time, do remember to let your accountant know).

>> If your business is going to have a company structure and you require the company to reimburse you straightaway for this asset, then, yes, include this asset in your start-up budget.

>> If your business is going to have a company structure but you're happy for the company to make use of an asset that you own while it's getting established, you don't need to include this asset in your start-up budget. Talk to your accountant, because they may recommend that you show this item as a company asset, and the debt to you as a company liability.

Adding enough to live on

Most businesses don't make any profit in the first six months and, in fact, many businesses make a loss during this time. For some businesses, the period before you see any profits may be even longer.

When budgeting for a new business, you not only need to budget for business expenses, but your own living expenses also. Quite how you do this depends on your circumstances, and whether you're continuing to work another job while your business gets established. Chapters 11 through to 13 explore business and personal budgets in detail, pulling together the different elements of your financial plan. When you complete this process, you should be able to ascertain whether you require any additional finance for living expenses.

TIP

While your budget for start-up expenses is an essential first step, this budget doesn't necessarily provide a clear indication of how much you need as start-up capital— you only know that for sure when you complete the rest of your business and personal budgets. See Chapters 11 to 13 for more on this.

Separating Start-Up Expenses from Operating Expenses

If you're new to business, you may find it hard to differentiate between start-up expenses and operating expenses. This difference is crucial in order to calculate how much start-up finance is required and to report business profitability accurately.

REMEMBER

A *start-up expense* is a one-off expense related to starting your business or purchasing an asset that your business requires. An *operating expense* is an ongoing expense that will feature as a regular part of running your business.

Purchasing materials and inventory

If you're a manufacturer, retailer or wholesaler, your start-up budget includes the initial purchase of products for resale. To create this budget, you need the following information:

>> **If you are a retailer:** Your start-up budget must include an estimate of the cost value of stock (including freight) you will need to have on your shelves on the first day you open.

TIP

Most retailers, other than those selling fresh produce, have at least two months' worth of stock at any one time. If you're importing goods from overseas, you will almost certainly require more than two months' worth of stock (either in your shop, or already in transit).

>> **Manufacturers:** The initial stock that you require entirely depends on whether you're doing custom manufacturing (in which case you probably only need to invest in display goods) or whether you're doing bulk production (in which case you may need a minimum initial volume in order to keep your costs down).

>> **Distributors/wholesalers:** The value of stock required depends on the lead time from your suppliers. If your suppliers can deliver to you overnight or within a couple of days, you'll need to hold much less stock than if you're importing goods from overseas.

TIP

From a bookkeeping perspective, when you buy goods that you plan to resell, or when you buy materials that you plan to manufacture into a finished product, these purchases aren't cost of goods sold, nor are they expenses. Instead, book-keepers allocate stock purchases to asset accounts called Inventory, Stock on Hand or Raw Materials. This distinction between an asset and an expense is crucial to understand when you're assembling your financial projections. If you show all the stock or raw materials required for starting your business as an expense, your projected Profit & Loss for the first period of operations could look very miserable indeed. (For more about the difference between cost of goods sold and expenses, see Chapter 9.)

Dealing with initial start-up expenses

One of the tricky questions in the first stages of a business plan is how to treat initial start-up expenses. For example, if you spend $500 painting the inside of your new office, does this count as a business start-up expense, or is it just repairs and maintenance?

The answer — in terms of your business plan and financial reporting, but not necessarily your tax return — is that if something's a one-off expense that's related to getting your business started and you don't expect to have this expense again as part of day-to-day trading (or not for a little while at least), you should treat this as a start-up expense.

For example, if you rent a new office or shop and you spend money on fitting out the premises, building shelves, adding carpet or painting, these are good examples of start-up expenses. However, if you repaint or re-carpet the office in a few years' time, this would count as repairs and maintenance.

Other items such as logo design, branding, marketing materials or packaging design are also good examples of start-up expenses. Sure, you'll almost certainly spend money on more marketing materials in the future, but you're unlikely to have such a big expense all in one go.

What you're trying to do is identify all those initial expenses that come in a rush when you first start up your business, and separate these from the ongoing expenses you're going to have with your business. This is the only way you can establish how profitable your business really is in those first financially delicate months of trading.

Putting theory into practice

I don't know about you, but despite the fact that *For Dummies* books are about as chirpy as can be when dealing with some pretty dry topics, I still tend to glaze over when reading about costs versus assets, profit and loss forecasts, and budget estimates. So I'm going to take a real-life business and show how a budget for start-up expenses interacts with financial forecasts.

In this scenario, Eva is starting up a small retail business. In Table 7-2, you can see what she reckons she's going to have to pay in the first four weeks of starting up her business (including the money she'll have to pay before she even opens her doors for trading).

TABLE 7-2   **First Four Weeks Budget for Retail Business**

Item	$
Eight weeks' rental bond	8,000.00
Four weeks' rent in advance	4,000.00
Signage and marketing	2,500.00
Website design including first month's hosting (hosting is $100 per month)	3,600.00
First lease payment for air-conditioning unit	400.00
Cost value of stock purchased for resale	35,000.00
Shop fit-out and computer equipment	20,000.00
Wages for the first month	6,000.00
Accounting fees for advice regarding starting a new business	2,600.00

(continued)

TABLE 7-2 *(continued)*

Item	$
Advertising for the first month	1,200.00
Insurance monthly premium	400.00
All other expenses for the first month (bank fees, electricity, internet, motor vehicle, telephone and so on)	1,800.00
TOTAL	**85,500.00**

Imagine that Eva sells $20,000 of goods in her first four weeks of trading. What do you think the projected Profit & Loss should be in her business plan for this period?

At a simplistic level, you could say that Eva is going to receive $20,000 as income, and she'll spend $85,500 in expenses, which would equate to a $65,500 loss. However, this basic approach doesn't give a true representation of what's going on, and no bank or investor is going to want a bar of a business that shows this kind of loss.

What Eva needs to do is separate her start-up expenses from her operating expenses. Table 7-3 shows how she does this.

TABLE 7-3   **Start-up Expenses versus First Four Weeks Operating Expenses**

Item	$
Start-up Expenses	
Eight weeks' rental bond	8,000.00
Signage and marketing	2,500.00
Website design	3,500.00
Cost value of stock purchased for resale	35,000.00
Shop fit-out and computer equipment	20,000.00
Accounting fees for advice regarding starting a new business	2,600.00
TOTAL	**71,600.00**

Item	$
Operating Expenses — First Four Weeks	
Four weeks' rent in advance	4,000.00
Website hosting	100.00
First lease payment for air-conditioning unit	400.00
Wages for the first month	6,000.00
Insurance for the first month	400.00
Advertising for the first month	1,200.00
All other expenses for the first month	1,800.00
TOTAL	**13,900.00**

Can you see how, if you view Eva's figures from this perspective, the projected Profit & Loss looks very different? If Eva makes 40 cents gross profit in the dollar, the business would have $20,000 in sales less $12,000 in cost of sales, making $8,000 net profit. Deduct $13,900 in operating expenses and the business would still show a loss of $5,900, but this is significantly less than a loss of $65,500.

TIP

Chapters 11 to 13 cover piecing your financial projections together in more detail, but at the early stages of your business, the thing that's vital for you to understand is the distinction between start-up expenses and operating expenses. This distinction is important not just from the perspective of creating a business plan that paints a positive picture for a prospective business, but also from a business management point of view. After all, if you don't understand this distinction, you won't be able to calculate your true profitability with any accuracy in the early months of trading.

By the way, your accountant will almost certainly treat start-up expenses differently for tax purposes, choosing to write off items that you've shown as start-up expenses (and which you're essentially treating as assets), so that you minimize your tax bills. However, the treatment of expenses from a tax-management point of view is different to how you should treat expenses from a business-management point of view.

Figuring Out How Much is Enough

Once you have a solid idea of how much start-up capital you require to get your business started, including funds to tide you over if your business takes a while to trade profitably, you can start thinking about three things:

>> If you don't have the necessary savings, will you be able to borrow the money? (See the following section for more information.)

>> How much will you need to borrow, and what will the likely repayments be? (See 'Estimating loan repayments', later in this chapter.)

>> If you need to take out a loan, will repayments be affordable in the first year or two of your business — or will this level of borrowing bring an unacceptable level of risk and/or stress? (See 'Thinking about whether you can really service this loan', later in this chapter.)

Depending on the answers to these questions, you may want to review your start-up budget. Although earlier in this chapter I stress the importance of giving your business every possible chance of success by budgeting enough (refer to the section 'Creating a start-up budget'), you may find that you can pull back on or delay some spending without the business suffering unduly.

Here are some tips for pruning your start-up budget:

>> **Consider leasing rather than buying assets outright.** Finance that's secured against an asset such as a vehicle is usually pretty easy to obtain and preserves your working capital.

>> **Be realistic.** Although you may really want that new vehicle or piece of equipment, it may be more prudent to delay such purchases, or hire equipment and tools as needed.

>> **Consider buying stuff second-hand.** Buying second-hand isn't as glamorous, but may do the job just as well.

TIP

Always guard your *working capital* (that is, the difference between your current assets and current liabilities) as a tigress guards her cubs. You may indeed have enough in the bank to purchase everything your business needs to get started. However, if your business is successful and grows at any kind of pace at all, the growth itself may put strain on your cashflow. (This concept of growth requiring additional cashflow is called the *limit of sustainable growth*, something I explore further in Chapter 13.)

Securing the Funds You Need

After deciding how much finance (if any) you require, the next task is to decide how best to secure this finance. In this section, I talk about different kinds of finance and the pros and cons of each. (In Chapter 15, I take this a step further, and talk about how best to pitch for the finance you require as part of your business plan, and how you may want to present information differently when seeking a loan from a bank versus seeking funds from an investor.)

Banks are often the easiest option, but one of the decisions you need to make is what kind of bank finance is right for you. Business loans operate very differently from credit cards, as do leases or overdrafts.

However, you may find that no bank is willing to offer you finance, especially if you have no steady income and no *collateral* (that is, assets such as your home against which the bank secures its loan). Other sources of funds include outside investors, equity partners, or borrowing from family or friends.

This chapter touches on all of these sources of finance, but I do suggest you seek external advice before proceeding with any of these options.

Getting a bank loan (if you can)

Before you jump into a long-term relationship with any lender, be clear what you're getting into. Here's a quick summary of the kinds of finance typically offered by banking institutions:

REMEMBER

>> A *business loan* usually works like an ordinary home loan — you borrow a fixed amount and commit to regular repayments over a certain number of years. A business loan is well suited for start-up finance, debt refinancing or financing business growth.

With business loans, the upside of structured repayments is that you're likely to pay off the loan relatively quickly. The downside is the bank usually offers a relatively short term on business loans (five years is quite standard), meaning that repayments are high in the early years when the business can least afford it.

>> A *business lease* can work in different ways depending on how you structure the lease. This kind of finance is almost always secured against a specific item of equipment or vehicle. Essentially, the finance company buys the asset on your behalf and then you make regular monthly payments for an agreed amount of time. Depending on the lease agreement, you will either own the

asset outright at the end of the loan term, or you will be able to purchase it for a reduced price.

TIP

Leases are relatively easy to obtain for existing businesses (because they're secured against the asset itself) and help preserve your valuable working capital for things that are harder to obtain finance for (such as an increase in inventory or financing of accounts receivable).

>> A *credit card* is the easiest type of finance to obtain, but is usually limited in how much you can borrow and involves the highest rate of interest. Generally, credit cards are best for short-term borrowing of relatively small amounts, and are a poor choice for start-up business finance.

>> A *microloan* is a small short-term small business loan, often provided by a non-profit organization or community bank that also offers support services for those just starting out.

>> A *line of credit* or *overdraft* works a little like a regular bank account, except the balance is in the red, not the black. You can use the loan for all your business banking, including both deposits and withdrawals. You have a credit limit on the account, and it's your choice whether you pay off the principal or pay interest only. Lines of credit are ideal for on-demand working capital and improved cashflow.

WARNING

Although a line of credit offers great flexibility for your business, you do need to have a disciplined nature to force yourself to pay off the debt. (If you never reduce the principal outstanding on your line of credit, you end up paying more interest than on a regular business loan.)

Offering up collateral

Almost all banks require some security against borrowings and, unless you're still renting, the most obvious security is usually your own home. While you probably feel reluctant to offer your home as security, you may find that you don't have much choice in the matter, or that a business loan secured against your home attracts substantially less interest than a business loan that's unsecured.

WARNING

Even if a business loan is in your name only, if you guarantee this loan against a property that's jointly owned, it's extremely likely that both parties (that is, both you and your best beloved) are jointly liable. This means that if the relationship breaks down, you get sick or even if you die, the other person may be legally obliged to repay the debt. For this reason, involving your better half in the decision about using the family home to secure a business loan is vital.

CROWD AROUND

Crowdfunding (also sometimes called *crowdsourcing, crowd financing* or *crowd fundraising*) can be a solid way to raise funds for your business idea.

With *equity crowdfunding*, backers receive equity or shares in the company in return for their investment; with *reward-based crowdfunding*, backers receive a product or service; with *debt crowdfunding*, backers receive interest payments.

Are you wondering whether crowdfunding is a possible way that you could raise funds for your business? New crowdfunding platforms launch almost every day, but GoFundMe, Indiegogo, Kickstarter, LendingClub, Pozible and SeedInvest are all platforms with solid reputations and high participation rates.

Seeking an outside investor

In the preceding sections, I talk only about *debt finance*, meaning that to get start-up capital for your business, you go into debt. However, the other major source of business finance is *equity finance*. With equity finance, you receive funding from an investor in exchange for a portion of ownership of your business.

The idea with most equity finance is that investors buy into your company, offering funds and expertise in return for part-ownership. The investors may receive low interest or minimal interest on these funds, with their goal being long-term capital gain. However, because such investors are exposed to the risk of your company failing, they usually look for businesses with a strong history of growth and higher-than-average returns.

The advantages of equity finance include the ability to raise funds even if you don't have security or collateral to offer, meaning that your financial structure is more stable. In addition, your business can hopefully benefit from the investor's management expertise. On the downside, an outside investor means that you no longer have complete control of your business. You may find it hard not being able to make decisions without consulting others first, especially if you're used to running your own show, and conflict between you and the investor becomes a real possibility.

Note that for the purposes of writing a business plan, an outside investor is going to be interested in how they can get an above-average rate of return from your business. Outlining this for a potential investor likely means returning to that question of what it is about your business model that's so special. Skip ahead to Chapter 15 for more about framing your business plan for the eyes of investors.

Borrowing from family and friends

Borrowing from family or friends can be both the easiest and the hardest way to secure finance, all at the same time.

TRUE STORY

When first writing this chapter, I drafted the next couple of paragraphs about borrowing from family and friends and then decided, 'Nah, I'll just delete this stuff — it's all so obvious.' And so I did. The very next day, I bumped into the sister of an old client of mine and we got chatting. The father of my client had lent my client a large sum of money many years ago, and my client had repaid his father assiduously in the intervening period until the debt was completely cleared. As far as I was concerned, this particular scenario was a happy one, where none of the stuff that so often goes awry with family loans had occurred. Little did I know, the sister of my client, many years after this loan had been offered and then repaid, was still upset. It turned out that she had approached her father for finance as well, but her father had said he couldn't, because he had no money left to lend. The sister had missed out on the purchase of the farm she wanted, and had nursed resentment against her brother for years.

WARNING

You will find many ways to make money in your lifetime, but you will only have one family, and your family relationships are probably more valuable than anything else you have in your life. (I'm including here the friends in your life that may be your substitute family.) If you're considering borrowing from friends or family, pause first to think how this could affect your friendships or how your siblings may feel. If these relationships would suffer if you fail to repay these funds (and failure in business, no matter how optimistic you currently feel, is always possible), then think again. You may be better to borrow from a different source.

Calculating Likely Loan Repayments

If you intend to take out a loan, your business plan needs to show how much you intend to pay each month in both repayments and interest expense.

You may be thinking you haven't gotten far enough yet with your plan to know how much finance you'll need. (After all, until you create budgets for your first year of trading, you won't know whether you'll require additional finance to pay for living expenses or cover for trading losses in those first few months.) The difficulty is, however, that you won't be able to create these budgets without having some idea of how much your loan repayments will be.

The answer to this chicken-and-egg dilemma is simple: Start by making an estimate of how much finance you require and what the likely loan repayments are going to be. (I explain how to calculate loan repayments next in this chapter.) Then assemble your financial projections, including your estimated loan repayments (which I explain in Chapters 8 to 13). If your projections predict that cash will be tight and these loan repayments unaffordable, return to your start-up budget and revise your plan.

TIP

This continual process of planning, budgeting, checking results and then adjusting your plan is part of what being in business is all about. Nothing is ever set in stone and you always have to be flexible about your plans and expectations, regardless of whether you're just starting out in business or you've been trading for 20 years.

Estimating loan repayment schedules

When estimating your business loan repayment schedule, keep in mind that the loan term for most business or personal loans is shorter than for home loans. (By *loan term*, I mean the number of years in which you agree to pay the loan back down to zero.) I mention personal loans here, not just business loans, because many small business start-ups find that banks are reluctant to lend money for a new business, but are happy to offer funds for a personal loan.

You can find oodles of loan repayment calculators online (simply type 'loan repayment calculator' into a search engine). However, for most situations I prefer the simple loan calculator that Excel offers, because I can not only view my loan repayment schedule at a glance, but also save my workings for future reference.

Here's what to do:

1. **Open up Excel.**

   If you don't have Excel, then Google Sheets also does the trick, although the instructions I list below may not be exact.

2. **Go to the File menu and select New. Or, if you're using a Mac, select New From Template.**

3. **Type** loan calculator **within the Search** Office.com **for Templates box and press Enter.**

4. **Look for the template called Simple Loan Calculator and Amortization Schedule and double click on it.**

   This popular template usually comes up early in the list.

5. **Enter the amount you want to borrow as the Loan Amount.**

6. **Enter the likely interest rate as the Annual Interest Rate.**

To find out the likely interest rate, go to the website for your bank and look up current variable interest rates for business loans. Banks often slap a premium of up to 5 per cent additional interest on business loans, compared to home loans, to allow for the additional risk involved.

7. **Enter 5 as the Loan Period in Years.**

You can enter a shorter period here if you prefer, but five years is a good estimate of the time in which you should aim to pay off a business loan. Note that banks are often reluctant to offer a longer loan term than this.

8. **Enter the Start Date for this loan and press Enter.**

In the blink of an eye, Excel calculates your monthly payments as well as the total interest and cost of the loan, similar to the workings shown in Figure 7-1.

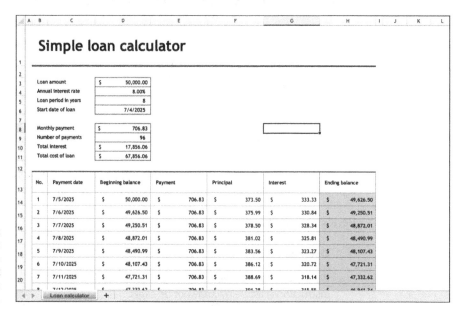

FIGURE 7-1: Excel provides a simple loan repayment template you can use at any time.

Calculating interest

When you do your financial projections (a spellbinding activity that I talk about in Chapters 11, 12 and 13), you have to split your loan repayments into *interest* and *principal*. Interest is the amount that the bank charges you each month for the pleasure of lending you money; principal (in this context) is how much you reduce the balance of your loan each month.

Looking at Figure 7-1, can you see how the monthly repayment is $706.83? Also, if you look at the first month's repayment, can you see how the interest is $333.33 and the principal is $373.50? This means that the first loan repayment reduces the balance of the loan by $373.50. As time goes on and the loan balance reduces, the monthly repayment stays the same but the amount of interest goes down and the amount of principal goes up.

In the context of your financial projections, the interest component is an expense in your Profit & Loss Projection. However, the whole value of the loan repayment shows as an outgoing in your Cashflow Projection.

If your business plan only includes a Profit & Loss Projection, you may be best to include the full value of the loan repayment in this report so that your projected net profit provides a better reflection of your likely cash position.

Thinking about whether you can really service this loan

After you calculate your predicted loan repayments, pause for a minute and ask yourself whether these repayments are realistic. The last thing you want to do while you're getting started is strangle your business with repayments that eat up your working capital and stifle growth.

TIP

If you're at all unsure about your calculated loan repayments, review your finance requirements carefully (refer to the section 'Figuring Out How Much Is Enough', earlier in this chapter). You may be better advised to plan on securing additional finance later down the track (when your business is hopefully growing and profitable) rather than saddling your new business with a high level of debt right from the start, or even postponing the launch of your business until you can be confident you have adequate start-up capital.

IN THIS CHAPTER

» Looking at different pricing strategies and thinking about what's best for you

» Mixing up price strategies so you can capture as wide a market as possible

» Applying price strategies to your business

» Calculating how much you're likely to sell this week, this month and this year

» Building a sales forecast for the next 12 months

Chapter **8**

Figuring out Prices and Predicting Sales

I f you're like most people starting out in business, you may be tempted to undercharge for your products or services. Maybe you're unsure about how much customers are willing to pay, or you're anxious that customers won't value your services. Maybe you're worried that you won't secure enough business to cover your expenses.

By undercharging, I'm talking about charging less than your customers are willing to pay. Precisely what this amount is can be tricky to judge, especially if you're pricing a service rather than a product. Calculating the value of your skills and expertise through the eyes of a customer is a very subjective process.

In this chapter, I talk about pricing strategies and how best to go about setting a price for your products or services. I also explain how to create your sales forecast for the next 12 months, one of the fundamental building blocks for any business plan.

Choosing a Pricing Strategy

Business educators use a heap of different terminology for price strategies, but essentially any price strategy boils down to one of three things: cost-based pricing, competitor-based pricing or value-based pricing. In the following sections I explore each strategy in turn.

Setting prices based on costs

Cost-based pricing is where you start by figuring out what it costs you to make a product or provide a service, and then you add an additional amount to arrive at the profit that you're after.

For example, imagine I decide to start a business selling sunhats at the local markets. The hats cost $8 each to buy, the stall costs $100 rent for the day and I reckon I can sell 50 hats a day. I want to make $250 profit to cover my time, so this means I decide to charge $15 per hat. (Sales of $15 × $50 = $750; less the $400 for the cost of the hats, less the rent of $100, and I'm left with $250 in my hot, sticky hand.)

This pricing model may sound like perfectly logical, good business practice, but it's not, because this way of working doesn't pause to consider how much customers are actually prepared to pay for these hats. Maybe another stall opposite is selling the self-same hats for only $12. Maybe the hats are a real bargain and I should be charging $20.

WARNING

From a strategic perspective, cost-based pricing is the weakest of all business models. On the one hand, if the resulting prices are too high in relation to the competition, the business will flounder; on the other hand, if resulting prices are less than people are prepared to pay, you'll miss out on the possibility of above-average profits.

Setting prices based on competitors

Competitor-based pricing is where you look at what your competitors are charging for similar products or services, and then set your prices accordingly. This pricing strategy is the most common strategy used by business.

As I mention in the introduction to this chapter, if you're just starting out in business, you may fall foul of the temptation to be cheaper than everyone else. However, unless everyone else in the industry is driving around in sports cars with money to burn, chances are your competitors' prices are the level they are for a very good reason. Unless you have a competitive advantage that enables you to produce products or provide your services cheaper than your competitors (refer to

Chapter 2), setting your prices lower than everyone else is likely to lead to poor profitability for you, as well as a risky business model.

Instead of trying to undercut competitors, look at the prices that your competitors are charging and use this analysis as a reflection of what the market is prepared to pay. Then pitch your pricing accordingly.

TIP

Competing on price alone is always a dangerous strategy. Sure, you need to be aware of competitor pricing and factor this information into your pricing decisions. However, how you position and sell your products and services should almost always be based on a combination of many different factors, such as quality of product or quality of service, delivery times, location, availability and ambience, and never just price alone. (For more about identifying your competitive strategy, refer to Chapter 3.)

Setting prices based on perceived value

Value-based pricing is where you reflect on the products or services you provide, look at the customer demand, and then set your price according to how much you think customers will be prepared to pay.

Here are a few examples of value-based pricing:

>> Apple use value-based pricing for many of their products (sought-after items such as iPads and iPhones), where no direct head-to-head competition exists and customers are prepared to pay premium prices for a brand on which they place a high value.

>> The stallholders selling umbrellas outside the city train station close to where I live push up the price of umbrellas by $3 or $4 every time it rains. Why? Because customers place a much higher value on staying dry when the rain is bucketing down.

>> I know of a very gifted and brilliant network engineer who has earned an almost god-like status among local businesses for being able to troubleshoot and solve network issues when everyone else has failed. He charges top dollar — significantly more than his competitors — but people will pay because they place such a high value on having reliable business systems, and getting those systems back up and running.

In many ways, value-based pricing represents the essence of good business sense and marketing. After all, how better to set your prices than by judging the maximum that customers are willing to pay? The only tricky thing about value-based pricing is that any judgment is subjective. For example, I love the design of Apple's gear and will happily pay premium dollars for a new iPhone. My son Daniel, however, doesn't place much value on Apple's design and prefers generic products. Therefore, the value Daniel places on an iPhone is significantly less than the value I place on the same item.

Building a Hybrid-Pricing Plan

So far in this chapter I've been talking about the theory of pricing and different pricing strategies. However, most successful businesses don't employ a single price strategy but instead employ a combination of strategies.

An example is a luxury inner-city hotel. Most of the time, the owners use *competitive-based pricing*, setting rates with the awareness of competitors' pricing very much in mind. However, with their premium rooms, they use *value-based pricing*, often improvising rates on the spot according to demand and what they think customers will be prepared to pay. Finally, for last-minute rates where they have a bunch of empty rooms and they know they won't be able to fill all of them, they use *cost-based pricing*, charging just enough above cost to make it worth their while to fill each room.

Using a combination of pricing strategies is called *hybrid pricing*, and is a key element in most successful businesses. The next part of this chapter explores ways to introduce hybrid pricing into your business, including premium products, no-frills products, package pricing and differential pricing.

Offering a premium product or service

With hybrid pricing, offering a premium product or service is only part of the picture. The idea is that as well as offering a premium product or service, you also offer a regular product or service. In other words, you target more than one type of customer.

Here are some examples:

>> Amazon offers a range of different pricing for freight, depending on how quickly you want your order delivered.

>> My butcher sells two types of minced beef: low-fat and not-so-low fat.

>> The guy who mows our lawns offers two services: regular just-with-a-lawnmower mowing, and premium all-grass-edges-trimmed-within-an-inch-of-their-life mowing.

PRICING GOODS THAT YOU MANUFACTURE YOURSELF

If you're manufacturing goods yourself, you must differentiate between what you charge at wholesale versus what you charge at retail. Even if you currently don't sell your goods at wholesale — maybe you're selling your wares at market stalls or direct to retail outlets — for your business model to be sustainable you almost certainly have to consider wholesale pricing at some point.

Why? Most manufacturers who work on a small scale (and I'm kind of assuming you do, because if you're the General Manager of Ford Motor Company you're probably not reading this book) don't have enough of a range or a broad enough sales team to service a wide range of retail stores. Range is always an issue for smaller businesses, because most large retailers don't want to bother with suppliers who only offer two or three products.

In addition, although you may be able to service retailers in your local area personally, chances are you won't be able to visit retailers interstate or in regional areas. Servicing these retailers almost always involves selling the products you make to some kind of distributor or wholesaler.

The crunch in regards to your pricing will be that your wholesale price ends up being a relatively small percentage of the retail price. For example, a shopkeeper selling an item for $20 probably doesn't want to pay much more than $10 wholesale for that item. The wholesaler who receives $10 probably won't want to pay much more than $7 to the supplier. So out of a possible revenue of $20 you only receive $7, and out of that $7 you need to pay all the costs of production. This is fair, and reflects the reality of doing business and the costs of distribution, but can sometimes put a damper on what you may have been thinking is a great business idea.

REMEMBER

Offering a premium product doesn't necessarily mean you compromise on the quality of your other products (a strategy that could risk your brand reputation). You can structure premiums in many different ways, such as faster service, guaranteed response time, additional services and complimentary extras.

Cutting back the frills

The flipside of premium pricing (refer to preceding section) is *no-frills pricing*. No-frills pricing doesn't necessarily mean inferior quality, but can include things such as off-peak pricing, lower service standards, longer response times or limited availability. Here are some examples:

>> Frequent-flyer programs place restrictions on what flights are available for frequent-flyer points.

>> Many gyms offer low-cost membership if you attend outside peak periods.

>> Tourism operators employ no-frills pricing for off-peak periods.

>> Supermarkets offer generic brands with basic product packaging.

Have a think about how you could offer a no-frills service or no-frills product. Would this fit with your branding? How could you ensure that this pricing model doesn't undercut sales from your existing client base?

Getting creative with packages

Package pricing, where one product or service is bundled together with something else, is another example of hybrid pricing. Package pricing can include things such as bundling two or more products or services together, offering bonus products, and extended warranties.

Examples of package pricing include

>> A day spa offering a pedicure, waxing and massage as a package.

>> A tourism operator offering flights, accommodation and meals as a package.

>> A club offering a free giveaway of some kind for every membership renewal.

TIP

If you're just starting up a new business, you may be pushed to think of how you could offer package pricing. Keep thinking creatively. Keep in mind that your business doesn't need to provide all elements of the package and that often the best approach is to team up with another business.

Charging different prices for the same thing

Yet another pricing strategy — and one that sounds a little dodgy at first — is to charge different prices for the same thing (this is also known as *differential pricing*). Don't worry — I'm not proposing you breach trade guidelines and regulations. Instead, I'm talking about charging different prices depending on the quantity ordered, the total size of an order, the costs of shipping to customers, how promptly customers pay, how much the customer orders in the course of a year, and so on.

FIXED RATE OR BY THE HOUR?

For many types of services, you get a conflict between customers who want a fixed fee and business owners who want to charge by the hour. For example, a contractor renovating a house would probably love to work on an agreed hourly rate, because they can be sure they'll be paid properly for all their time and don't risk being out of pocket if they underquote. However, the homeowners almost certainly want a fixed quote for this job, because they need to budget and can't afford for the costs to blow out.

On the other hand, a fixed rate can be a win–win, offering the consumer certainty about the price, and the business a chance to charge a premium. Many bookkeepers operate in this way, charging businesses a fixed price each month to keep accounts in order; similarly, many fixed-fee lawyers operate in a similar fashion.

For you as a businessperson, no right or wrong answer exists as to whether to charge a fixed fee or charge by the hour. However, be aware that you'll often find a natural tension between what customers prefer and what business owners prefer. If you're in an industry where you feel you're able to offer a specific service for a fixed fee, this can be an excellent marketing edge, especially if your competitors are charging by the hour.

Differential pricing works really well for almost any business because it enables you to maintain your margins for regular sales, but generate extra income by selling to other customers at a discount.

Here are a few ways to implement differential pricing:

» **Pricing based on customer location:** Charging different rates (either for shipping or for on-site service) depending on where the customer is located makes good sense, although you still want to keep your pricing structure pretty simple.

» **Pricing based on loyalty:** Offering special pricing to customers who are members of your loyalty program or members of an affiliate organization is a good marketing strategy and rewards customer loyalty.

» **Pricing based on order size or quantities ordered:** This kind of pricing makes intuitive sense straight off the bat. Almost any business will charge a different price for someone who buys 1,000 units rather than 10. (When you structure pricing according to quantity, this is called *quantity-break pricing*.)

» **Pricing based on payment terms:** Offering credit terms is expensive, not just in terms of using up working capital but also because of the risk of bad debt. Consider offering higher discounts for payment upfront or payment within 7 days.

>> **Pricing based on total spending:** Providing reward incentives for total spending often features as part of loyalty programs and makes good business sense. For example, if customers spend more than $500 over the course of the year, they get something for free or a discount on their next purchase.

>> **Pricing based on customer commitment:** Another clever strategy is to offer discount pricing but make the customer jump through hoops to get it. Money-back coupons where you have to post proof of purchase to the supplier, or price-match guarantees are examples of this kind of pricing.

Forming Your Final Plan of Attack

Previously in this chapter, I talk in detail about different pricing strategies. Thinking in this way may spark new ideas and creative thinking, but you might also feel a little overwhelmed and wonder where to start. So, here's my specific recommendation for the process to follow:

1. **Do some research as to what you think customers will be prepared to pay.**

   This research will involve looking at what competitors are charging as well as thinking about how your product or service is different and what value customers are likely to place on this difference.

2. **Think about how you could vary your product or service to provide two or three 'levels' of pricing (no-frills, regular and premium).**

   Not every business can offer multi-level pricing (for example, I don't know that I'd seek out a surgeon offering a no-frills service), but you'd be surprised how many types of businesses can. (Refer to the section 'Building a Hybrid-Pricing Plan', earlier in this chapter, for more on pricing levels.)

3. **Investigate at least two ways to bundle or package your offering with other products or services.**

   'Getting creative with packages', earlier in this chapter, provides a few ideas on this topic.

4. **Find two or three ways to charge your customers different prices for the same things.**

   This pricing strategy (differential pricing) is probably the most crucial of all. Even if you can't figure out how to have more than one level of pricing, or you can't come up with a method to create a package, you should be able to incorporate some form of differential pricing in your strategy. 'Charging different prices for the same thing', earlier in this chapter, provides some pointers as to how you can do this.

Although the upside of a hybrid pricing strategy is that you maximize the number of customers you can reach, and hopefully make premium profits on at least some of your sales, you can risk confusing customers if you offer too many options. As your business grows and changes, experiment with different pricing combinations to see what works best and gets the best response from your customers.

Monitoring and changing your price

If you've already been in business for a while, you may feel that your price strategies are pretty well settled and working just fine. That's good, but regardless of whether you're just starting out in business or you're running a 50-year-old family legacy, you still want to keep an eye on your pricing.

The biggest indication that your pricing may need to shift is if you have poor financial results. (Of course, poor results can be caused by many factors, not just pricing.) However, if you know that your competitors have just raised their price, your customers are commenting what good value you are, or you haven't raised your price in more than a year or two, it's probably time to do a price review.

Changing prices doesn't only mean raising prices. Always be open to new pricing plans, special offers, package pricing and so on. If you do decide to raise prices, try to do so incrementally and avoid big price hikes that may scare your customers. Alternatively, find ways to sneak price rises through the back door, such as only increasing prices on certain low-profile products or services, or getting rid of discounts.

Ensuring you value yourself and your time

When you first start a new enterprise, you probably can't charge for all the time you spend working on your business. After all, you're still setting up systems and building up goodwill in the first few months, testing what works and what doesn't, and trying to secure new customers.

However, once you've established a business model and started trading in earnest, it pays to monitor how many hours you're working. If you regularly spend upwards of 50 hours or so a week on your business and you're only yielding an average income, this may well indicate that your business model — and, by implication, your pricing structures — aren't working as well as they should.

Valuing your time properly also helps you to sell your business when you're ready to do so. When a business broker calculates how much a business is worth, they not only look at how much income the business generates, but also how many hours a week the owner(s) work. If the hourly rate generated by the business is low, the goodwill will probably be valued at zero, or even a negative amount.

DISCOUNT DRAMAS

WARNING

If you build discounts into your pricing strategies, be careful that when you offer discounts, your business receives something tangible in return. For example, offering a discount for cash payments rather than credit card often makes sense because you normally pay merchant fees on credit card transactions. Similarly, offering a discount for prompt payment probably makes sense (depending on how much discount you offer) if you're currently in debt to the bank and paying interest.

Another example is if you discount overstocked or end-of-season items. This makes sense because these slow-moving items are taking up valuable shop or warehouse space that could be better used for product that actually sells.

However, if you routinely offer discounts without receiving something that benefits your business in return, you risk eroding your profitability model. In addition, regular customers may get used to these discounts and come to expect them.

Building Your Sales Forecast

Once you have figured out your pricing strategy (what you intend to charge per hour, per unit or per service rendered), the next step in your business plan is to create a sales forecast for the next 12 months (or, if your business hasn't started yet, create a sales forecast for the first 12 months of operation).

Creating sales forecasts prompts all kinds of questions. If you're charging by the hour, what's a reasonable number of hours to bill for each week? If you're selling items, how do you know how many you'll sell? What if you sell lots of different items, at different prices? In the following sections, I talk about the details behind creating this kind of projection.

Calculating hours in a working week

If your business charges by the hour or by the session (maybe you're a book-keeper, consultant, counsellor, electrician, gardener, physiotherapist, plumber, private tutor, or some similar business), one of the first questions is how many hours can you reasonably charge for per week, per month or per year.

Imagine a recent music graduate (I'll call her Maddie) wants to set up a business as a tutor. Maddie reckons she can teach about 48 students a week in lesson blocks of 30 minutes (that's 24 hours of teaching), and that she's going to charge $60 per hour. With this in mind, she reckons that she'll earn $74,880 per year. (That's 24 multiplied by 52 weeks multiplied by $60.)

Is Maddie correct in her estimate of income for the next 12 months? I'm going to test her calculations using the following step-by-step method, which you can use as well:

1. **Estimate how many days you're going to work each week, and how many hours you can realistically charge for each day to arrive at your average number of billable hours per week.**

   When doing this calculation, remember to include billable hours only. Don't include travel time between locations, non-billable time due to administration/paperwork, or time spent running your business (bookkeeping, customer phone calls, marketing and so on).

2. **Estimate how much holiday you're going to take (or be forced to take) each year.**

   Here, don't think in terms of lying on the beach watching the surf, but include both holidays where you go away and breaks where you may be available to work, but you can't. (For example, a school tutor probably won't get much work in school holidays, a gardener may find it hard to work in heavy rain or snow, or a consultant may find that work grinds to a halt before and after Christmas.)

   In Table 8-1, I've included 12 weeks against the holiday Maddie will take annually, because that's the number of weeks of school holidays each year where she lives.

3. **Make an allowance for public holidays.**

   Most people don't work public holidays. If you don't plan to (or maybe you can't because your customers will be unavailable), you have to allow for public holidays as well. Public holidays of ten days a year equates to an equivalent of two weeks per year. In Maddie's case, many public holidays also coincide with her local school holidays, so she only allows for five days (one week) of public holidays per year.

4. **Think of what will happen if you get sick.**

   My observation is that being a freelancer is one of the best possible ways of ensuring good health. Knowing that you won't get paid if you don't show up is a real incentive to getting out the door, however you're feeling. However, most people do get sick from time to time, and it's realistic to make an allowance for this.

5. **Calculate how many weeks per year you will be able to charge for.**

In Maddie's case (see Table 8-1), after taking out holidays, public holidays and sick days, she can likely work a full week (that's 24 billable hours) for only 38 weeks of the year. (Most businesses that aren't dependent on school terms can probably work more weeks per year than this, however.)

6. **Multiply the number of working weeks per year by the number of weekly billable hours, to arrive at your maximum billable hours per year.**

As shown in Table 8-1, for Maddie this equals 38 weeks per year multiplied by 24 hours per week, making a total of 912 hours.

7. **Multiply your maximum billable hours per year by your hourly rate.**

The result for Maddie is $54,720 per year, quite different from her initial estimate of $74,880.

TABLE 8-1

Calculating Maximum Billable Hours per Year

Number of days worked per week	4
Average number of billable hours per day	6
Total billable hours per week	*24*
Number of holiday weeks per year	12
Number of public holidays per year, expressed in weeks	1
Number of sick days per year, expressed in weeks	1
Total working weeks per year	38
Maximum possible billable hours per year	**912**
Hourly rate	$60
Maximum possible income per year	*$54,720*

Note: The method shown in Table 8-1 only gives you the maximum billable hours per year for an example business. If you're still getting your business established, not only will your calculations be very different but it also may be some time until you have enough customers to reach your maximum billable hours.

Increasing sales by hiring staff

If your business is primarily service-based, don't forget to think beyond your own time and how many hours you can pack into a week. Instead, expand your thinking to include delegating some of the work involved to employees or subcontractors.

Building a plan that involves employees servicing your customers (rather than just you servicing customers) is a vital part of any entrepreneurial conception. For example, don't just think of how many lawns you can mow, kids you can tutor or companies you can consult to. Instead, picture a team of people mowing lawns, a whole school of tutors or an entire posse of consultants.

REMEMBER

If your business is service-based, leveraging your expertise in this way is the only possible method by which you can hope to earn more than the industry average. For example, if you start up a business as a gardener, tutor or physiotherapist, you can only work so many hours in the week. However, with a team of employees working for you, all delivering this service, you may be able to make a decent profit.

Predicting sales for a new business

If a business is still getting established, making an estimate of your first 12 months' sales can be really hard. Maybe people are going to flood through the door, maybe you're going to be a ten-week wonder, or maybe your business will grow steadily and organically over time. However, in order to build a business plan, you're going to have to make some kind of estimate.

TIP

To ensure your sales forecast is as realistic as possible, the more detail the better. Try to slice up sales targets by *market segment*, *product* or *region*:

>> **Market segment targets:** *Market segment* is a fancy word that really means type of customer or type of work. For example, a building contractor may split his market into new houses and renovations, a musician may split her market into weddings, private functions and pub gigs. A handyman may split his market into private clients and real estate agents.

>> **Product-based targets:** Product-based targets work best if you sell products rather than services. You can set sales targets according to units sold, or dollars sold, of each product. For example, a car yard could aim to sell at least 20 cars a month, a real estate agent could try to sell five houses every month, and a lawnmowing business could set sales targets of 80 lawns per month.

>> **Regional targets:** With regions, you set sales targets according to geographic regions. This works best for slightly larger businesses that typically have a dedicated salesperson or sales team in each region.

If you take on board any of the pricing strategy stuff I talk about earlier in this chapter (refer to the section 'Building a Hybrid-Pricing Plan' for more), chances are you're going to have a few different prices or packages on the go. This makes your sales forecast even more complicated. However, in Table 8-2, you can see how a few different businesses make a stab at constructing their initial estimates.

TABLE 8-2   **Initial Sales Estimates**

	Unit Price	Unit Sales per Week	Sales per Week
Cake Business			
Friands	$5.00	100	$500.00
Muffins — regular	$4.00	100	$400.00
Muffins — wholesale	$2.50	50	$125.00
Chocolate brownies	$5.00	130	$650.00
Teacakes	$12.00	60	$720.00
Total			**$2,395.00**
Kid's parties			
Flip Out Package	$350.00	5	$1,750.00
Trees About Package	$490.00	3	$1,470.00
Adventure Package	$650.00	1	$650.00
Total			**$3,870.00**
Naturopath			
Short consultation	$95.00	20	$1,900.00
Long consultation	$140.00	5	$700.00
Consult + massage	$250.00	2	$500.00
Herbs	$60.00	15	$900.00
Phone consultation	$70.00	3	$210.00
Total			**$4,210.00**
Retail fashion			
Clothing $11 to $20	$15.00	88	$1,320.00
Clothing $21 to $30	$25.00	32	$800.00
Clothing $31 to 40	$35.00	48	$1,680.00
Clothing $41 to 50	$45.00	30	$1,350.00
Clothing $51 to $60	$55.00	18	$990.00
Clothing $61 to $70	$65.00	6	$390.00
Total			**$6,530.00**

The idea behind any detailed sales forecast is that you start by itemizing the different items you sell or the different prices you charge, and you try to make an estimate of weekly sales against each of these items.

TIP

Try to incorporate a decent level of detail into initial sales estimates, including all items you sell or services you provide.

Predicting sales for an established business

If you've been running your business for a while, one of the most accurate ways of predicting sales is to analyze what sales have been for the last 12 months, and then build from there. Sure, you may have changed things — maybe you've switched to a new location, introduced new products or increased your pricing — but, nonetheless, your historical sales results are always going to provide you with the best indicator for future sales.

REMEMBER

When basing sales forecasts on historical data, consider the following:

>> When looking at sales figures for previous months, check whether these figures are shown including or excluding sales/consumer tax. (Most salespeople think in terms of the final value of each sale; accountants tend to look at sales figures net of any taxes collected on behalf of the government.)

>> Does your business have significant seasonal variations? If so, have you factored these into your monthly forecasts?

>> If you examine the trends, is the business growing or declining? Ideally, you should analyze trends over two or more years to truly get a sense of what's happening.

>> Have any changes to pricing or product range occurred between last year and this year?

TIP

When looking at sales forecasts, also factor in personalities. Salespeople are often very buoyant with their predictions (this optimism tends to be part of the job), while accountants are typically gloom and doom. Hopefully, your business plan can arrive at a happy medium.

Creating Your Month-by-Month Forecast

At the simplest level, creating a forecast for the next 12 months can be as simple as listing the names of the months in one big row and writing an estimate underneath each one. However, this method is somewhat unsophisticated, to put it mildly.

One trick to improving the accuracy of sales forecasts is to maintain a good level of detail. Start by looking at your weekly sales forecasts (something I talk about earlier in this chapter in the section 'Building Your Sales Forecast') and extrapolate these figures to create monthly forecasts, bearing the following in mind:

>> If you've been thinking about your sales in terms of weeks, keep in mind that some months have four weeks and others have five.

>> Most business plans include sales projections for at least the next 12 months, if not 24 months.

>> You need to factor in holidays and other seasonal events. For example, unless you run a Santa Claus for hire business, Christmas and early January are quiet months for most businesses.

>> Show your sales before any consumer tax (sales tax, GST, VAT and so on) that you're obliged to charge to customers but have to then remit to the government.

TIP

>> If you run a service business and intend to deliver some services yourself, and some using contractors, consider separating the income generated by each, similar to what I've done in Figure 8-1. Categorizing sales in this way helps you to be realistic about what you can achieve, demonstrates how much more income you can generate if you use subcontractors or employees, and also assists in calculating costs (a topic I cover in Chapter 9).

	A	B	C	D	E	F	G
1		Price					
2	Flip Out Package	$ 350.00					
3	Trees About Package	$ 490.00					
4	Adventure Package	$ 650.00					
5							
6		Jul	Aug	Sep	Oct	Nov	Dec
7	**Parties with owner's labour**						
8	Flip Out Package	8	8	8	8	8	8
9	Trees About Package	4	4	4	4	4	4
10	Adventure Package	2	1	1	1	1	1
11							
12	**Parties with subcontract or employee labour**						
13	Flip Out Package	12	12	13	8	12	12
14	Trees About Package	8	6	8	10	12	12
15	Adventure Package	2	3	4	4	5	4
16							
17	**Income Generated**						
18	Flip Out Package	$ 7,000	$ 7,000	$ 7,350	$ 5,600	$ 7,000	$ 7,000
19	Trees About Package	$ 5,880	$ 4,900	$ 5,880	$ 6,860	$ 7,840	$ 7,840
20	Adventure Package	$ 2,600	$ 2,600	$ 3,250	$ 3,250	$ 3,900	$ 3,250
21	Total Sales	$ 15,480	$ 14,500	$ 16,480	$ 15,710	$ 18,740	$ 18,090

FIGURE 8-1:
A monthly sales projection.

TRUE STORY

ARE YOU DREAMING?

I have a friend who trained as a naturopath, spending years of study with the expectation that this was how she would make her living in the years to come. However, after she graduated and started out on her own, she found it very difficult to make much money out of her practice. After a year or two, she started attending monthly network meetings with fellow naturopaths. Through these meetings she learnt that it wasn't just her who was having a hard time building up her practice, and that the pickings naturopaths typically survive on can be scant indeed.

If you're starting a new business, how can you assess how realistic your sales forecasts are? If your business is something that has been done before, I suggest you do some research first. Research industry benchmarks (something I discuss in more detail in Chapter 10), talk to your accountant, chat to people already working in the industry, join online networking groups or go to industry conferences. So long as the quality of your product or service is up to scratch and you have a decent marketing strategy, you can probably expect to achieve similar results to those already working in the industry.

Things are trickier if you've invented a new product or you're launching a specialist service of some kind. In this situation, it's very hard to measure customer acceptance or interest in your product without first testing the market in some way. Ways of testing the market may include consumer focus groups, launching your service or product on a small scale locally or experimenting with online sales.

Chapter **9**

Calculating Costs and Gross Profit

T he summer just past stretched into weeks of long, sunny days. The next-door kids, Callum and Rhys, hatched a plot to make homemade lemonade and sell it to thirsty passers-by. Most days I'd stop and buy a glass and the kids would happily announce how much profit they'd made so far. The school holidays were almost at a close the afternoon I bumped into their dad in the supermarket. He had a trolley piled high with lemons. 'This profit the boys are making is costing me a fortune,' he laughed.

Chances are that such halcyon days belong only to childhood and that, in your business, you're going to have to be seriously realistic about what everything costs. No more lemons for free.

In this chapter, I talk about calculating the costs for each sale that you make, and how to relate these calculations to your gross profit margins. And I show you how to build on your sales projections to include these costs so that you can create a forecast of your gross profit for the year ahead. This forecast forms the basis of your Profit & Loss Projection, a report essential to any business plan.

Calculating the Cost of Each Sale

The focus of this chapter is the costs that go up and down in direct relation to your sales. For example, if you manufacture wooden tables, your costs include timber. If you sell books, your costs include the purchase of books from publishers.

If you run a small service-based business and you have no employees, you may find that you have no costs of this nature (and, hence, most of this chapter is irrelevant to you). However, before abandoning this chapter willy-nilly, do read through the first couple of sections ('Identifying your variable costs' and 'Costing your service'), just to make sure.

Identifying your variable costs

In order to complete the expenses part of your Profit & Loss Projection for the next 12 months in your business plan, you first need to grasp the difference between variable costs and fixed expenses. *Variable costs* (also sometimes called *direct costs* or *cost of goods sold*) are the costs that go up and down in direct relation to your sales.

This theory may seem all very well, but you need to understand how it applies in the context of your own business. Here are some examples that may help:

>> If you're a manufacturer, variable costs are the materials you use in order to make things, such as raw materials and production labor. (For the boys next door making lemonade, their variable costs were lemons and sugar.)

>> If you're a retailer, your main variable cost is the costs of the goods you buy to resell to customers. Other variable costs, particularly for online retailers, may include packaging and postage.

>> If you're a service business, you may not have any variable costs, but possible variable costs include sales commissions, booking fees, equipment rental, guest consumables or employee/subcontract labor.

Fixed expenses (also sometimes called *indirect costs* or *overheads*) are expenses that stay constant, regardless of whether your sales go up and down. Typical fixed expenses for your business may include accounting fees, bank fees, computer expenses, electricity, insurance, motor vehicles, rental, stationery, and wages.

TIP

Not sure which variable costs apply to your business? Figure 9-1 provides a question-based checklist to prompt you to think about your business and what variable costs it may have.

FIGURE 9-1:
Identifying variable costs for your business.

Costing your service

I mention near the beginning of this chapter that if you're providing a service, you may not have any variable costs associated with your business. However, you may well have some minor costs associated with providing your service and, as soon as your business grows, you will have the cost of hiring employees or contractors to provide the service on behalf of your business.

Table 9-1 shows some examples where variable costs apply.

TIP

If you're unsure whether something is a variable cost or a fixed expense, ask yourself this: Do you spend more on this item as sales increase? If your answer is yes, chances are this item is a variable cost.

TABLE 9-1

Variable Costs Examples for Service Businesses

Type of Business	Likely Variable Costs
Contract cleaning	Cleaning staff wages, cleaning materials
Holiday house	Guest consumables, booking commissions
Massage therapist	Daily room hire
Home maintenance business	Building materials, cost of subcontractors
Medical practitioner	Medical supplies, pathology

Costing items that you buy and sell

When calculating costs for items that you buy and then sell you have two types of costs to consider:

>> **Incoming costs:** These are the costs involved in getting the goods to your door. Incoming costs often include freight and, for importers, may also include customs charges, duties and tax. Incoming costs may also vary significantly depending on the quantity you order.

>> **Outgoing costs:** These are the costs involved in making the sale and getting the goods to your customer. Outgoing costs include ecommerce fees, merchant fees, outwards freight, packaging and storage.

In Table 9-2, I show a costings worksheet for a wholesaler. You can see that, at first glance, the wholesaler's buy price is $9.00 and the sell price is $18.00, making for a handsome margin of 50 per cent. Browse through the figures in more detail, however, allowing for freight, storage, commissions and so on, and you can see that the final margin is something much closer to a paltry 24 per cent. (For more on gross profit and gross profit margins, see the section 'Understanding Gross Profit', later in this chapter.)

Adding import costs

If you decide to import goods from overseas, doing your product costings carefully is particularly important. Even if current exchange rates make your prices look cheap as chips, this rosy picture may soon fade when you add the costs of e-commerce fees, freight, customs, distribution and taxes. Work through your final product costings *before* you consider exporting or importing anything anywhere.

TABLE 9-2

Calculating True Costs and Margins

Description	Percentage of Sell Price	$
Sell Price (Before Taxes)		**$18.00**
Less **Variable Costs**		
Buy price for this item	50%	$9.00
Inwards freight to warehouse	5%	$0.90
Storage costs warehouse	2%	$0.36
E-commerce fees	10%	$1.80
Outwards freight to customer	8%	$1.44
Packaging	1%	$0.18
Total costs of selling		**$13.68**
Gross Profit		**$4.32**
Gross Profit Margin	*24%*	

WARNING

A whole scad of jargon goes hand in hand with export and import. Terms such as FOW (Free on Wharf), FOB (Free on Board) and CIF (Costs, Insurance and Freight) are all there ready to trap the unsuspecting novice. For importers, understanding what price your suppliers quote is vital because the extras of freight, insurance, agent commissions and duty can easily add a further 40 or 50 per cent to the cost of product.

TIP

If you're restricted to buying and selling in different currencies — maybe you buy in US dollars but sell in Euros — take the time to generate multiple pricing models and make sure you can still be profitable even if the exchange rate changes substantially.

Creating product costings for manufacturers

If you manufacture products, one of the most crucial steps in your business plan is to create an accurate costing worksheet for each product that you sell. This process can be pretty tedious, but without knowing exactly what everything costs, you can't move forward and plan.

Tables 9-3 and 9-4 show two possible product costings and the kind of information to include. I've taken both of these examples from businesses that I've mentored — the first example is a family member who started a business making homemade gourmet sauces, the second example is a friend who made kid's clothing and sold it at the markets.

TABLE 9-3

Cost of Producing One Bottle of Pickle

Item	$	Notes
100g fresh tomato	$0.80	Based on seasonal average
30g onion	$0.05	
20g sugar	$0.03	Based on buying in bulk 50kg bags
5g salt	$0.01	Based on buying in bulk 10kg bags
Cost of labor	$0.88	Average 400 bottles per day, with labor $350 per day
Kitchen rental	$0.38	Average 400 bottles per day, with rental $150 per day
Bottle plus lid	$0.45	
Label	$0.35	
Packaging	$0.40	$3.20 per custom box, 8 bottles per box
Total	**$3.35**	

TABLE 9-4

Cost of Producing Children's Dungarees

Item	$	Notes
Corduroy fabric	$ 2.50	Based on 0.8 square meter of fabric
Labor	$20.00	Average 40 minutes labor per dungaree set
Thread	$ 0.05	
Label	$ 0.03	
Packaging	$ 0.10	
Total	**$22.68**	

Can you see how both examples in Tables 9-3 and 9-4 put a value on labor? You may think this doesn't apply to you, because chances are if you're just starting out in business, you're contributing your own labor for free. However, when creating a product costing, you're best to include a realistic allowance for how much the labor would cost if you were to pay for someone else to create the product. This way, you can see the 'true' profitability of each product, and you get a better sense of the long-term potential of your enterprise.

The other interesting thing to consider is volume discounts. For example, in the product shown in Table 9-3, the cost of sugar is based on buying 50 kilograms at a time. However, how much would this business save if the owner was able to buy 100 kilograms at a time? (Even if your business can't afford to buy in large quantities yet, just knowing that your costs may reduce dramatically as your business grows is an important part of the business planning process.)

TIP

If you use accounting software, you can usually set up 'kits' or 'assemblies' for each product you manufacture. In other words, you can create an inventory item that's made up of several other items. The benefit of working in this way is that the software calculates product costs automatically; the downside, especially for a small business, is that this method of accounting for every gram of salt or squirt of glue used can be hideously time-consuming.

WARNING

THE DANGERS OF CUSTOM MANUFACTURE

Over the years, I've observed that almost any business doing custom manufacture struggles to make a profit. Why? The very nature of creating one-off pieces — whether these are original sculptures, handmade furniture, custom spiral staircases or hand-built guitars — means that you are engaging with the unknown.

The unknown factor may be materials that cost more than you expect, a customer who isn't happy with the first prototype, underestimating the cost of labor, or many other factors. The time taken up discussing a job with a customer, drawing up designs, communicating changes and working out how to do something is almost always more than you expect.

When you create one-off items, you don't have the same ability to control your costs in the way that you do when you make the same item over and over again.

Am I warning you never to engage in this kind of business? No, not quite. After all, without custom manufacturers our society would be without potters and artists, sculptors and artisans, furniture makers and craftspeople. However, if you're planning this kind of business and you want to make a profit, you will need to be particularly brutal about quotations and costings, and you need to be prepared to reject jobs where the margins are too slight.

Understanding Gross Profit

You've almost certainly heard of the terms *gross profit* or *gross profit margins* but are you entirely clear what these terms mean and why an understanding of these terms is so crucial to your business plan? If you have even a moment's hesitation in answering 'yes' to this question, then read on . . .

Calculating gross profit

Put simply, gross profit is equal to sales less variable costs. A few examples may help bring this concept to life:

>> A clothing retailer buys a skirt from the wholesaler for $20 and sells it for $50. Their gross profit is $30.

>> A massage therapist charges $80 per massage but the therapy center takes $25 as a booking and room fee. Their gross profit is $55.

>> A carpenter charges $800 for fixing a veranda. Materials cost $200 and labor for their apprentice costs $100. Their gross profit is $500.

Sounds okay so far? Just bear in mind:

REMEMBER

>> Gross profit equals sales less variable costs.

>> Gross profit is always more than net profit.

>> The more you sell, the more gross profit you make.

Figuring gross profit margins

Following on from the examples in the preceding section, if a clothing retailer buys a skirt for $20 and sells it for $50, the gross profit is $30. Sounds easy, but how do I figure out the *gross profit margin*? As follows:

Gross profit margin = gross profit divided by sales multiplied by 100

In this example, the retailer's gross profit margin equals $30 divided by $50 (that's gross profit divided by sales) multiplied by 100, which is 60 per cent.

As I mention earlier, the more you sell, the more gross profit you make. However, if your costs stay constant, your gross profit margin stays the same, regardless of how much you sell. For example, if this retailer sells four skirts, their sales would be $200, their costs would be $80, their gross profit would be $120, but their gross profit margin would still be the same, at 60 per cent.

Table 9-5 shows the gross profit and gross profit margins for the three examples from the preceding section.

TABLE 9-5   **Calculating Gross Profit and Gross Profit Margin**

	Clothing Retailer	Massage Therapist	Carpenter
Sell price	$50.00	$80.00	$800.00
Costs	$20.00	$25.00	$300.00
Gross Profit	$30.00	$55.00	$500.00
Gross Profit Margin	**60%**	**69%**	**63%**

TIP

Unless you know that something cost more to buy or to make than what you sold it for, both your gross profit and your gross profit margin should always be a positive figure.

Looking at margins over time

So far in this chapter, the examples I use talk about gross profit per unit sold or hour worked. However, in real life gross profit margins often vary from one transaction to the next (shopkeepers make a higher margin on gourmet jams than they do on milk, for example).

For this reason, it's good to be able to calculate your average gross profit margins over a period of time. Here's how some different kinds of businesses go about calculating their gross profit:

>> A builder constructs a house that then sells for $500,000. He spends $360,000 on materials and labor to build this house. His gross profit on the job is $140,000, and his gross profit margin is 28 per cent.

>> A couple making homemade chili sauce that they sell in all different shapes and sizes, and at different prices, can see that they made $80,000 in sales over the last 12 months and spent $20,000 on ingredients, bottles, labelling and freight. Their gross profit for the year is $60,000, and their average gross profit margin is 75 per cent.

>> A teenager buys secondhand clothes and resells them online. Last month, they sold $2,500 and spent $1,300 on buying clothes and postage. Their gross profit for the month is $1,200, and their average gross profit margin is 48 per cent.

Analyzing Margins for Your Own Business

Have you been reading this chapter and thinking to yourself that this theory is all very well, but you're not a retailer, a carpenter or a massage therapist? If so, never fear. In the following sections, I explain how to apply the principles of gross and net profit to your own business.

Calculating margins when you charge by the hour

If you have a service business and you charge by the hour, calculating your gross profit can be blindingly easy. Why? Because sometimes, a service business has no variable costs, and gross profit equals 100 per cent of income. Read on to find out more.

Here's how you work out your gross profit and gross profit margin if you have a service business:

1. **Write down your hourly charge-out rate, not including any taxes that you charge to customers (such as GST, VAT or sales tax).**

2. **Ask yourself whether any variable costs are associated with your service and, if so, calculate how much these costs are per hour.**

   The most likely cost for a service business is employees or subcontract labor. For example, when I ran a contract bookkeeping service, I paid my contractors an hourly rate for doing bookkeeping. This was a variable cost associated with my service.

   If you're a sole owner-operator with no employees, you may find that no variable costs are associated with your service.

3. **Subtract the cost you calculated in Step 2 from the hourly rate from Step 1.**

   This is your gross profit for this service. If you have no variable costs associated with your service, your hourly gross profit is the same as your hourly charge-out rate.

4. **Divide the gross profit you calculated in Step 3 by the hourly rate from Step 1, and divide your result by 100.**

   If you have no variable costs associated with your service, your gross profit margin will be 100 per cent.

5. **Consider the profitability of your service model.**

   Most service businesses need a decent gross profit margin in order to survive. If you're subcontracting out your services, don't underestimate the margin you'll need in order to cover all your business expenses. For example, if you're charging customers $100 per hour but paying employees $70 per hour, leaving yourself with a slim gross profit margin of 30 per cent, you're almost certainly going to be doing things tough.

Calculating margins when you sell products

If you buy or manufacture items that you sell to others, each item has a separate gross profit margin. If you use accounting software to track your inventory, you'll be able to generate reports that calculate gross profit margins for you. However, if you don't have this resource, grab a calculator and work through the following for each item you sell:

1. **Write down the sell price of this item, not including any taxes that you charge to customers (such as GST, VAT or sales tax).**

   If the sell price varies depending on the customer, do the analysis for each price you sell this item for.

2. **Write down the cost of this item.**

   If you buy this item from someone else, write down the total cost of purchasing this item, including freight but not including any taxes that you can claim back from the government (such as GST or VAT). If you manufacture this item, write down the total cost of all materials and production labor.

3. **Subtract the cost you calculated in Step 2 from the sell price you calculated in Step 1.**

   This is your gross profit for this item.

4. **Divide the gross profit you calculated in Step 3 by the sell price you calculated in Step 1, and divide your result by 100.**

5. **Consider the results and your fate in life.**

   Number crunching is not an end in itself. Does this margin seem reasonable? If you're not sure, ask around other people who work in the same industry as yourself, and try to get a sense of what margins you should expect.

TIP

Always bear in mind that, so long as your pricing policies remain consistent, your gross profit margin should stay relatively constant, no matter how much you sell.

Calculating margins if you do big projects

If you do lots of big projects over the course of a year — maybe you're a builder, you do custom manufacturing or you do big contract consultancy jobs — you're going to find it tricky to calculate your hourly gross profit, or your gross profit per unit sold. A different tack is required:

1. **Look at your total sales for 12 months, not including any taxes charged to the customer (such as GST or VAT).**

   I'm talking about total sales for all the different products that you sell, combined. If you're looking at a Profit & Loss report to get this figure, don't include things such as interest income, or sundry income from services.

2. **Add up your total variable costs for 12 months, not including any consumer tax paid (such as GST or VAT).**

   If you're an owner-operator with no employees running a service business, you may find that no variable costs are associated with your service. Otherwise, if you're unsure how to figure out what your variable costs are, refer to 'Identifying your variable costs', earlier in this chapter.

3. **Subtract the total costs you calculated in Step 2 from the total sales you calculated in Step 1.**

   This is your gross profit for the past 12 months.

4. **Divide the gross profit you calculated in Step 3 by the total sales you calculated in Step 1, and divide your result by 100.**

5. **Review your overall profitability.**

   What makes an acceptable gross profit margin varies from business to business. However, what's important for you is to be aware of your gross profit margin and ensure that it stays consistent over time.

Building Your Gross Profit Projection

In the earlier chapters in this book, I talk about clarifying your business idea and competitive strategies (Chapters 2 and 3), creating a budget for start-up expenses (Chapter 7), and setting prices and creating your first sales projection (Chapter 8).

Next on the road map is expanding your sales projection to add an estimate of direct costs so that you can arrive at a projection of your gross profit for the next 12 months.

Note: I'm assuming here that you've already made a stab at predicting sales for the next 12 months. If you haven't, scoot back to Chapter 8 to complete this process. What you're aiming for is a monthly estimate of total sales for the next 12 months. This could be a single total for each month, or you may choose to split sales into several categories (similar to the first few rows of Figure 9-2).

What you do next depends on what kind of business you're working on.

If you have a service business with no employees and no variable costs

This type of business has the simplest of financial forecasts. Simply enter the heading 'Variable Costs' and leave the figures in this row blank. However, note that if you forecast substantial growth for your business, you may not be able to do all the work yourself, and you may need to hire subcontractors or use employee labor. In which case, you'll need to show the variable costs of this labor (read on to find out more . . .).

If you have a service business and you use employee or subcontract labor

In this section, I'm talking about a service business that uses employee or sub-contract labor to provide at least some of the services. In this context, the employee or subcontract labor becomes a variable cost because the cost of this labor goes up or down in direct relation to sales. (I'm not talking about a service business where the owner provides all the services but maybe has an admin employee working in the office. This scenario is different, because the business isn't actually hiring out the admin worker to clients.)

Examples of this kind of business could be a plumber who subcontracts out some work, a party business that pays employees a casual rate to go to parties, a builder who uses a laborer, or a consultant bookkeeping service that hires lots of bookkeepers.

	A	B	C	D	E	F	G
1		Price	Materials	Labor			
2	Flip Out Package	$ 350.00	$ 45.00	$ 175.00			
3	Trees About Package	$ 490.00	$ 60.00	$ 175.00			
4	Adventure Package	$ 650.00	$ 85.00	$ 240.00			
5							
6	**Total Parties Sold Using Owner's Labor**	**Jul**	**Aug**	**Sep**	**Oct**	**Nov**	**Dec**
7	Flip Out Package	8	8	8	8	8	8
8	Trees About Package	4	4	4	4	4	4
9	Adventure Package	2	1	1	1	1	1
10							
11	**Total Parties Sold Using Subcontract or Employee Labor**						
12	Flip Out Package	12	12	13	8	12	12
13	Trees About Package	8	6	8	10	12	12
14	Adventure Package	2	3	4	4	5	4
15							
16	**Income Generated**	**Jul**	**Aug**	**Sep**	**Oct**	**Nov**	**Dec**
17	Sales - Flip Out Package	$ 7,000	$ 7,000	$ 7,350	$ 5,600	$ 7,000	$ 7,000
18	Sales - Trees About Package	$ 5,880	$ 4,900	$ 5,880	$ 6,860	$ 7,840	$ 7,840
19	Sales - Adventure Package	$ 2,600	$ 2,600	$ 3,250	$ 3,250	$ 3,900	$ 3,250
20	**Total Sales**	$ 15,480	$ 14,500	$ 16,480	$ 15,710	$ 18,740	$ 18,090
21							
22	**Variable Costs**						
23	Materials & Labor - Flip Out Package	$ 3,000	$ 3,000	$ 3,220	$ 2,120	$ 3,000	$ 3,000
24	Materials & Labor - Trees About Package	$ 2,120	$ 1,650	$ 2,120	$ 2,590	$ 3,060	$ 3,060
25	Materials & Labor - Adventure Package	$ 820	$ 1,060	$ 1,385	$ 1,385	$ 1,710	$ 1,385
26	**Total Cost of Sales**	$ 5,940	$ 5,710	$ 6,725	$ 6,095	$ 7,770	$ 7,445
27							
28	**Gross Profit**	$ 9,540	$ 8,790	$ 9,755	$ 9,615	$ 10,970	$ 10,645

FIGURE 9-2:
Building a gross profit projection for a service with employees or subcontractors.

Here's how to create a gross profit projection for this kind of business:

1. **Complete your sales projections for the next 12 months.**

   You should have a spreadsheet file with the months along the top, details regarding sales below, and a grand total sales forecast for each month along the bottom. In Figure 9-2, the first 20 rows show this information. (Refer to Chapter 8 for more information on sales projections.)

2. **If you haven't done so already, separate out sales where you're going to do the work, and sales that you'll get employees or subcontractors to do the work.**

   Figure 9-2 shows how this is done. The reason you separate the two is because you're going to have variable costs associated with the services that employees or subcontractors provide.

TIP

If you have a company structure, rather than a sole trader or partnership structure, you will receive some kind of salary. Usually in financial projections, director salaries are shown in the expenses part of the projection, not as a variable cost, but if you feel strongly that you want to show the cost of your labor here, you can do so. The format of a business plan has no absolute rights or wrongs; the only condition is that the structure needs to be logical and make sense not just to yourself, but also to others.

3. **Insert costs next to each of your prices.**

   Can you see how I've inserted the costs both for materials and for labor for each service in the first few rows of columns C and D in Figure 9-2?

4. **List your variable costs below the sales.**

   I've inserted a separate row for each service provided here, because the cost is different for each one.

5. **Calculate the value of variable costs by multiplying the number of times the service is sold by the cost of each service.**

TIP

   I often add names to cells, rather than specifying cell references. For example, in the spreadsheet for Figure 9-2, I give cell B2 the name 'FlipOut'. I talk more about naming cells in Chapter 11.

6. **Add a row that calculates gross profit.**

   Gross profit is equal to sales less variable costs. For example, in Figure 9-2, the gross profit for July equals $15,480 less $5,940, equaling $9,540. The formula for this gross profit in July is **=B20-B26**.

7. **Save this spreadsheet with the name 'Gross Profit Projection'.**

   Of course, you can save this spreadsheet with any name you like. However, I do refer to this file in Chapter 11 and so if you save the file by this name, you'll find my instructions in that chapter make more sense.

If you buy and sell a small number of products

For this kind of business, I'm talking about someone who buys or manufactures a few specific products and then resells them. Examples could include someone making homemade jams, a baker selling pastries, a cafe selling a limited range of items or a cabinet-maker producing a limited range of furniture.

In the next example, I show how to create a gross profit projection for this kind of business:

1. **Complete your sales projections for the next 12 months.**

   You should have a spreadsheet file with the months along the top, details regarding sales below, and a grand total sales forecast for each month below. In Figure 9-3, the first 17 rows show this information. (Refer to Chapter 8 for more information on sales projections.)

2. **Insert costs next to each of your products.**

   I've inserted the costs for each of my products in the first few rows of column C in Figure 9-3.

A	B	C	D	E	F	G
1		**Cost of**				
	Sell Price	**Ingredients**				
2 Friands	$ 5.00	$ 0.66				
3 Regular Muffins	$ 4.00	$ 0.80				
4 Wholesale Muffins	$ 2.50	$ 0.80				
5						
6	**Jul**	**Aug**	**Sep**	**Oct**	**Nov**	**Dec**
7 Friands - Units Sold	430	430	410	450	490	550
8 Regular Muffins - Units Sold	445	445	430	470	510	540
9 Wholesale Muffins - Units Sold	210	210	190	230	270	290
10						
11 Friands - Total Sales	$ 2,150	$ 2,150	$ 2,050	$ 2,250	$ 2,450	$ 2,750
12 Muffins - Total Sales	$ 1,780	$ 1,780	$ 1,720	$ 1,880	$ 2,040	$ 2,160
13 W/sale Muffins - Total Sales	$ 525	$ 525	$ 475	$ 575	$ 675	$ 725
14 **Total Sales**	$ 4,455	$ 4,455	$ 4,245	$ 4,705	$ 5,165	$ 5,635
15						
16 Friands - Cost of Ingredients	$ 284	$ 284	$ 271	$ 297	$ 323	$ 363
17 Muffins - Cost of Ingredients	$ 356	$ 356	$ 344	$ 376	$ 408	$ 432
18 W/sale Muffins - Cost of Ingredients	$ 168	$ 168	$ 152	$ 184	$ 216	$ 232
19 **Total Variable Costs**	$ 808	$ 808	$ 767	$ 857	$ 947	$ 1,027
20						
21 **GROSS PROFIT**	$ 3,647	$ 3,647	$ 3,478	$ 3,848	$ 4,218	$ 4,608

FIGURE 9-3: Building a gross profit projection for a business selling a small number of different products.

TIP

Earlier in this chapter, I talk about creating detailed product costing worksheets for each product (refer to 'Creating product costings for manufacturers'). If you're feeling clever, you may want to link each of the costs at the top of this worksheet to your product costing worksheets. This would mean that the moment you update a product costing, your gross profit projection is automatically updated as well. Chapter 11 talks more about linking one worksheet to another.

3. **List your variable costs below the sales.**

   I've inserted a separate row for each product provided in Figure 9-3, because the cost is different for each one.

4. **Calculate the value of variable costs by multiplying the number of units sold by the cost of each item.**

   For example, the formula in cell B18 is **=B9*C4**.

TIP

   I often add names to cells, rather than specifying cell references. For example, in the spreadsheet for Figure 9-3, I give cell C2 the name **CostFriands**. I talk more about naming cells in Chapter 11.

5. **Add a row that calculates gross profit.**

   Gross profit is equal to sales less variable costs. For example, in Figure 9-3, the gross profit for January equals $4,455 less $808, equaling $3,647. The formula for this gross profit in January is **=B14-B19**.

6. **Save this spreadsheet with the name 'Gross Profit Projection'.**

   Of course, you can save this spreadsheet with any name you like. However, I do refer to this file in Chapter 11 and so if you save the file by this name, you'll find my instructions in this chapter make more sense.

If you sell many different products or your variable costs are a percentage of sales

Sometimes, the idea with variable costs is that they are a stable percentage of income. For example, if you pay commissions on sales, these commissions are normally a certain percentage. Or if you're a retailer, the cost of the goods you buy is probably a similar percentage of sales each time you make a sale.

If your variable costs are always a pretty stable percentage of sales, the trick is to set up your gross profit projection so that your variable costs calculate automatically. In other words, set up your worksheet so that if you increase sales, variable costs automatically increase as well.

For example, in Figure 9–4, the bookseller knows that for every $100 of full–price books he sells, it costs him $60 to buy the books. In other words, his variable costs represent 60 per cent of sales. Similarly, he knows that remainder books cost him, on average, 20 per cent of the sale value.

Here's how to build your gross profit projection if you sell lots of products, meaning the easiest way to calculate variable costs is as a percentage of sales:

1. **Complete your sales projections for the next 12 months.**

   You should have a spreadsheet file with the months along the top, details regarding sales below, and a grand total sales forecast for each month along the bottom. In Figure 9-4, the first 11 rows show this information. Notice that in contrast to a business that only sells a handful of different products, in this example the bookseller calculates sales projections according to the type of goods he's selling, and the average profit on each. (Refer to Chapter 8 for more information on sales projections.)

2. **Think of how much it costs you to buy each kind of item that you sell, and express this is a percentages of the sale value next to each price.**

   For example, if a footwear retailer always doubles the cost when pricing shoes, their variable costs for shoes would be 50 per cent.

3. **List your variable costs below the sales.**

   Insert a separate row for each kind of product that you sell.

4. **Calculate the value of variable costs by multiplying the average value of each sale by the percentage that this item normally costs.**

For example, the formula in cell B14 is **=B8*C2**.

5. **Add a row that calculates gross profit.**

Gross profit is equal to sales less variable costs. For example, in Figure 9-4, the gross profit for July equals $42,750 less $19,788, equaling $22,963. The formula for this gross profit in July is **=B11-B17**.

6. **Save this spreadsheet with the name 'Gross Profit Projection'.**

Of course, you can save this spreadsheet with any name you like. However, I do refer to this file in Chapter 11 and so if you save the file by this name, you'll find my instructions in this chapter make more sense.

FIGURE 9-4:
Building a gross profit projection for a business selling lots of different kinds of products, or calculating costs on a percentage basis.

	A	B	C	D	E	F	G
1		**Average Sell Price**	**Cost as a % of sales**				
2	Full-price books	$ 24.99	60%				
3	Remainder books	$ 19.99	20%				
4	Gift and other products	$ 17.99	65%				
5							
6							
7		**Jul**	**Aug**	**Sep**	**Oct**	**Nov**	**Dec**
8	Full-price books sales	$ 25,000	$ 25,750	$ 26,500	$ 27,500	$ 35,000	$ 45,800
9	Remainder book sales	$ 15,000	$ 15,450	$ 15,900	$ 16,500	$ 21,000	$ 27,480
10	Gifts & other sales	$ 2,750	$ 2,833	$ 2,915	$ 3,025	$ 3,850	$ 5,038
11	**TOTAL SALES**	$ 42,750	$ 44,033	$ 45,315	$ 47,025	$ 59,850	$ 78,318
12							
13							
14	Purchases full-price books	$ 15,000	$ 15,450	$ 15,900	$ 16,500	$ 21,000	$ 27,480
15	Purchases remainders	$ 3,000	$ 3,090	$ 3,180	$ 3,300	$ 4,200	$ 5,496
16	Purchases gifts	$ 1,788	$ 1,841	$ 1,895	$ 1,966	$ 2,503	$ 3,275
17	**TOTAL VARIABLE COSTS**	$ 19,788	$ 20,381	$ 20,975	$ 21,766	$ 27,703	$ 36,251
18							
19	**GROSS PROFIT**	$ 22,963	$ 23,651	$ 24,340	$ 25,259	$ 32,148	$ 42,067

TIP

The neat thing about showing variable costs as a percentage in the top-left corner of your worksheet is that if you change one of these percentages, your variable costs change automatically too. In addition, working in this way enables you to experiment with different scenarios. For example, imagine that this is your business and you're thinking of switching suppliers. The service is much better, but the cost of books from this supplier will be 65 per cent of sales, rather than 60 per cent. By changing one figure in the top of your worksheet, you can see instantly the impact this change would make to your profitability.

GROSS PROFIT, CANARIES, FRAUD AND MORE

Understanding and monitoring your gross profit margin is an essential part of managing almost any business.

At the early stages of a business plan, understanding your gross profit margin is crucial for creating accurate budgets and experimenting with different business models. For example, look at your sales figures and ask yourself, what difference would a 5 per cent increase in gross profit make to the bottom line of your Profit & Loss? Often an increase of just 5 per cent can make the difference between business survival and death.

As your business becomes more established, your gross profit margin becomes an indicator of the health of your business. Similar to a canary down the mine, an unusual result in profit margins on your Profit & Loss report is often the first indicator that something is astray.

I remember getting a call a few years ago from a private investigator who'd been asked to investigate an alleged fraud in a computer retail company. The owner of the company suspected his bookkeeper of siphoning off funds, but couldn't identify how it was happening. The reason for these suspicions? The gross profit margin of his company had always been stable at 35 per cent, but in recent months it had fallen to 32 per cent. (I did assist with the investigation and, sadly, we were able to confirm the owner's fears.)

IN THIS CHAPTER

» **Creating a 12-month forecast for business expenses**

» **Tweaking your forecast so it's as accurate as can be**

» **Comparing your business with others similar to you**

» **Understanding where taxes and loan repayments fit into the picture**

» **Figuring out how much money you need to keep that hungry wolf at bay**

Chapter **10**

Managing Expenses

Although a business plan takes many shapes and sizes, pretty much every business plan includes a projection of both income and expenses for the next 12 months ahead. (Some business plans extend further than this, for three or even five years; however, for most purposes, 12 months usually does just fine.)

In this chapter, I focus on the expenses element of this 12-month forecast. Estimating future expenses isn't some idle form of crystal-ball gazing where you pluck some figures out of the air until you arrive at a final prediction of profit that makes you sleep easy. Instead, planning each expense in detail provides you with an opportunity for a reality check, even if this reality can prove rather chilling at times.

In this chapter, I suggest that if you're creating your first business plan, you look at your personal expenses as well. After all, in the absence of benevolent fairy godmothers or inheritances from wealthy great-aunties, starting a business that requires your full-time input but doesn't generate enough profits for you to survive is never going to fly.

Concentrating on Expenses

I accept that this book provides no gripping plot, murders or sex scenes, and that few people picking up this book are going to start at Chapter 1 and read through to the end. Instead, you'll probably flick through the pages, picking and choosing the bits you're interested in, which is generally okay. However, when you're working on financial projections, simply jumping in at whatever chapter catches your eye can be a time-wasting exercise.

As I explain in Chapter 1, the typical financial planning cycle involves creating a start-up budget, followed by estimating prices, costs and expenses. You then use this information to create Profit & Loss Projections, break-even analysis reports and Cashflow Projections.

If you've been working through this cycle chapter by chapter, you'll be about half-way through this process. (Chapter 7 focuses on budgeting for start-up expenses, Chapter 8 on prices and rates, Chapter 9 on product costs and gross profit and Chapter 10 — that's this chapter — on expense budgets. Chapters 11, 12 and 13 then complete the financial planning process.)

So, if you've just picked up this book and plunged in at this chapter, pause for a moment and check that you've already covered the initial stages of your financial plan (that is, creating a start-up budget, setting prices and calculating product costs). If you haven't, take the time to get these foundations in place first.

Separating start-up expenses and variable costs from ongoing expenses

When planning for business expenses, always separate *start-up expenses* from *ongoing expenses*:

» *Start-up expenses* are one-off expenses that you encounter when you first start a business, such as new equipment, company formation expenses, legal expenses and signage. I talk lots about start-up expenses in Chapter 7.

» *Ongoing expenses* are the kind of expenses that occur year in and year out, and which form a regular part of everyday trading. Ongoing expenses are the focus of the next part of this chapter.

When you're working with Profit & Loss Projections in your business plan, you only include ongoing expenses. Start-up expenses — if relevant to you — are shown separately.

Similarly, remember the difference between *variable costs* and *fixed expenses*.

>> *Variable costs* (also sometimes called *direct costs* or *cost of goods sold*) are the costs that go up and down in direct relation to your sales.

>> *Fixed expenses* (also sometimes called *indirect costs* or *overheads*) are expenses that stay constant, regardless of whether your sales go up and down.

This chapter focuses on fixed expenses only. For more about creating a worksheet that forecasts variable costs, refer to Chapter 9.

Thinking of what expenses to include

If you've been running your business for a while, you already have a good idea of what your expenses are going to be. However, if you're just getting started with your business plan, thinking of the types of expenses you may encounter can be tricky. Are you going to take out insurance? What about accounting fees? Will you need to pay any professional memberships? What expenses could you face that you haven't even thought of yet?

TIP

Figure 10-1 shows a Business Expenses worksheet that lists expenses in the first column, how often they occur in the second column, an estimate of the amount in the third, and a monthly estimate in the fourth. To create a Business Expenses worksheet similar to this one, here's what to do:

1. **Open up a new worksheet in Excel or Google Sheets and list business expenses in the first column, followed by the months of the year in the first row.**

   Remember to only include ongoing business expenses at this point, and not variable costs or start-up expenses. For the months of the year, you're usually best to project at least 12 months ahead. (I only show six months in Figure 10-1 due to lack of space.)

2. **Estimate the amount of each expense, and in a separate column, specify whether this expense occurs weekly, fortnightly, quarterly, monthly or annually. Show all amounts exclusive of value-added tax (such as GST or VAT).**

CHAPTER 10 **Managing Expenses** 163

If you haven't started trading yet and you're still creating a business plan, estimating expenses can be very tricky. See 'Using AI to Secure Business Intelligence', later in this chapter, for ways to improve the accuracy of your estimates.

If your business is already trading, the best way to make estimates is to look at what you've spent in the past. Supplier invoices and Profit & Loss Statements are all good sources for this information.

Round all amounts to the nearest $100 or so — forecasts aren't meant to be an exact science.

3. **Based on the frequency of this expense, enter monthly estimates for each one.**

WARNING

Be super careful with any expenses that you pay weekly. For example, if you rent is, say, $500 a week, your monthly budget is not four times this amount.To calculate a monthly budget for something you pay weekly, you need to first multiply the weekly amount by 52, and then divide it by 12. In this example, $500 a week rent multiplied by 52 equals $26,000. Divide this by 12 and you get just over $2,166 a month (not $2,000).

For more about showing weekly or irregular expenses, see 'Allowing for irregular payments', later in this chapter.

4. **Think carefully about the timing of any expenses you pay only quarterly or annually.**

For example, Figure 10-1 only shows a single amount in February for accounting fees, because these are only paid once a year.

5. **Review the totals in the Total Expenses row.**

The Total Expenses row should automatically add up the rows above it. This means that if you change a figure, the total recalculates automatically. In Excel, the easiest way to do this is to press your AutoSum button (the one with a Greek symbol that looks a bit like an 'E').

6. **Save your work and ponder.**

With your final worksheet complete, spend a generous amount of time checking it over, ensuring it makes sense and is realistic.

	A	B	C	F	G	H	I	J	K
1	**Type of Expense**	**Freqency**	**Estimate Per Period**	**Jan**	**Feb**	**Mar**	**Apr**	**May**	**Jun**
2	Accounting Fees	Annually	$2,000	$0	$2,000	$0	$0	$0	$0
3	Bank Charges	Monthly	$100	$100	$100	$100	$100	$100	$100
4	Communication Expenses	Monthly	$380	$380	$380	$380	$380	$380	$380
5	Consultant Expenses	Quarterly	$300	$300	$300	$300	$300	$300	$300
6	Insurance	Monthly	$280	$280	$280	$280	$280	$280	$280
7	Interest Expense	Monthly	$520	$520	$520	$520	$520	$520	$520
8	IT Expenses	Monthly	$450	$450	$450	$450	$450	$450	$450
9	Lease Expenses	Monthly	$800	$800	$800	$800	$800	$800	$800
10	Marketing Expenses	Annually	$14,400	$1,200	$1,200	$1,200	$1,200	$1,200	$1,200
11	Merchant Fees	Monthly	$1,200	$621	$709	$823	$729	$945	$964
12	Motor Vehicle Expenses	Monthly	$350	$350	$350	$350	$350	$1,800	$350
13	Office Supplies	Annually	$1,800	$150	$150	$150	$150	$150	$150
14	Rental Expense	Fortnightly	$1,500	$3,250	$3,250	$3,250	$3,250	$3,250	$3,250
15	Repairs and Maintenance	Annually	$6,000	$500	$500	$500	$500	$500	$500
16	Staff Amenities	Monthly	$300	$300	$300	$300	$300	$300	$300
17	Travel Expenses	Monthly	$350	$350	$350	$350	$350	$350	$350
18	Utilities	Quarterly	$2,400	$600	$0	$0	$600	$0	$0
19	Wages and Salaries	Weekly	$900	$3,600	$3,600	$4,500	$3,600	$3,600	$4,500
20	Wages oncosts	Weekly	$108	$540	$540	$675	$540	$540	$675
21	**Total Expenses**			$14,291	$15,779	$14,928	$14,399	$15,465	$15,069

FIGURE 10-1: Forecasting expenses for the months ahead.

A BUDGET, PROJECTION OR CASHFLOW?

People tend to use the words 'budget', 'projection' and 'cashflow' synonymously, but subtle differences do exist. A *budget* is about setting sales targets and expense limits. In larger businesses, for example, part of the responsibility for each manager is to meet agreed sales budgets, and ensure spending doesn't exceed allocated expense budgets.

On the other hand, a *projection* often looks further into the future than a budget. Rather than being a document that sets out expectations and responsibilities, a projection is more a statement of what might be possible. I often use projections to experiment with 'what-if?' scenarios, looking at what would happen to my profits if sales were to slump by 10 per cent, or expenses increase by a similar amount. (In this chapter, when I talk about building an expenses worksheet, I'm still really at the projection stage. Later on, if the plan shows that the business model is viable, I can take these projections and use them to create budgets.)

A *cashflow* is a different report again, and looks at the actual cash flowing in and out of a business. For example, if you receive a $20,000 loan from the bank, this appears on your Cashflow Projection but doesn't show on your budget or Profit & Loss Projection. (Why not? Because a loan doesn't count as income.) Chapter 13 talks lots more about cashflow reports and how they work.

Fine-tuning Your Worksheet

With the first draft of your expenses worksheet complete, you're ready to fine-tune it so you can be sure that your projections are as accurate as possible. Look at relationships between expenses, think about irregular payments, and focus on large expenses in a bit more detail.

Recognizing relationships

Are any of your expense categories directly related to one another? For example, staff oncosts usually go up or down in direct proportion to wages.

TIP

The trick is to tell your spreadsheet about relationships so that it calculates them for you automatically. In Figure 10-1, for example, you can see a figure for wages in Row 19. I know that wages oncosts average 15 per cent of wages, so my formula for wages oncosts in January is **=F19*15%**. The neat thing about specifying relationships in this way is that when you change one figure in the spreadsheet, other figures change automatically, too.

Allowing for irregular payments

When creating expense projections, take a while to consider expenses that vary from month to month or change with the seasons. Here are a few specifics to consider:

» Utility bills, such as electricity and gas, often fall due every two or three months, rather than every month.

» If you pay wages every week, bear in mind that every third month you'll get a month with five paydays, not four.

» Think about seasonal variations. Depending on your business, expenses can increase or decrease dramatically at different times of year.

» If you're a small owner-operated business, think about when you may take holidays, and whether you need to increase your wages expense during this time.

» If you don't know when an expense will fall due, you can average this expense across the year. For example, I know that my car usually clocks in at approximately $2,000 of repairs per year, but I never know when these bills are going to fall due. With these kinds of expenses, I just use my annual estimate and leave a monthly amount in place.

Playing with the 10 per cent rule

I have a technique that I've developed over the years as a way of ensuring that my expense estimates are more likely to be accurate. What I do is go through the worksheet and identify any expenses that make up around 10 per cent, or more, of the total expenses. For example, if you look at Figure 10-1, you can see that marketing expenses make up almost 10 per cent of total expenses each month. For such a small business, this expense makes up a significant proportion of outgoings.

TIP

Next, for any expense that makes up around 10 per cent of total expenses, I see if it makes sense to dissect this expense in more detail. In the example shown in Figure 10-1, I would suggest to the business that they add more detail about marketing expense in the worksheet — for example, listing different types of marketing expenditure separately.

Using AI to Secure Business Intelligence

You can find out how other businesses in your industry are faring by using something called *business benchmarking*. Business benchmarking results are compiled using survey results from other business owners. Individual results are always kept confidential, and it's only the averages (or highs and lows) that are reported, as well as percentages. For example, if I'm planning to open a boutique bar and I'm working on my business plan, I could look at the benchmarks for bars and clubs and see what percentage of sales I could expect to spend on alcohol, food, rental, wages and so on, or how much profit an average bar in a city suburb makes each year.

TIP

Business benchmarks provide an excellent way for you to check whether your financial projections are realistic, especially if you haven't started your business yet.

Locating benchmarks for your business

How best to locate benchmarks for your business depends on your location and industry. A good starting point for resources is to ask AI (using ChatGPT or a similar tool). For example, you might ask 'Where can I find business benchmarks for an auto-mechanic business in the UK?' or 'How can I find business benchmarks for a café in regional Australia?' or 'What gross profit does an average physiotherapist business in North America make?'

You can also find benchmarks from a few other sources:

>> **Banks:** Banks often have industry-specific information useful for benchmarking.

>> **Benchmarking services:** Search online using the word 'benchmarks' or 'benchmarking' to find organizations specializing in the collation and resale of benchmarking data. IBISWorld and Statista are two of the best known services providing industry-wide reports and data. If your business is based in Australia, Benchmarking Data & Research (www.benchmarking.com.au) also sell benchmarking data.

>> **The 'big 5' accounting practices:** The major accounting and consulting firms, such as KPMG, PWC or EY, usually publish reports on key industries that are available for a fee. Call to find out what reports are available for your industry.

>> **Boutique accounting practices:** Some accountants specialize in particular industries. For example, I know of someone who has a boutique accountancy practice specializing in medical practitioners and dentists. Specialist accountants will be very conversant with their industry and can quickly advise you whether your financial projections fall within industry standards.

>> **Government departments:** Government departments such as the Bureau of Economic Analysis (US) or Companies House (UK) can be a great resource; Companies House in particular allows you to view filed accounts for any registered UK company. The Canadian government is also a great resource (search for 'Government of Canada, financial performance data').

>> **Industry associations:** Industry associations almost always have some reference materials regarding benchmarks and are usually willing to advise members.

>> **Networking meetings:** If you have colleagues working in the same industry but not in direct competition (maybe you're all in professional practice of some kind but specializing in different areas), you may find these colleagues are willing to share information regarding rent, wages or other expenses as a percentage of sales. (However, most business owners will be reticent regarding the actual amount paid for these items.)

Using benchmarks as part of your plan

With a topic such as benchmarking, I like to use a detailed example to bring the whole concept to life.

In this fictional example, imagine a doctor (I'll call her Kate) has recently opened a new medical practice. As part of her business plan, she has purchased a set of benchmarks from a benchmarking organization (see Table 10-1).

In Table 10-1, you can see that the average medical practice has a turnover of $822,000. The lowest practice in the survey has a turnover of $294,600 and the highest has a turnover of $1,691,500. Sounds interesting enough, but the really practical aspects for you — in planning your business — are the percentages. For example, can you see that the average medical practice spends 25.3 per cent on wages and 5.5 per cent of turnover on rent?

TABLE 10-1   **Using Business Benchmarks**

Indicator	Average	Low	High
Total income (thousands)	$822.2	$274.6	$1,691.5
Drugs, supplies, consumables	2.16%	0.76%	3.59%
Wages and salaries (staff only, not owners)	25.30%	15.10%	39.34%
Rent of premises	5.52%	1.92%	9.09%
Staff oncosts	2.23%	1.11%	3.87%
Non-vehicle depreciation/lease/hire purchase	2.70%	0.56%	5.18%
Net profit	49.22%	30.21%	67.31%
Support staff per practitioner	1.52	1.00	2.35
Average consult length (minutes)	15	10	19
Average no. of consults per doctor per week	156	105	200
Opening hours per day	9.51	8.00	11.00
Opening days per week	5.50	5.00	6.10

Now look at Figure 10-2, which shows Kate's first year's Profit & Loss report. Can you see how in the final column, Kate has calculated how much each expense is as a percentage of sales? For example, her rent at $18,200 per year is 6.4 per cent of income (that's $18,200 divided by $285,000 multiplied by 100). Compare this rent against other medical practices, and you can see that Kate is paying slightly above the average rent of 5.5 per cent. Similarly, Kate is spending 32.6 per cent on wages, well above the average of 25.3 per cent.

	A	B	C	D
1		My Business	Expenses as % of Sales	Benchmark Expenses % of Sales
2	Total Sales	$ 285,000.00		
3				
4	Drugs, supplies, consumables	$ 9,300.00	3.3%	2.2%
5	Wages and salaries	$ 93,000.00	32.6%	25.3%
6	Staff oncosts	$ 13,950.00	4.9%	2.2%
7	Rent of premises	$ 18,200.00	6.4%	5.5%
8	Depreciation/lease/hire purchase	$ 12,200.00	4.3%	2.7%
9	All other expenses	$ 22,050.00	7.7%	13.1%
10	Total Expenses	$ 168,700.00		
11				
12	Net Profit	$ 116,300.00	40.8%	49.2%

FIGURE 10-2: Looking at expense percentages is part of the benchmarking process.

TIP

You may be wondering how to apply the preceding example to your own business — after all, chances are that you're not a medical practitioner. Here's what to do:

1. **Complete your sales, cost of sales and expenses projection for the next 12 months.**

   For more detail on how to do these projections, refer to the first part of this chapter, along with Chapters 8 and 9. Alternatively, if your business has already been trading for a while, you could generate a Profit & Loss report for the most recent 12 months of trading, and send this report to a spreadsheet.

2. **Add a column for % of sales, and create a formula for % of sales against each row.**

   Can you see the column of percentages in Figure 10-2? You can create this column by inserting a formula against the first cost of sales row and then copying this formula to all the other rows. For example, the formula that I type in cell C4 (next to Drugs, supplies, consumables) is '**=B4/B2**'. (The dollar signs in B2 mean you can copy this formula to other rows and the cell reference stays the same.) I then click the % button on my menu bar to show this figure as a percentage.

3. **Get hold of benchmarks for your industry.**

   I talk about how to find benchmarks earlier in this chapter (refer to 'Locating benchmarks for your business').

4. **Compare your business plan against the industry averages.**

   For example, if you're running a cafe and benchmarks show that the average cafe spends 30 per cent on wages, compare this percentage with your projections and see whether you're spending, relatively speaking, more or less.

You may find it tricky to find benchmarks that are relevant to you. Maybe you've invented a totally new product or maybe your business is an unusual combination of many different activities. In this scenario, try to locate a set of benchmarks for a business type that's at least similar to yours in some way or other.

TIP

If you've already been trading for a couple of years or more, you can also benchmark your financial projections against Profit & Loss reports from your own business for previous years. For example, if results from previous years show that your wages usually average 30 per cent of sales, but your Profit & Loss Projection for next year shows that wages only equal 25 per cent of sales, you have probably made an error in your projections.

Thinking about Taxes and Loan Repayments

Spend a while browsing any reading matter about business planning and you soon stumble across righteous statistics about how the 30 per cent or so businesses with formal business plans do a squillion times better than the 70 per cent that don't. Sounds wonderful, but these statistics fail to mention the suffering that at least another 25 per cent endured before they gave up on the whole planning process.

In the following sections, I touch on some of the pain points that you're likely to encounter at this stage of your plan, hopefully supplying straightforward answers to some of the more complicated of questions.

Allowing for personal and company tax

One of the questions people often ask is whether to include personal or company tax in their business expense worksheet. The answer depends on whether your business is structured as a sole trader, partnership or company.

If you're a sole trader or partnership, you're responsible for paying tax on any profit that the business makes. The amount of tax you pay depends on many factors, including whether you have any sources of income other than the business. Generally, I don't include personal income tax as an expense on any business plan.

If your business has a company structure, you do need to include company tax expense on your expenses worksheet. In Chapter 11, I explain how to pull all the different elements of your business plan together, starting with your income worksheet, deducting your cost of sales and business expenses, calculating net profit, and finally adding two rows called Company Tax Expense, and Net Profit After Company Tax.

Understanding where other taxes fit in

What about taxes such as sales tax, VAT or GST? The answer depends on where you live.

If your business is subject to any kind of value-added tax (known, for example, as VAT in Canada and the United Kingdom, or GST in Australia and New Zealand), you don't include this tax in any of your expenses. Instead, you show the value of each expense before tax is applied. (Why? Because this kind of tax applies only to the final sale to the consumer — as a business, you're entitled to claim back any tax of this nature that you pay.) On the other hand, if your business pays a sales tax (something that applies in almost every state within the United States), you should include sales tax in your expenses, showing the value of each expense inclusive of the tax that you pay. (Why? Because this tax forms part of the cost of this expense — you can't claim this tax back from the government.)

Dealing with loan repayments and interest

If your business has borrowed money and you're paying off a business loan, deciding how to show loan repayments in your expenses worksheet can be quite tricky.

Imagine that you have a bank loan and your repayments are $1,000 per week. You've almost paid off this loan, and you currently have only $15,000 left to repay. The interest on this loan equals only about $15 per week.

Any accountant will gladly explain that in terms of the profit of your business, the only expense that you can claim is the interest. However, when you're doing a business plan, this kind of analysis is too simplistic. The interest may be inconsequential, but budgeting $1,000 a week in repayments is not.

The best way to show loan repayments in your business plan depends on the circumstances:

>> If you decide to include both a Profit & Loss Projection and a Cashflow Projection in your business plan (and if you're not sure yet, skip ahead to Chapter 13), you should show the value of the interest expense in your Profit & Loss Projection, and the value of the whole loan repayment in your Cashflow Projection.

>> If your business plan only requires a Profit & Loss Projection, err on the side of caution and show the full value of the loan repayment in your expenses worksheet. This way, the final net profit that you arrive at in your projections will be as close as possible to your likely surplus in cash.

Keeping the Wolf from the Door

If you're starting a new business and you have very little savings or start-up capital, you may find you have very little to live on while building up your business. In this scenario, I can't stress enough how important it is to create a budget not only for business expenses, but also for personal expenses.

TRUE STORY

I remember one of the students in a business start-up course I was running. Dave had recently been retrenched from a high-stress high-income job in construction management. Disillusioned and disheartened, he had decided to leave the corporate world and instead start up a handyman business. His business concept seemed solid enough and, when working on his income projections, he was realistic that it could take some time to build up clients and a good income base. However, when we worked on his personal budget, my hair stood on end. Dave's commitments were huge. He had two car leases, three kids at private school and whopping mortgage repayments. With his savings, he only had about six weeks to go before everything would come crashing down around his ears. When Dave weighed everything up, he realized that he (and his partner) couldn't bear to downsize, shift his kids to public school and sell his cars. Besides, he didn't have time to make all these changes in the six weeks he had left until his savings ran out. Instead, he went back to the corporate world, with a plan to maybe return to his idea of a handyman business at a point when his commitments weren't quite so scary.

Even if your business is already up and running, creating a budget for personal expenses is usually still a good idea. You must ensure that your business is going to generate enough income to cover your personal expenses. If not, you may need to make changes to your business plan (such as adjusting expenses or increasing income) or, alternatively, make some changes to your personal spending patterns.

Identifying income

When building a personal budget, the first step is to make a list of all your non-business sources of income. (Of course, if you're already running your own business rather than in the start-up phase, you may have no income that doesn't come from your business.)

If you still earn income from employment, remember to factor in this income after tax, and not before tax, when doing a personal budget. In other words, if your pay is $1,600 a week but your employer deducts $400 a week in taxes, only include $1,200 as your income. Also, if you receive wages weekly and you're doing an expenses budget on a monthly basis, you need to multiply your wages by 52 then divide them by 12 to arrive at how much income you receive each month.

Figuring how much you need to live

Your budget for personal expenses works in much the same way as your budget for business expenses, except that the kinds of expenses in your private life are very different.

You can find a heap of free personal budgeting apps for use on your smartphone. Unless you already have a personal budgeting system in place, I suggest you download one of these apps and use it as a prompt to analyze how much you currently spend on what, and how much you need each week to survive.

The app you use will have its own approach, but the aim of the game is this:

1. **For every category of personal expense, calculate how much you spend, and whether this expense occurs weekly, fortnightly, quarterly, monthly or annually.**

    TIP

    If you're at all unsure how much an expense is, document every single cent you spend for at least the next four weeks. Recording every itsy-bitsy bit of spending can be tedious, but if you spend a few weeks doing this, you'll end up with a very incisive insight into your financial affairs.

2. **Use the totals provided by the app to calculate how much money you spend every month.**

3. **Calculate any income you receive, or will receive, that's independent of your business, after tax (if you have any, that is).**

    I talk about what income to include earlier in this chapter (refer to the section 'Identifying income').

4. **Look at the difference between your monthly income and monthly expenses.**

    Unless you plan to change your spending habits, the shortfall between monthly income generated from non-business sources and monthly expenses is the *minimum* after-tax profit that your business must generate in order for you to be able to survive.

5. **Write this figure down and ponder!**

WHAT IF I CAN'T BEAR TO DO A PERSONAL BUDGET?

Scrutinizing personal spending has to be one of the more depressing ways to spend a rainy afternoon. Alternatively, a rough-and-ready way to figure out how much you need to live is to write down how much you've earned the last 12 months, look up how much you've saved or how much savings you've used, and calculate the difference. Unless your personal circumstances have changed, this difference is going to be approximately the same as how much you need to live.

However, if you're starting or growing a business and you're willing to live a little leaner while things get off the ground, this method isn't good enough. The only way to really get a handle on your finances is to make a budget, try to live by it, and see if you're spending more than you can afford.

TIP

When you look at each month for the next 12 months, can you see any months where expenses are particularly high or income particularly low? (For people working casual jobs, Christmas can be one of these times.) If you can plan ahead for these times, maybe slotting some money away into a savings account, this can make life less stressful and help you feel that your personal budget is under control.

Setting goals and budgets

In the preceding section, I suggest you write down everything you currently spend each week or each month, and analyze how much your expenses are going to be each month. However, this is a very different process from creating a budget for each type of expense.

For example, maybe you've been monitoring your spending for the last eight weeks and you can see you spend an average of $200 per week eating out. The question you need to ask yourself is this: Given your overall financial goals, is this amount reasonable?

TIP

One way to identify where you can save money is to categorize each expense as to whether it's essential or optional, and whether it's a fixed amount or variable. Table 10-2 provides examples for each of these categories. Generally, you won't have much influence — certainly in the short term — over essential expenses that are a fixed amount each month. However, you will almost certainly have room to save money on all other kinds of expenses.

TABLE 10-2

Categorizing Different Kinds of Personal Expenses

Type of Expense	Examples
Essential expense, no flexibility to decrease	Rent, mortgage payments, loan payments, insurance premiums
Essential expense, possible flexibility to decrease	Food, utility bills, phone plans, internet
Optional expense, flexibility to decrease	Eating out, takeaways, alcohol, cigarettes, clothing, gym membership, holidays, streaming services

What you're trying to develop here are good habits regarding personal spending. These habits are more important at some stages of life than others (a family with young children and a mortgage probably need to be much more careful about money than a young person with no commitments in a big share house). However, the skills you develop in regards to your personal spending tend to spill over into skills you can use in your business, and vice versa.

As part of this planning process, I recommend you set a clear goal for what you want to achieve financially. Do you want to save $10,000 within the next 12 months? Get rid of all your debt within three years? Or be a millionaire by the time you're 40?

REMEMBER

Goals can be short term or long term. Short-term goals are things you can achieve in the next couple of weeks or months. Long-term goals are what you want to achieve in the next one to five years. And, of course, even longer term goals are what you want to achieve in the next 10 to 20 years.

Recognizing why personal and business budgets connect

You may be wondering why I devote so much space in this chapter to talking about personal budgets when this is meant to be a book about business. I do so because I've seen many new businesses flounder because of a failure by the owners to understand their personal spending. Here are the kinds of traps you want to avoid:

TRUE STORY

>> I knew a couple who started a business at the beginning of the holiday season and had a few bumper months of trading. Filled with confidence, they drew all the available cash out of the business and spent it on an overseas holiday. Later on, when the business needed cash to get it through lean times, they had no reserves.

>> Former clients of mine started up a business that did very well right from the start. However, they hadn't created a realistic budget for personal spending, and despite the business thriving, it didn't generate enough profit in that first year to cover mortgage repayments and school fees. Although they did muddle through in the end, that first year of trading was very stressful and left a legacy of huge credit card debt.

>> A friend of mine started up a business that soon built to generate a steady but modest income. Being a happy-go-lucky personality, she spent money from her business pretty much as soon as it came in. However, 18 months after she opened doors for trading, she lodged her first tax return. She hadn't set any money aside for tax, and had to take out a personal loan to cover the debt.

As I mention in the introduction to this section, if your personal expenses look as if they're likely to exceed the profit your business generates, and you don't have any other source of income or savings, one of your options is to see if you can cut back on your personal expenses.

You may be surprised to find how cheaply you can live if you really have to. Your flexibility depends on your stage of life — announcing that you're about to start a business as a street performer two weeks before your partner is due to give birth to twins is never going to go down well — but, mostly, you'll be surprised how you can simplify even the most complicated of lives.

REMEMBER

Sometimes a business can survive, but leave a broken relationship in its wake. One reason business plans are so important is that they can help you to understand the risks involved not just on a financial level, but on a personal level also.

And on that cheery note, this chapter comes to a close.

4

Checking Your Idea Makes Financial Sense

Chapter **11**

Assembling Your First Financial Forecast

n this chapter, I pull together all the information that goes into the financial forecast known as your Profit & Loss Projection, including pricing and sales projections, costs and gross profit projections, and expense projections. This helps you arrive at an estimate of just how much profit your business is likely to generate over the next 12 months.

Looking at your likely profits can be an emotional turning point when creating a business plan, especially if this is the first Profit & Loss Projection you've ever made. Few of us go into business without wanting to make a profit and, if the Profit & Loss Projection shows limited profits for what's likely to be a heap of work, you'll probably feel rather discouraged.

Feeling discouraged is okay. If your business model is a dud, you're better to quit now while you're still ahead than spend another year or two on an idea that will never fly. On the other hand, if you suspect that your essential idea is still strong, this part of the planning process gives you another chance to look at all your figures and experiment with pricing, costs and expenses.

Of course, you may find that your financial projections predict a business with a rosy future. That's great. Nothing is better than a promising business plan. However, in the last part of this chapter, I spend a bit of time explaining how you can use AI to perform scenario analysis. What if sales were 10 per cent less, or expenses 10 per cent more? AI is an incredibly efficient way to assess how robust your plan is, and the likely risks involved.

Understanding More About Spreadsheets

If you're already comfortable with using spreadsheets, and getting spreadsheets to share data, feel free to skim read (or skip) the first few pages of this chapter. Otherwise, stick around for a quick theory lesson. The concepts may be a little tricky at first, but I promise you that 30 minutes spent now understanding spreadsheets will save you countless hours in the months ahead.

Of course, if you're using a business planning app to assemble your financial projections, you may prefer to skip this section.

Naming worksheets within a single workbook

When you're in business, you often end up with different bits of information in different places or files. For example, maybe you have your product costings in one spreadsheet file, your expense budget in another, and your sales projections in another.

TIP

With Excel or Google Sheets, as with any other spreadsheet software, you can link data between different worksheets, so that updating one bit of information automatically updates the same bit of information in another worksheet. For example, imagine you have detailed product costings in one worksheet, and the bottom line of each worksheet calculates the final product cost. Then imagine you have a separate worksheet that calculates gross profit, and simply refers to the final product cost when calculating profit. By linking these two worksheets, you can automatically update gross profit projections every time you update your product costings. Working in this way saves time and reduces the chance for error.

The easiest way to get your head around this concept is to give it a go, starting with naming worksheets in a single workbook:

1. **Open up Excel (or any other spreadsheet software).**

   Any new spreadsheet file consists of single worksheets within a workbook. A *workbook* is the file that you create using spreadsheet software and, by default, every new workbook in Excel contains three *worksheets*, each one of which is a single page.

2. **Look at the tabs running along the bottom which say Sheet1, Sheet2 and Sheet3.**

   You're currently in Sheet1, so this tab appears in white, not grey.

3. **Rest your mouse on the tab that says Sheet1 and right-click.**

   Or, if you're using a Macintosh, hold down the control button and then click with your mouse.

4. **Click Rename and then type** Sales Detail **as the name.**

   You have now renamed this tab.

5. **Now rest your mouse on the tab that says Sheet2 and right-click to rename this tab to become** Sales Summary.

   Or, if you're using a Macintosh, hold down the control button and then click with your mouse.

   All done? Great. You have now created and named two separate worksheets within a single workbook. The first worksheet is called SalesDetail and the second worksheet is called SalesSummary, similar to the worksheets shown in Figure 11-1.

6. **Go to the File menu and save this workbook.**

   For this example, give the workbook an easy-to-remember file name such as 'testing'.

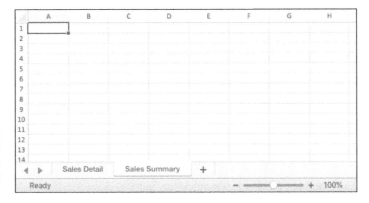

FIGURE 11-1: Renaming the first two worksheets in Excel.

Linking one worksheet to another

Once you've created two worksheets within a single workbook (refer to the preceding section if you're wondering what I'm talking about), you're ready to link one worksheet to another. Here goes:

1. **Open up your file with the Sales Detail and Sales Summary worksheets.**

   Refer to the preceding section for how to create this file. You may still have this file open, of course, in which case you don't need to do anything.

2. **Type the information you can see in Figure 11-2. When you get to the total, click the AutoSum symbol so that the total calculates automatically.**

	A	B	C	D	E	F
1	Sales Product A	$ 3,000				
2	Sales Product B	$ 1,000				
3	Sales Product C	$ 20,000				
4	Total Sales	$ 24,000				
5						
6						
7						
8						
9						
10						
11						

Sales Detail | Sales Summary | +

Ready — ●————— + 120%

FIGURE 11-2: Entering data into the Sales Detail worksheet.

   If you can't see the AutoSum symbol, type this formula instead: **=SUM(B1:B3)**.

3. **Highlight the data in row 4 (cells A4 and B4) and click Copy.**

   You can find the Copy and Paste commands by right-clicking with your mouse on a PC, pressing the command button and clicking the mouse on a Mac, or by clicking the Copy and Paste buttons on the top menu bar.

4. **Click the Sales Summary tab to move to that worksheet.**

   The worksheet will be completely blank at this stage.

5. **Click Paste Special.**

TIP

   You can find the Paste Special commands by right-clicking with your mouse on a PC, pressing the command button and clicking the mouse on a Mac, or by selecting Paste Special from the Paste button on the top menu bar.

   You'll see a dialogue box similar to Figure 11-3.

FIGURE 11-3:
The Paste Link
command
appears in the
bottom-left of the
Paste Spe-
cial window.

6. **Click the Paste Link button that appears in the bottom-left of the Paste Special window.**

   Check Figure 11-3 if you can't spot the Paste Link button. In a heartbeat, your total sales now appear in row 1.

7. **Check out the formula that shows in the formula bar for cell B1 (=SalesDetail!B4).**

   This formula tells Excel to go to the worksheet called Sales Detail, find whatever value is in cell B4 and then dump it in this cell in the Sales Summary worksheet. (If you can't see the formula bar, go to the View menu and ensure that the Formula Bar option is clicked.)

Feeling underwhelmed? Don't be. Flick back to the Sales Detail tab, and change one of the sales figures. Then return to the Sales Summary tab and you'll see that the total has updated automatically. Seems simple, but this concept will help to connect your Gross Profit and Expenses Projections into a single dynamic document.

Using names to identify important cells

I want to share one more spreadsheet concept before leaping into the practicalities of your business plan, and that is how to name important cells.

The idea of naming cells is that when you open up a workbook a few weeks or months later and you're trying to remember what on earth you were trying to do, the formulae that use names make much more sense than formulae that use cell references. Cell names also provide an efficient way to copy formula from one worksheet to another.

Here's an example of how cell naming works:

1. **Open up the file where you've linked two worksheets.**

   Refer to the preceding section for more on this file. You may still have this file open, of course, in which case you don't need to do anything.

2. **Go to the Sales Detail tab. Right-click on cell B4 and click Define Name.**

   The Define Name window appears, similar to that shown in Figure 11-4.

FIGURE 11-4:
Naming cells makes your worksheets easier to understand.

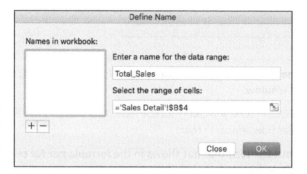

3. **As the Name, type** Total_Sales, **then click OK.**

   Note that you can't have a space in the name (so I can't call this cell 'Total Sales').

4. **Click in cell A6 and type** Cost of Sales.

5. **Click in cell B6 and type** =Total_Sales*50%. **Then press the Enter key.**

   For this example, in the blink of an eye, B6 should show as $12,000 (50 per cent of the total sales of $24,000).

You may be wondering what the big deal is. After all, I could have typed =B4*50% rather than =Total_Sales*50%. However, cell names work well for two reasons: The first reason is that cell names are easier to understand if someone else tries to use this worksheet (for example, the term 'Total_Sales' is way more meaningful than 'B4'). The second reason is that if you want to refer to this cell more than once (maybe many costs will end up being a percentage of total sales), copying formula from one cell to another is much more efficient if you use cell names.

TIP

For more details about naming cells, and how cell names can help you create worksheets with a minimum of fuss, go to YouTube and search 'naming cells in Excel'.

Building Your Profit & Loss Projection

So you're ready to create your first Profit & Loss Projection for the next 12 months? Then make yourself a hot cup of something and get ready to see how all the bits of your plan fit together.

Step one: Insert your projected sales forecasts

The top of any Profit & Loss Projection always starts by showing income, then cost of sales, then gross profit. I talk about calculating gross profit in detail in Chapter 9, so if you haven't already worked through your gross profit projections, scoot over to Chapter 9 first. With these workings in place, you're ready to go.

Here's how to add sales to your Profit & Loss Projection:

1. **Using Excel (or any other spreadsheet software), open up your Gross Profit Projection worksheet.**

   Refer to Chapter 9 for more about this worksheet. The idea is that you've already created a worksheet estimating both your sales and your cost of sales for the next 12 months.

   Note: If your sales projections are very simple and you don't have any cost of sales, you may not need to create a Gross Profit Projection. In this case, you can simply start with a Profit and Loss Projection and enter your sales estimates from scratch.

2. **Rest your mouse on the tab at the bottom of this worksheet that says Sheet1 and right-click.**

   Or, if you're using a Macintosh, hold down the control button and then click with your mouse.

3. **Click Rename and then type** GrossProfit **as the name.**

4. Rest your mouse on the tab that says Sheet2 and right-click.

5. Rename this tab to become ProfitLoss.

You have now created and named two separate worksheets within a workbook. The first worksheet is called GrossProfit and the second worksheet is called ProfitLoss.

6. On the ProfitLoss worksheet, label the months along the top (in row 1).

7. Go to your GrossProfit tab, and highlight the row where you recorded the grand total for sales each month. Right-click with your mouse (or control then click if you're on a Mac) and select Copy.

8. Return to the ProfitLoss tab and click on cell B2.

Cell B2 is where the first month of total sales is going to show.

9. Right-click (or control then click for Mac users) and select Paste Special.

10. Click the Paste Link button that appears in the bottom-left of this dialogue box.

Before your eyes, the sales for each month should appear right across row 2, similar to Figure 11-5. (I just show the first few months here, but you get the general idea.)

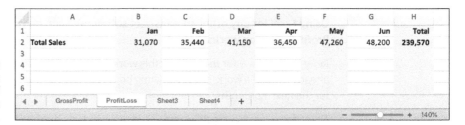

	A	B	C	D	E	F	G	H
1		Jan	Feb	Mar	Apr	May	Jun	Total
2	Total Sales	31,070	35,440	41,150	36,450	47,260	48,200	239,570
3								
4								
5								
6								

FIGURE 11-5:
Total sales form the first line of your Profit & Loss Projection.

GrossProfit | ProfitLoss | Sheet3 | Sheet4 | +

140%

TIP

Are you wondering why I've gone to all the trouble of creating multiple worksheets and linking one sheet to another, rather than just copying and pasting the estimated total sales? The reason I suggest you work in this way is so your total sales will update automatically whenever you tweak your detailed sales. For example, maybe I want to see what would happen if I lift my pricing by 10 per cent. All I have to do is tweak the pricing in my Sales Projection worksheet and this flows automatically through to my Profit & Loss Projection.

Of course, if you're a very small business and you don't want to go to the trouble of splitting up your income in any kind of detail — you just want to type in an estimated dollar total for each month — then you don't need to bother creating a separate worksheet for sales projections.

Step two: Bring across variable costs

If your business has no variable costs, you can skip this step entirely. However, if your business has variable costs (and refer to Chapter 9 if you're not sure whether this is the case), then the next stage is to bring these figures across.

Again, you need to have your gross profit projections complete before you do this step. If you haven't, you may need to have a quick look through the last few pages of Chapter 9 before you continue.

1. **Open up your Gross Profit Projection worksheet.**

   I'm following on from the instructions in the previous section of this chapter ('Step one: Insert your projected sales forecasts') and I'm assuming you've already inserted a row showing projected sales.

2. **Go to the GrossProfit tab, and highlight the rows where you recorded the total for cost of sales and gross profit for each month. Right-click with your mouse (or control then click if you're on a Mac) and select Copy.**

3. **Return to the ProfitLoss tab and click on cell A4.**

4. **Right-click (or control then click for Mac users) and select Paste Special.**

5. **Click the Paste Link button that appears in the bottom-left of this dialogue box.**

   Your total cost of sales for each month, as well as Gross Profit, should now appear below your sales. (If a bunch of zeros appear in row 5, which may happen because row 5 is blank in the Gross Profit worksheet, simply delete these zeros.)

6. **Format the cells if necessary.**

   Sometimes the formatting doesn't come across when you link one worksheet to another. So feel free to add bold to your headings and format the amounts to include dollar signs.

7. **Check your results.**

   By the time you're done, your worksheet should look similar to Figure 11-6, showing total sales, cost of sales and gross profit for the next 12 months. This worksheet has exactly the same figures as your gross profit projection, but with the difference that it displays much less detail. This less detailed format is what many investors or bank managers would expect to see as an overall financial projection.

FIGURE 11-6:
Cost of sales and
gross profit show
below total sales
on your Profit &
Loss Projection.

	A	B	C	D	E	F	G	H
1		Jan	Feb	Mar	Apr	May	Jun	Total
2	**Total Sales**	31,070	35,440	41,150	36,450	47,260	48,200	**239,570**
3								
4	**Total Cost of Sales**	12,428	14,176	16,460	14,580	18,904	19,280	95,828
5								
6	**Gross Profit**	**18,642**	**21,264**	**24,690**	**21,870**	**28,356**	**28,920**	**143,742**
7								

GrossProfit ProfitLoss Sheet3 Sheet4 +

140%

Step three: Add your expenses budget

Step three in building your Profit & Loss Projection is to add detail regarding your expenses. Chapter 10 explains how to create a worksheet that accurately forecasts business expenses on a monthly basis, and I'm going to assume here that you've already completed this worksheet.

Here's how to add expenses to your Profit & Loss Projection:

1. Open up your expenses worksheet.

Refer to Chapter 10 for details on how to create this spreadsheet.

2. Highlight every single cell that has anything in it.

In other words, click in the top-left cell and drag your mouse down to the bottom-right cell.

3. Right-click and select Copy.

Or press the command button and then click if you're a sensible Macintosh person.

4. Go to your Profit & Loss Projection workbook and click the ProfitLoss tab.

5. Click cell A8 in this worksheet, then right-click and select Paste.

What I'm meaning here is you click in the first column below the Gross Profit totals. When you click Paste, you're copying everything from your expenses worksheet into your Profit & Loss worksheet.

6. At the bottom of the expenses, insert a row called Total Expenses. Add a Sum formula so that Total Expenses automatically calculates the expenses listed above.

Figure 11-7 shows what this will look like. You now have a Profit & Loss worksheet that starts with sales, then shows cost of sales and gross profit, and finally lists all your expenses.

	A	B	C	D	E	F	G	H	I
1		Jan	Feb	Mar	Apr	May	Jun	Total	
2	Total Sales	31,070	35,440	41,150	36,450	47,260	48,200	239,570	
3									
4	Total Cost of Sales	12,428	14,176	16,460	14,580	18,904	19,280	95,828	
5									
6	Gross Profit	18,642	21,264	24,690	21,870	28,356	28,920	143,742	
7									
8	Accounting Fees	-	2,000	-	-	-	-		
9	Bank Charges	100	100	100	100	100	100	600	
10	Communication Expenses	380	380	380	380	380	380	2,280	
11	Consultant Expenses	300	300	300	300	300	300	1,800	
12	Insurance	280	280	280	280	280	280	1,680	
13	Interest Expense	520	520	520	520	520	520	3,120	
14	IT Expenses	450	450	450	450	450	450	2,700	
15	Lease Expenses	800	800	800	800	800	800	4,800	
16	Marketing Expenses	1,200	1,200	1,200	1,200	1,200	1,200	7,200	
17	Merchant Fees	621	709	823	729	945	964	4,791	
18	Motor Vehicle Expenses	350	350	350	350	1,800	350	3,550	
19	Office Supplies	150	150	150	150	150	150	900	
20	Rental Expense	3,250	3,250	3,250	3,250	3,250	3,250	19,500	
21	Repairs and Maintenance	500	500	500	500	500	500	3,000	
22	Staff Amenities	300	300	300	300	300	300	1,800	
23	Travel Expenses	350	350	350	350	350	350	2,100	
24	Utilities	600	-	-	600	-	-		
25	Wages and Salaries	3,600	3,600	4,500	3,600	3,600	4,500	23,400	
26	Wages oncosts	540	540	675	540	540	675	3,510	
27	Total Expenses	14,291	15,779	14,928	14,399	15,465	15,069	89,931	
28									
29	Net Profit	4,351	5,485	9,762	7,471	12,891	13,851	53,811	
30									
31									

GrossProfit　ProfitLoss　Sheet3　Sheet4　+

140%

FIGURE 11-7:
Your completed
Profit & Loss
Projection.

TIP

Are you wondering why I suggest you copy across all the expense totals from your worksheet, rather than just a single total for expenses in the same way as you did for sales and cost of sales? The reason is partly historical. Accountants, business advisors and investors are accustomed to a standard format for Profit & Loss projections, and this format typically provides a summary of sales and cost of sales, and more detail for expenses.

7. **Add a line for Net Profit at the bottom of your worksheet, inserting a formula that subtracts Total Expenses from Gross Profit.**

In Figure 11-7, the formula for January's net profit would be **=B6-B27**. Your formula will be different because you're bound to have a different number of rows for your expenses, but I'm sure you get the general idea.

Notice that in Figure 11-7, I also added a final column showing the total for each row, so that I can see the total sales, gross profit, expenses and net profit for the whole period combined.

Step four: Think about tax

If you're a sole trader or partnership, the amount of personal tax you pay depends on many factors, including whether you have any other sources of income other than the business. For this reason, I suggest that you don't include personal income tax as an expense on your Profit & Loss Projection, but that you make an allowance for tax when calculating how much you require in personal drawings. (See 'Assessing whether your net profit is reasonable, or not' later in this chapter for more info.)

However, if your business has a company structure, you need to include company tax as an expense on your Profit & Loss Projection based on the profits you make. To do this, simply add a final line to your Profit & Loss report called Company Tax Expense. Calculate this expense at the correct percentage of company tax and then add a final line to your worksheet called Net Profit After Tax.

Step five: Check you've got it right

You're not quite done yet. The last step is to check that you got everything right. (Spreadsheets are great in the way they calculate everything for you, but get one formula wrong, and the error can spread like a dropped stitch on a knitting project.)

REMEMBER

So here's your checklist:

>> Save your workings and then make a copy of your Gross Profit Projection worksheet. On the copy, change your prices to $10 for every product, change

your unit costs to $1, and change the unit sales to 100 units per month. Check that your gross profit comes out at $900 every month.

>> Grab a calculator and manually check the sums for the first and the last month in your forecast. Check total sales, gross profit, total expenses and net profit.

>> If your business is already up and running, review your Profit & Loss report for the most recent month. Plug in the figures from this report into the first month of your Profit & Loss Projection and check that the net profit in your projection matches with the report.

All good? Then you're ready to move onto the next part of your business plan, which is where you get to ponder whether the forecasted profit is what you need it to be . . .

Analyzing Net Profit

As I mention in the preceding section, one of the primary purposes of your Profit & Loss Projection is to figure out how much profit you'll be left with at the end of the day. This result enables you to decide whether you want to continue with this business, whether you need to change your business model in some way, and whether you're making a reasonable rate of return on your investment.

Calculating net profit margins

So, to do a quick recap:

>> Gross profit equals sales less variable costs.

>> Net profit equals gross profit less fixed expenses.

>> Gross profit is always more than net profit.

>> The more you sell, the more gross profit you make.

>> The more you sell, the more net profit you make.

To calculate your net profit margin, you first calculate your net profit, and then you divide this amount by the value of total sales and multiply the result by 100. For example, if my sales are $200,000 a year and my net profit is $6,000, my net profit margin is 3 per cent (that's $6,000 divided by $200,000 multiplied by 100).

Assessing whether your net profit is reasonable, or not

A specific percentage rate at which you can say that a net profit margin is reasonable doesn't exist, because too many variables affect this judgment. However, you should be able to establish for yourself a rate that you think is reasonable, and run with that.

The biggest factor to take into account is whether the net profit on your Profit & Loss Projection includes payment for your time. If your business has a sole trader or partnership structure, the final net profit on your Profit & Loss Projection represents the profit that your business generates before you see a single cent in payment for your time. Therefore, the net profits (and hence the net profit margins) need to be much higher than for an equivalent business with a company structure. (In contrast, if your business has a company structure, you need to include your monthly wages as part of your expenses, and so payment for your time is already accounted for.)

Another approach is to think about how much you need to live comfortably. If the net profit of your business is more than what you require to live (or, if you're a company, the net profit plus your wages), this figure is probably reasonable. However, if the net profit doesn't cover your personal expenses, your business has a problem. (For more about budgeting for personal expenses, refer to Chapter 10.)

TIP

When looking at your projected net profit, I recommend that you look at the margin for error. If your Profit & Loss Projection shows a high level of sales and a similarly high level of expenses, with only a narrow net profit margin left at the end of the day, you must ask yourself whether you have enough room for error. (I talk about this topic later in this chapter, in 'Using AI to Assess the Risk Involved'.) For example, if a reduction of only 10 per cent in sales could mean you can't pay your rent or make your mortgage repayments, this net profit is probably not quite enough.

Thinking ahead further than 12 months

In this chapter (and most other chapters in this book) I suggest you work on financial projections for the next 12-month period only. I make this suggestion for two reasons: First, if you're just getting started in business, trying to make financial projections for two, three or even five years into the future can quickly feel like a make-believe exercise, because so much about what lies ahead is unknown. Second, what I'm trying to do in this book is to get you to create financial projections yourself, and I don't want to discourage you by making things any trickier than they need to be.

However, if you only do financial projections for 12 months into the future, you may not get a true picture of what lies ahead, particularly if you have strong growth patterns or your business is just getting started. Sometimes, you need to extend your forecasts for 24 or even 36 months ahead in order to predict at what point your business will really start to flourish and generate decent profits.

Extending your Profit & Loss Projection is easy — simply copy and paste the results from the 12th month across to additional columns, and then change the figures as need be. All the same principles apply — you're simply extending the forecast for another year or two.

Looking at your rate of return

One final factor that I think is worth considering when you look at your net profit is your *return on investment ratio*. This ratio calculates the return that you make on any money that you're investing (or have already invested) in the business, and answers the all-important question of whether this rate of return is reasonable.

For example, imagine that to get your business going you're going to put in $200,000 of your personal savings and you plan to work full-time on the business. You calculate that a reasonable wage in return for your time is $75,000 per year. In this scenario, you would ideally want your business to generate profits of at least this amount plus a return of, say, 5 per cent on the funds you've invested.

The formula for calculating your return on investment (ROI) is this:

ROI = Net profit (after wages) divided by investment in the business

To continue with the example, imagine that in the last three years, after paying yourself a decent wage for the hours you spend working in the business, you've averaged a net profit of $5,000 per year. Your return on investment is $5,000 divided by $200,000 multiplied by 100, which equals 2.5 per cent.

In theory, if the interest rates for term deposits are more than 2.5 per cent — and they almost always are — you could spare yourself the hassle and risk of running a business and instead make more by investing your assets elsewhere.

Although number crunchers love this kind of pillow talk, I don't always agree. Looking at percentage rates of return doesn't take into account some of the more intangible benefits of being in business for yourself, such as the work–lifestyle balance, being your own boss, doing something you're passionate about, or being able to live in a regional area where jobs are scarce.

WHAT IF THE FIGURES AREN'T GOOD ENOUGH?

I've been called many things in my time, but one of the nicknames that I'm fond of, in a perverse kind of way, is 'the smiling assassin'. I earned this title for my ability to deliver bad news in a warm and fuzzy way that leaves people wondering what the hell just happened.

As someone who spends a lot of time looking at the financial performance of businesses, and interpreting results for business owners, this smiling assassin role is very familiar. Too often businesspeople slog away at their business, earning just enough to survive, too busy to face the reality that their trading model is flawed, the future is gloomy, or that they're sinking ever quicker into debt. They ask me for advice, because they know that something has to change, but in their heart of hearts they often don't want to hear what it is I have to say.

I can't sit with you, dear reader, and look at your financials with a beady eye. However, I can encourage you to take a long, hard look at your financial projections and ask yourself whether the projected final profit is likely to be enough to justify the work you're going to put in.

When I work on business mentoring courses, probably one quarter of the class decide not to proceed with their business idea at the end of the course, and another quarter of the class end up making major changes to their plan. To me, even for the people who ditch their business idea completely and return to their day job, the business plan has been successful. Why? Because that person hasn't wasted a whole load of time and money on a dud idea.

Of course, maybe all your business idea needs is some tweaking at the edges. What if you could increase sales or prices by just 10 per cent, decrease costs by a similar amount, and cut expenses to the bone? Would your idea work then? Or do you need additional products, a different distribution model, a revised manufacturing process, or a new location?

In Chapter 1, I show an image of the financial planning cycle, commencing with your start-up budget, moving on to prices, then calculating costs and expenses, and finally calculating net profit, break-even and cashflow. At the end of this cycle, I return to reviewing your business model and competitive strategy.

Keep this cycle in mind when working on the financials of your plan. Don't think of your financial projections as being the culmination of the planning process, but rather look at these projections as an opportunity to return to your business model and make improvements.

Using AI to Assess the Risk Involved

If you're doing a plan for a new business or a business that's currently undergoing significant change, one of the major challenges is how unknown everything is. For example, maybe you're planning to open up a new retail outlet, a dentistry practice or a health spa. When it comes to forecasting your sales, you may feel that you're just plucking figures out of the air.

Figure-plucking (a highly technical term that I'm particularly fond of) is a dangerous thing. In an attempt to discourage this process, in Chapter 8 I focus on planning for sales in detail, analyzing the number of items or services you have to sell in order to reach projected monthly sales totals. In Chapter 10, I also talk about benchmarking, and explain how important it is to research industry averages. (I suggest talking to your accountant, looking up benchmarking services, using AI apps, or contacting industry associations.) However, even with all this solid groundwork in place, you may still be wondering about the accuracy of your financial projections.

In this situation, I recommend you do a bit of scenario analysis, varying your income, cost of sales and expenses upwards or downwards by 10 or 20 per cent to see what happens. Playing with percentages in this way is a good method for assessing how robust your plans are, and how much wriggle room you have to play with.

TIP

The most thorough way to complete your scenario analysis is to make a copy of your financial projections and modify the figures. However, this process can be quite time-consuming, and a quicker approach is to use AI to help.

The exact requests you need to use will vary, depending on your AI app; however, for example, at the time of writing, I was able to go to ChatGPT and type in the following question: 'Can you look at a financial forecast and see what would happen if sales decreased by 5%?'

I was prompted to copy and paste my spreadsheet results and, once complete, ChatGPT provided the answer. Next, I asked, 'What if sales decreased by 5%, my gross profit margin decreased by 5%, and my expenses increased by 8%?' In a few seconds, I was able to see what financial impact these variations would have on my bottom line.

While perhaps chilling in the accuracy and speed of its results, this particular use of AI is undeniably efficient.

Chapter **12**

Calculating Your Break-Even Point

U nderstanding your break-even point is as essential to your business toolkit as food is to a teenage boy. (Or to myself, for that matter.)

Break-even calculations help you to decide prices, set sales budgets and assess the health of your business plan. You can figure out how far sales can drop before you start to make a loss, how much extra you have to sell before you turn a profit, how changing sales impact profits, and how much you need to lift sales in order to compensate for an increase in costs.

Sounds handy? In this chapter, I explain how you can calculate the break-even point for your own business. So grab your calculator, hang a 'do not disturb' sign around your neck and get ready to go . . .

Identifying Your Tipping Point

Your *break-even point* is the number of dollars you need to earn in any given period in order to cover your costs. Or, to put it differently, the total sales you have to make in order that you make neither a loss nor a profit.

Most business textbooks talk about your break-even point only in terms of *the business* breaking even. In other words, the break-even point is the point at which sales are high enough to cover the costs of your business. However, you can also think of your break-even point not only in terms of covering the costs of your business, but your living expenses too.

In real life, I find that people use the word *break-even* to refer to three totally different things:

>> **Business break-even point:** When you calculate your business break-even point, you calculate the sales the business has to make in order to meet its business expenses. In other words, if the business breaks even, it neither makes a profit nor a loss. This calculation is most relevant for businesses with a company structure where directors' salaries (owner salaries) are factored into the fixed expenses of the company.

>> **Business/personal break-even point:** When you calculate your business/personal break-even point, you calculate the sales the business has to make in order to meet business expenses and pay you — as the business owner — enough to cover your personal expenses.

   Most business plan books don't include any reference to personal expenses when calculating break-even, but I think that doing so is important for small businesses with single owner-operators or for small partnerships. After all, even if your business does make a profit, this profit may not be enough if the business is your sole source of income and the profit generated isn't enough to cover your basic living expenses.

>> **Cash break-even point:** When you calculate your cash break-even point, you calculate the sales you have to make in order for your cash out to match your cash in over a specified period of time (usually 12 months). In this scenario, cash out could include things such as new equipment or business start-up costs, and cash in could include business loans or money that you have set aside in savings.

   Calculating your cash break-even point provides a simpler approach to doing a proper cashflow (a topic I cover in detail in Chapter 13). However, a cashflow is a more accurate and detailed approach and is preferable if your business offers credit to customers or has inventory.

In the first part of this chapter, I cover how to calculate business break-even, and business/personal break-even. I look at break-even from a cash perspective towards the end of this chapter (see the section 'Looking at Things from a Cash Perspective').

Calculating business break-even

The basic formula for calculating your business break-even point is easy:

Break-even point = Fixed expenses divided by gross profit margin

Imagine I have a friend (I'll call her Annie) who has a cafe on the main street. Her fixed expenses are $4,500 per week (one wait staff, one kitchen assistant, insurance, rent and so on). Overall, on average she makes a gross profit margin of about 60 per cent. (In other words, if she sells a panini sandwich for $10, the ingredients cost her $4; if she sells a coffee for $6, the ingredients cost $2.40.)

Annie's business break-even point is going to equal fixed expenses (that's $4,500 per week) divided by her gross profit margin (60 per cent) which is $7,500. In other words, she has to generate $7,500 in sales just to break even and cover her basic expenses. Figure 12-1 shows this principle in action.

FIGURE 12-1:
Calculating
business
break-even point.

	A	B	C	D
1				
2	Average Gross Profit Margin	60%		Based on ingredients costing 40 cents for every dollar sold
3				
4	Fixed Expenses Business	$ 4,500.00		Staff, rent, insurance and so on
5				
6	Break-even Point	**$ 7,500.00**		Equals fixed expenses divided by gross profit margin
7				

Think this through to see how it works out. If Annie generates $7,500 in income, she'll have to pay out $3,000 in supplies (that's the cost of food at 40 cents in the dollar). This leaves $4,500 gross profit, which is exactly the amount she needs to cover her fixed expenses. This figure is Annie's business break-even point.

Factoring personal expenses into the equation

The break-even chat in the preceding section is all very well, but if your business has a sole trader or partnership structure, you probably need to do more than cover your business expenses — in that you'll need to generate enough income to cover personal expenses as well. (I'm assuming that if your business has a company structure, you already pay yourself a wage, and so your wage forms part of your fixed expenses.)

To bring personal expenses into the picture, you need to repeat the business break-even calculation, but this time include the amount of income you need to generate to cover personal expenses.

Building on the example earlier in this chapter, what do you think break-even would be in the following situation?

>> Annie has a cafe with fixed expenses of $4,500 per week. These expenses don't include any wages for herself.

>> She needs to generate a minimum of $1,000 per week in order to cover her personal living expenses.

>> She makes an average gross profit margin of 60 per cent.

The formula is the same; however, this time fixed expenses need to include not just business expenses but personal expenses also.

Break-even point = Fixed expenses (including personal expenses) divided by gross profit margin

You could see how the sums pan out in Figure 12-2. Annie needs to earn an additional $1,666 per week (that's $9,166 in total) in order for her business to break even and for her to generate enough to live on.

FIGURE 12-2: Calculating break-even point to cover both business and personal expenses.

	A	B	C	D
1				
2	Average Gross Profit Margin	60%		Based on ingredients costing 40 cents for every dollar sold
3				
4	Fixed Expenses Business	$ 4,500.00		Staff, rent, insurance and so on
5	Fixed Expenses Personal	$ 1,000.00		The minimum personal funds Annie needs to survive
6	Total Fixed Expenses	$ 5,500.00		
7				
8	Break-even Point	$ 9,166.67		Equals fixed expenses divided by gross profit margin
9				

Calculating break-even for your business

Are you ready to calculate the break-even point for your own business? Just before I launch into a step-by-step explanation, I'm going to quickly recap the difference between variable costs and fixed expenses. (For more on this topic, scoot back to Chapter 9.)

» *Variable costs* (also sometimes called *direct costs* or *cost of goods sold*) are the costs that go up and down in direct relation to your sales, and typically include commissions, the cost of the goods you buy to resell to customers, raw materials, subcontract labor and so on.

» *Fixed expenses* are expenses that stay constant, regardless of whether your sales go up and down. Typical fixed expenses for your business may include accounting fees, bank fees, IT expenses, electricity, insurance, marketing expenses, motor vehicle expenses, rental and wages.

Got all that straight? Then here goes:

1. **Open a new worksheet in Excel (or any other spreadsheet software).**

   You can either start a whole new workbook or, if you have already created sales and profit projections, you can add a new worksheet to this workbook.

2. **Enter your gross profit margin on the first line, similar to Figure 12-2.**

   To calculate your gross profit margin, grab your average gross profit (per unit, product, service provided, month or per year), divide this by sales (again, per unit, product, service provided, month or per year) and multiply by 100. If you're not sure how to do this calculation, make your way back to Chapter 9, where I explain how to calculate your gross profit margin in lots of detail.

   If you are an owner-operated service business with no employees and no variable costs, your gross profit margin will be 100 per cent.

   Format your gross profit margin as a percentage. To do this, simply click the % button on the main toolbar.

TIP

3. **Add the fixed expenses for your business to the next line of the worksheet.**

   If you're not sure how much your fixed expenses are, Chapter 10 focuses on calculating the fixed expenses for your business. I usually like to calculate break-even and think of fixed expenses on a monthly basis, but you can choose any period of time that makes sense to you.

   If you have already created a worksheet for fixed expenses, similar to what I suggest in Chapter 10, you can link the fixed expenses cell on your break-even worksheet to your expenses worksheet. This way, whenever you update your expense projections, your break-even point will recalculate automatically.

TIP

4. **If your fixed expenses don't include any wages for yourself, add whatever you need for living expenses to the next line of the worksheet.**

   Again, Chapter 10 has lots of tips about building a personal budget so that you're realistic about how much you need to survive.

5. **Total up your business and personal fixed expenses.**

   Figure 12-2 shows the general idea.

6. **Add a row that calculates break-even point, dividing total fixed expenses by the average gross profit margin.**

   In Figure 12-2, the formula for the break-even point is **=B6/B2**. Simple. You now know what you have to achieve in sales in order to meet your business expenses.

TIP

If it suits, you can express the break-even point in a different time period. In Step 3 in the preceding steps, if you express your fixed expenses as total expenses for a month, consequently your break-even point calculates what you need to achieve in sales per month. However, maybe it makes more sense to you to look at your break-even point per day, per week or per year. Another option (again, if relevant to your business), is to express the break-even point in units sold, or the number of services provided, rather than dollars. For example, if your break-even point is $10,000 a week and you're selling custom-built handmade guitars at $5,000 a pop, you know you have to sell two guitars a week to break even. Or if your break-even point is $4,000 a month and you're mowing lawns at an average of $50 a lawn, you know you have to mow 80 lawns a month to break even.

WARNING

Calculating a break-even point using the method shown in the preceding steps gives you a general indication of how much income your business needs to generate in order to make neither a profit nor a loss over a sustained period of time. However, this calculation doesn't take into account the cash requirements for a business. A business can make a profit but still have negative cashflow (and vice versa), because of factors such as start-up costs, extending customer credit or building inventory. For a more detailed explanation of cashflow management, see Chapter 13.

Changing Your Break-Even Point

If you find that your business is trading unprofitably, and despite your best efforts you can't get your sales high enough to meet your break-even point, your only option may be to change your break-even point.

Using the principles of break-even calculations, you have three possible solutions:

>> Raise your prices (which is often not an option if you're finding it hard to make enough sales)

>> Cut your variable costs (that is, the costs of production or providing your service)

>> Cut your fixed costs

For example, if I go back to the cafe owner whose calculations are shown in Figure 12-2, I can see that Annie needs to generate $9,166 per week just to pay expenses as well as her own wage. Imagine that the city council is planning major road works and Annie knows that her turnover is going to be affected. She reckons she'll probably generate only about $6,000 a week while the work is going on.

Annie goes to the worksheet where she calculated her break-even and experiments with the different scenarios, shown in Figure 12-3.

>> In Strategy One, Annie can see that she'd have to increase gross profit margin to 92 per cent in order to break even if sales dropped to $6,000 per week. She knows she can't cut food costs or increase prices this much, so this strategy doesn't seem practical.

>> In Strategy Two, she keeps her margins the same but cuts her expenses by $1,900 a week. This seems to work, but she doesn't know if she can cut expenses by this much and still stay open.

>> In Strategy Three, Annie increases her margin by 10 per cent and cuts her expenses by $1,300 a week. She can see that this will work, and thinks that cutting her expenses by this much is probably possible, especially if her landlord agrees to a temporary reduction in rent.

FIGURE 12-3: Understanding break-even enables you to plan ahead for changes in trading conditions.

	A	B	C	D	E
1	**CURRENT BREAK-EVEN POINT**			**STRATEGY ONE**	
2	Average Gross Profit Margin	60%		Average Gross Profit Margin	92.0%
3					
4	Fixed Expenses Business	$ 4,500.00		Fixed Expenses Business	$ 4,500.00
5	Fixed Expenses Personal	$ 1,000.00		Fixed Expenses Personal	$ 1,000.00
6	Total Fixed Expenses	$ 5,500.00		Total Fixed Expenses	$ 5,500.00
7					
8	Break-even Point	$ 9,166.67		Break-even Point	$ 5,978.26
9					
10	**STRATEGY TWO**			**STRATEGY THREE**	
11	Average Gross Profit Margin	60%		Average Gross Profit Margin	70%
12					
13	Fixed Expenses Business	$ 2,600.00		Fixed Expenses Business	$ 3,200.00
14	Fixed Expenses Personal	$ 1,000.00		Fixed Expenses Personal	$ 1,000.00
15	Total Fixed Expenses	$ 3,600.00		Total Fixed Expenses	$ 4,200.00
16					
17	Break-even Point	$ 6,000.00		Break-even Point	$ 6,000.00
18					

WHAT DOES SOMETHING REALLY COST?

One of the things that can do your head in when working with costings is the question of how to apportion the fixed costs of your business across every item sold or every service provided.

Think of a business selling homemade fudge. The cost of ingredients for fudge stays the same for every packet sold, but the fixed costs (premises rental, equipment rental, insurance and so on) per packet go up or down depending on the number of packets of fudge made.

If the fixed costs are $700 a week and the business makes 700 packets of fudge that week, the fixed costs are $1 per packet. But if the business makes 1,400 packets of fudge, the fixed costs are only 50 cents per packet.

For this reason, it can sometimes be hard to arrive at the 'true' cost of an item. For you as a business owner, the challenge in this respect is twofold: First, be ever vigilant about controlling your fixed costs; second, always try to maximize production to make as full use of resources as you can. This may mean making full use of rented premises, keeping staff productive and, of course, ensuring that sales are as high as they can possibly be given this level of expenses. By maximizing resources in this way, you keep the fixed costs per unit as low as possible.

TIP

The handy thing about understanding your break-even point in this kind of detail is that you can take pre-emptive action if you know that costs are going to increase or sales are going to decrease.

Looking at Things from a Cash Perspective

When I was teaching at our local business college, one of the exercises teachers were asked to do with the students (all of whom were planning their new businesses) was to do a break-even analysis from a cash perspective for the first 12 months of trading.

At first I was a bit skeptical of this somewhat simplistic approach, because the only way to be really sure how things stand from a cash perspective is to do a proper cashflow, a topic I cover in Chapter 13. However, if you don't offer credit to customers and you don't carry inventory, this cash break-even analysis can be a very powerful and relatively simple-to-use technique.

The idea is that you don't look simply at business profitability, but also at how much cash you have in the bank to begin with, how much cash you intend to spend on setting up and how much money (if any) you intend to borrow.

You can see how this analysis looks in Figure 12-4, where I take the figures for Annie's cafe business (the example I use earlier in this chapter), but imagine that she's in her first 12 months of trading. You can see that when I factor in her existing savings and the fact that she's borrowing slightly more than she needs to spend for the start-up, her weekly break-even point drops from $9,166 to $7,467. What this means, in practical terms, is that although in the long-term Annie does need to generate $9,166 in sales every week in order to break even, she only has to average $8,301 per week in the first 12 months. This is probably a good thing, because most businesses need some time to build up trading.

Here's how to create your own cash break-even analysis:

1. **Identify the capital you intend to contribute in the first 12 months of trading and list these sources in a spreadsheet.**

   Figure 12-4 gives you a general idea.

2. **List setup expenses, fixed expenses, wages and working capital requirements in the next section of the spreadsheet.**

   By working capital, I mean the balance that you always need to have in your business bank account. I've shown $3,000 in Figure 12-4, which is probably scarily low!

3. **Using Figure 12-4 as an example, calculate your weekly and annual break-even point.**

   To arrive at my weekly break-even point, I divide the Total Income Required to Break Even by 52 (the number of weeks in the year).

4. **Look at the break-even point and see how this compares to your projected sales for the first 12 months.**

   If your break-even point is greater than what you've forecasted in sales, you almost certainly have a problem. You need to reduce start-up expenses, increase finance, change profit margins, reduce fixed expenses or stop eating.

   If your break-even point is less than what you've forecasted in sales, things are looking good. (Although if you offer customers credit or have stock on hand, I still recommend that you work through a more detailed cashflow, as explained in Chapter 13.)

	A	B
1	**Calculating Your 'Cash' Break-Even Point for the First 12 Months of a New Business**	
2		
3	Personal savings contributed	$ 20,000.00
4	Other non-business sources of income	$ 5,000.00
5	Proceeds from business loan	$ 80,000.00
6	**A: Total Capital Contributed to Business in first 12 months**	**$ 105,000.00**
7		
8	Money required for setup expenses	$ 75,000.00
9	Total fixed expenses (business) for the first 12 months	$ 234,000.00
10	Total wage required for yourself for the first 12 months	$ 52,000.00
11	Balance required in the bank (working capital)	$ 3,000.00
12	**B: Total Capital Required Plus Fixed/Personal Expenses in first 12 months**	**$ 364,000.00**
13		
14	**C: Equals B minus A**	**$ 259,000.00**
15		
16	**D: Average Gross Profit Margin**	60%
17	**E: Total Income Required to Break Even (C divided by D)**	**$ 431,666.67**
18	Monthly break-even point	$ 35,972.22
19	Weekly break-even point	$ 8,301.28
20		

FIGURE 12-4: Calculating what you need to do in order to break even in the first 12 months.

IN THIS CHAPTER

» **Ruminating on the many reasons cashflow is different from profit**

» **Looking at a Cashflow Projection report and how it's different from a Profit & Loss Projection**

» **Analyzing how much money is going to flow in and out the door**

» **Creating your all-singing, all-dancing Cashflow Projection report**

» **Designing a budget that works hand-in-hand with cash demands**

» **Working on a Balance Sheet Projection**

Chapter **13**

Creating Cashflows and Building Budgets

O f all the perils of business, one of the most disheartening has to be a promising enterprise that grows so fast that it starves itself of funds. However, if you have an eye to the future, not to mention the ability to create a Cashflow Projection report, you should be able to predict when a cashflow crunch is going to occur. You can then plan accordingly, maybe approaching the bank for additional finance, timing expenses differently or consciously slowing growth.

Not all business plans require a Cashflow Projection report, but this chapter will help you decide whether to include this report, or not. Indeed, even if you don't include this report in your final plan, the process of building it can help you understand why having a healthy bank balance doesn't necessarily relate to profit, and vice versa.

I also explore the need to create ongoing budgets. Budgets enable you to set goals for income and limits on expenses, imposing a gentle discipline on the day-to-day running of your business that helps you meet the predictions of your Cashflow Projections and ensure that everything stays on track. Whether or not you include a Budget Report as well as Profit & Loss Projection in your business plan depends on the nature of your business, a decision for which this chapter provides lots of guidance.

Understanding Why Cash Is Different from Profit

I wish I had a dollar for every time a client asks, 'Veechi, my reports say I'm making a heap of profit, so how come I have nothing in the bank?' Similarly, I occasionally witness clients who have rosy bank balances and who are living the high life, even though their Profit & Loss reports are decidedly gloomy.

In the first part of this chapter, I explain why profit doesn't always equal money in your bank account, and vice versa.

Five reasons your projections may look rosy, but funds could be tight

Even if your Profit & Loss Projection for the next 12 months looks rosy as can be, you may still find yourself short of funds during this period. Here are a few of the reasons:

>> **You need to pay tax:** A tricky habit to avoid (do tell me if you discover how), but the truth is that as soon as you make any profit, you have to pay tax.

>> **You buy new equipment or have major start-up costs:** As I explain in Chapters 6 and 9, start-up costs for your business aren't usually shown as an expense in your Profit & Loss Projections. You need to allow for these costs separately.

>> **You make loan repayments:** If you only show interest expense on your Profit & Loss Projection (rather than the whole value of each loan repayment), then your actual expenditure will exceed your projected expenses.

>> **You offer customer credit:** If you bill a customer in April, your Profit & Loss Projection will show this income in April, even though you may not actually

receive payment until weeks or months later. Therefore, any increase in what customers owe you will reduce the funds you have available, and increase your need for working capital.

>> **You increase inventory levels:** If you buy or manufacture goods for resale, as your business grows, your stock levels will increase, quickly using up funds.

In this chapter, I show you how to allow for all of these things (tax, new equipment, customer credit, loans and inventory) using a Cashflow Projection report, so that you can plan not just for profit, but make a prediction as to your bank balance also.

WARNING

Many a business has floundered due to lack of working capital, even though it has been trading profitably. This is the reason creating a Cashflow Projection in addition to a Profit & Loss Projection can be crucial in many situations.

Five reasons your projections may look grim, but your bank account may be healthy

It may be easy to grasp why a business may not have any funds available even though it's turning a profit. However, what about the opposite scenario, where the Profit & Loss Projection looks gloomy but you still have plenty of money in your bank account? Here are some reasons this situation can occur:

>> **You receive a loan:** Your Profit & Loss Projection shows only income from trading, and doesn't include money received from loans.

>> **Your receive credit from suppliers:** In the short-term, you can keep your bank account stable while making a loss simply by receiving credit from suppliers, or paying suppliers more slowly than normal.

>> **You reduce the value of inventory:** If your stock levels go down, you will have more funds available. Simple as that.

>> **You reduce customer credit:** If customers owe you less at the end of a trading period than they do at the beginning, this will be a source of funds.

>> **You haven't yet paid taxes to the government:** If you charge consumer tax to customers (GST, VAT or sales tax) or pay consumer tax on expenses, and you have to pay the difference between tax collected and tax paid to the government, then your Profit & Loss Projection should show all income and expenses not including this tax. However, if you only submit a return to the government every three or six months, you may end up with additional funds in your bank account as the due date for lodging this return approaches.

WARNING

Having a comfortable amount in your business bank account when trading unprofitably can be quite dangerous, because the availability of funds can lull you into a false sense of security, and encourage you to spend beyond your means.

Summarizing what's different about a cashflow report

A Cashflow Projection is very similar to a Profit & Loss Projection, but with a few notable differences. I summarize these differences in Table 13-1.

TABLE 13-1   **Differences between a Profit & Loss Projection and a Cashflow Projection**

A Profit & Loss Projection . . .	A Cashflow Projection . . .
Shows sales in the month that they're made	Provides additional detail to show sales in the month that payment is received
Doesn't include incoming funds from loans or other sources of finance	Includes additional detail showing all sources of funds, including loans and capital contributions
Doesn't include consumer taxes (GST, VAT or sales tax) but shows all figures net of tax	More complex Cashflow Projections may show figures including tax, and then show tax payments separately
Shows only the interest on loan repayments, not the full value of the loan repayments	Shows the full value of loan repayments
Shows cost of sales (the cost of materials and so on) at the time a sale is made, regardless of when materials were purchased	Provides additional detail to show the purchase of materials in the month payment is made
Doesn't include capital expenditure or start-up costs	Includes all cash outflows, including capital expenditure and start-up costs
Doesn't include owner drawings (relevant for sole traders and partnerships only)	May include owner drawings (relevant for sole traders and partnerships only)
Includes no information regarding likely cash available	Forecasts the closing bank balance for the end of each month

To see how these differences play out, have a look at the Cashflow Projection in Figure 13-1. Can you see how the first half of the report mirrors the format of a Profit & Loss Projection? (Except for the fact that I've hidden the detail of the expense rows, so that everything can fit on this page.) Cash inflows reflect cash collected from sales (as opposed to actual sales generated) as well as incoming funds from loans. Cash outflows include the purchase of new equipment, purchase of stock (as opposed to the actual cost of goods sold), expenses and loan repayments.

FIGURE 13-1:
A Cashflow
Projection
predicts the
closing balance
of your
bank account.

	A	B	C	D	E	F	G	H	I
		Dec	Jan	Feb	Mar	Apr	May	Jun	Total
1									
2	**Total Sales**		31,070	35,440	41,150	36,450	47,260	48,200	**239,570**
3	Payments Collected from Sales		25,000	31,070	35,440	41,150	36,450	47,260	216,370
4									
5	**Total Cost of Sales**		12,428	14,176	16,460	14,580	18,904	19,280	**95,828**
6	Purchase of Stock		15,000	15,000	17,000	15,000	19,000	20,000	101,000
7	Inventory at Month End	25,000	27,572	28,396	28,936	29,356	29,452	30,172	
8									
9	**Gross Profit**		**18,642**	**21,264**	**24,690**	**21,870**	**28,356**	**28,920**	**143,742**
10									
52	**Total Expenses**		14,291	15,779	14,928	14,399	15,465	15,069	**89,931**
53									
54	**Net Profit**		**4,351**	**5,485**	**9,762**	**7,471**	**12,891**	**13,851**	**53,811**
55	Less: Company Tax		1,305	1,646	2,929	2,241	3,867	4,155	16,143
56	**Net Profit After Tax**		**3,045**	**3,840**	**6,833**	**5,230**	**9,024**	**9,696**	**37,667**
57									
58	**INCOMING CASHFLOW**								
59	Payments Collected From Sales		25,000	31,070	35,440	41,150	36,450	47,260	**216,370**
60	Loan Finance		85,000						**85,000**
61	Total Incoming Cashflow		110,000	31,070	35,440	41,150	36,450	47,260	**301,370**
62									
63	**OUTGOING CASHFLOW**								
64	Purchase of New Equipment		76,000		25,000				**101,000**
65	Purchase of Stock		15,000	15,000	17,000	15,000	19,000	20,000	**101,000**
66	Expenses (See Row 52)		14,291	15,779	14,928	14,399	15,465	15,069	**89,931**
67	Company Tax				5,879			10,264	**16,143**
68	Loan Repayments		2,500	2,500	2,500	2,500	2,500	2,500	**15,000**
69			107,791	33,279	65,307	31,899	36,965	47,833	**323,075**
70									
71	Opening Bank Balance		1,000	3,209	1,000 -	28,868 -	19,617 -	20,132	
72	Incoming Cashflow less Outgoing Cashflow		2,209 -	2,209 -	29,867	9,251 -	515 -	573	
73	Closing Bank Balance		**3,209**	**1,000 -**	**28,868 -**	**19,617 -**	**20,132 -**	**20,705**	

In Figure 13-1, you can see that although the Net Profit for this business is very positive for the six months ahead ($53,811 before tax, or $37,667 after tax), the projected Closing Bank Balance is not so positive. By March, the account is $28,868 overdrawn, and although this eases, the business still has a negative balance of $20,705 by the end of June. This is because the business has invested money in equipment, and increased receivables and inventory.

Looking at Cashflow Coming In

If your business sells to other businesses (as opposed to direct to the consumer), you will almost certainly be expected to offer credit to your customers. The amount of credit depends very much on whom you're selling to and the industry you're in. Some industries are lucky enough to have 7-day accounts as standard, but most industries expect at least 30 days from date of invoice, if not 30 days from end of month. (Invoices paid 30 days from end of month means that all April invoices will be paid by 30 May, all May invoices by 30 June, and so on. With these terms, an invoice dated 1 April doesn't fall due for payment until 30 May, meaning the customer effectively receives 59 days credit on this invoice.) Some large supermarket chains and department stores may even negotiate for special payment terms of up to 120 days.

Customer credit is a brutal drain on cashflow, especially for growing businesses. If your business is growing, more customers will demand credit, and this will require increased funds. For example, if I offer credit terms that are 30 days from date of invoice, and my sales average $25,000 a month, I will always be owed $25,000 or so (probably more actually, given that many customers try to extend credit terms beyond the due date). If my business grows and in 12 months' time I average $40,000 sales per month, I need an additional $15,000 in funding or excess profits in order to keep my head above water.

REMEMBER

When creating a Cashflow Projection, you need to look not only at money collected from sales, but also at any other sources of funds, such as loan finance or capital contributions from the owners.

Calculating collections versus sales

If you offer credit to your customers, creating a Cashflow Projection in addition to a Profit & Loss Projection is important if either one of the following situations apply:

>> Your business is growing and your sales are increasing each month.

>> You have seasonal variations with bumper months and lean months.

In Figure 13-1, can you see how the first row under Incoming Cashflow on my Cashflow Projection shows a row called Payments Collected From Sales? In this row, I show when I think I'm likely to receive the payments from sales.

In this example, you can see that the value of credit extended to customers is growing each month. This growth translates to a demand for additional funds, meaning that planning for cashflow is crucial.

REMEMBER

When adding a Payments Collected row to your Cashflow Projection, don't forget to include the value of payments you will receive from customers who currently owe you money. In Figure 13-1, the Payments Collected From Sales amount for January is $25,000, which is the value of debtors outstanding as at the end of December.

Thinking about loans and other sources of funds

Bank loans or any other source of finance also make a big impact on cashflow. When you receive a loan, your Cashflow Projection will show the full amount of this loan, yet your Profit & Loss Projection won't show a cent. (Why? Because a loan isn't income, and your Profit & Loss Projection only shows actual business income.)

You generally show loan finance at the bottom of your Cashflow Projection report, in the section that summarizes all cash inflows. In Figure 13-1, you can see $85,000 in loan finance coming in during January.

Your Cashflow Projection is also the spot to record any other sources of funds, such as personal funds you or your business partner plan to contribute. Again, personal contributions of funds don't count as business income (which is why you don't show these contributions on your Profit & Loss Projection) but they certainly do count as incoming cashflow (which is why these contributions show on your Cashflow Projection).

Thinking about Outgoing Cashflow

The four biggest things that chew up cashflow in a new business, yet don't actually count as expenses, are the purchase of new equipment, the purchase of stock, the payment of tax bills and the repayment of loans. You need to consider all of these factors when summarizing the Cash Outflows in your Cashflow Projection.

Allowing for the purchase of new equipment (or other start-up items)

In Chapter 7, I go into a whole load of detail about creating a budget for your new business, talking about start-up costs such as new equipment, vehicles, IT systems, and rental bonds. I also explain how these start-up costs aren't really expenses in terms of your Profit & Loss. For example, if you spend $50,000 in setting up a new business and in the first month of trading you make $1,000 worth of sales and you have $500 of expenses, you've still made $500 profit in your first month, not a $49,500 loss.

So, having explained that you don't include start-up costs in your Profit & Loss Projections, you may have been wondering where it is that you *do* show your start-up costs. The answer is in your Cashflow Projection report.

Back in Figure 13-1, check out how Purchase of New Equipment shows as the first row under the Outgoing Cashflow heading. Of course, you can change this heading to whatever is most relevant for you (labelling this row as New Vehicle, Start-up Costs, Shop Fit-out Costs or whatever).

Looking at payment for stock versus cost of sales

If you buy or manufacture goods for resale, you almost certainly carry stock. (Possible exceptions would be if you make custom one-off items, or if you make fresh goods, all of which you sell each day.)

If you carry stock, creating a Cashflow Projection in addition to a Profit & Loss Projection is important if the value of the stock that you carry is likely to exceed the value of credit you can obtain from creditors. (For example, if you need to carry eight weeks' worth of stock at any one time, but your suppliers only offer you four weeks' credit.) What this means is that as your business grows, you need to finance the increase in the value of stock you have to carry.

A Cashflow Projection is also helpful if you need to order goods in bulk. For example, maybe you can only secure decent volume discounts if you order 1,000 units or more of something at a time. This may mean you need to order only once every three months or so, but you need to budget accordingly so that you can finance three months' worth of stock with each order.

In Figure 13-1, I used my Profit & Loss Projection as a starting point, and then modified the cost of sales section to include additional information about when I need to pay for stock. The row called Inventory at Month End calculates automatically, based on the value of inventory at the end of the previous month plus Purchase of Stock less Cost of Sales. I enter the figures against Purchases of Stock manually, ensuring that the order is timed so that I always have at least one month's worth of stock on hand at any one time.

TIP

Adding a row to your Cashflow Projection that predicts your stock levels at the end of each month is a great way to keep yourself 'honest' and test how realistic your stock purchase figures really are. For example, in Figure 13-1, predicted inventory at the end of May is $29,452 but predicted total sales in June are $48,200. Depending on lead times for delivery and the number of stock lines, such lean inventory levels may be impossible in real life.

Deciding where to show tax payments

One of the questions people often ask is whether to include personal or company tax in their Cashflow Projection. The answer depends on whether your business is structured as a sole trader, partnership or company:

» **If you're a sole trader or partnership:** The amount of personal tax you pay depends on many factors, including whether you have any additional sources of income other than the business. For this reason, I suggest that you don't include personal income tax as an expense on your Cashflow Projection, but that you do make an allowance for personal drawings in the Cash Outflows section of your Cashflow Projection, and that this allowance is enough to cover any personal tax you may have to pay.

WARNING

If you have a sole trader or partnership structure, you may still need to pay tax on profits made even if you don't draw any funds from the business. For example, maybe your business has made a $30,000 profit and you've used this profit to buy new equipment (which you can't claim as an outright tax deduction, but must instead claim back over several years). Even if you haven't drawn a cent out of the business, you still need to pay tax on this $30,000 profit.

>> **If your business has a company structure:** You need to include company tax expense on your Profit & Loss Projection. I explain how to do this in Chapter 11, where you make a monthly allowance for company tax based on profits made. However, if you only pay company tax once a year, you may want to adjust your Cashflow Projection to remove the monthly allowance for company tax and instead only show tax in the month in which it's due.

>> **If your business is subject to any kind of value-added tax, such as VAT or GST:** You don't include this tax in any of your expenses. Instead, you show the value of each expense before tax is applied. (Why? Because this kind of tax applies only to the final sale to the consumer — as a business, you're entitled to claim back any tax of this nature that you pay.)

>> **If your business pays a sales tax on purchases (something that applies in almost every state within the United States):** You should include sales tax in your expenses, showing the value of each expense inclusive of the tax that you pay. (Why? Because this tax forms part of the cost of this expense — you can't claim this tax back from the government.)

Factoring in loan repayments

As I explain in Chapter 10, loan repayments and loan interest are two entirely different things. For example, if you have a bank loan with repayments of $1,000 per week, but you have only $15,000 outstanding on this loan, the interest on this loan will be only about $15 per week. In terms of the profit of your business, the only expense that you can claim is the interest.

If you decide to include both a Profit & Loss Projection and a Cashflow Projection in your business plan, you should show the value of the interest expense in your Profit & Loss Projection, and the value of the loan repayment in your Cashflow Projection. You show this amount as a separate row under Outgoing Cashflow, as per Figure 13-1.

WHAT ABOUT SUPPLIER CREDIT?

In the same way as you may receive payments from customers several weeks after sales are made, you may also not have to pay suppliers until several weeks after you receive the goods you purchase. In terms of Cashflow Projections, adjusting expenses to allow for supplier credit can get quite tricky, especially given that only some expenses will be subject to credit. (For example, most energy suppliers probably offer you 30 days credit, but your staff wages need to be paid weekly, with no credit terms.)

I've created lots of Cashflow Projections for different businesses over the years, many of which have been hideously (and probably unnecessarily) complex. I now try to keep Cashflow Projections as simple as possible. For this reason, unless a business is importing goods and operates on extended credit terms of 90 or 120 days, I take a financially conservative approach and don't adjust figures to allow for supplier credit.

Predicting the Bottom Line

In the earlier sections in this chapter, I talk about why profit is different from your bank balance, and I explore how to calculate likely cash inflows and outflows for your business. The final step is to predict the balance of your bank account at the end of each month.

TIP

The easiest way to create a Cashflow Projection is to use a spreadsheet (have a look at Figure 13-1 for an example). The most straightforward approach is usually to start with your Profit & Loss Projection, save it under a different name, and then make all the necessary changes, adding several lines to modify the Profit & Loss Projection so it becomes a Cashflow Projection.

Setting up a worksheet in Excel

Although creating a Cashflow Projection can be quite complex, please don't be discouraged: A simple cashflow is relatively easy to create and, once you learn how to do it, can be an enormously powerful tool.

Here's my step-by-step guide:

1. **Make a copy of your Profit & Loss Projection.**

   I'm assuming here that you have already created a Profit & Loss Projection. If not, skedaddle back to Chapter 11.

TIP

Incidentally, Chapter 11 also explains how you can copy and paste links to data, rather than just copying the data. If you're comfortable with these technicalities, you can create a new worksheet that links back to your Profit & Loss worksheet, meaning that if you update a figure in your Profit & Loss, it will automatically update your cashflow.

2. **Set up Incoming Cashflow and Outgoing Cashflow to match the headings in Figure 13-1.**

   If any of these headings aren't relevant to your business (maybe you don't offer customers credit or you're not planning to take out a loan), skip this information.

REMEMBER

   If your business has a sole trader or partnership structure, you also need to allow for any drawings that you plan to take out of the business. In this scenario, include an additional row for Owner's Drawings under Outgoing Cashflow.

3. **Complete the detail required in order to get an accurate picture of Incoming and Outgoing Cashflow.**

   I explain how to show payments collected from sales, loan finance, new equipment, payment for stock, tax bills and loan repayments earlier in this chapter (refer to 'Looking at Cashflow Coming In' and 'Thinking about Outgoing Cashflow' for more details).

4. **Add rows for Opening and Closing Bank Balance.**

   Again, check out the format of Figure 13-1 for how this looks.

5. **Enter your Opening Bank Balance in the first column.**

   In Figure 13-1, my Cashflow Projection starts in January. Therefore, in the January column next to Opening Bank Balance, I enter the opening balance of my bank account (or what I think the opening balance is likely to be). For simplicity's sake, if I have more than one bank account, I combine the balance of them all.

6. **Calculate your Closing Bank Balance.**

   Nice and easy. The balance of your Closing Bank Balance is equal to your Opening Bank Balance plus Incoming Cashflow less Outgoing Cashflow. Type in a formula to this effect. For example, the formula in Figure 13-1 for January would be **=C71+C72.**

REMEMBER

7. **Review the predicted Closing Bank Balance for each month.**

   Look at the predicted Closing Bank Balance for each month and ponder whether any problems are looming. If necessary, you may need to time expenses differently or secure additional finance. (Read on to find out more.)

Making a pre-emptive strike

So what should you do if your Profit & Loss Projection looks hunky dory, and you're happy with the whole concept of your business model and strategy, but your Cashflow Projection shows you don't have enough funds, or that you're going to hit a few months of cashflow difficulties?

The good thing about being able to predict a future cashflow squeeze is that you'll have more options if you act early than if you wait until creditors are pounding at the door and you can't supply customers because you have no stock. Here are some ideas:

>> If your business is profitable, you may well be able to secure a business loan or a short-term overdraft. (The loans manager is going to be much more amenable if you ask for finance before you hit troubled times.)

>> If the profitability of your business is really marginal, you may want to revisit your whole business model, review your pricing and look at what you can do to reduce costs.

>> If you'd planned to buy any equipment outright, think about leasing instead, so that you preserve your precious funds for working capital.

>> If you have control over the timing of your expenses and the predicted cashflow shortfall is only temporary, see if you can shift some expenses to later months.

The example in Figure 13-1 is interesting in terms of cashflow requirements and the need for forward planning. You can see that although the business is profitable over the first six months, generating total profits of $37,667 after company tax, by the end of the six months the bank account is in the red by $20,705. Indeed, this peaks in the month of March with a predicted overdrawn balance of $28,868. This cashflow not only shows a business in need of additional finance to see it through the next 12 months of trading, but also a business that may want to delay expenses if at all possible in the months of March through to June.

Calculating sustainable growth

One of the paradoxical things about being in business is that if you get too successful too quickly, you can actually send yourself down the gurgler. Just in case you think I'm talking out of my ear, here's my logic.

As your business grows, you need more *working capital* (that is, the difference between your current assets and your current liabilities). In order to increase working capital, you need to first make a profit and then invest this profit back into the business. However, if you grow too fast, you need working capital faster than you can make and invest your profit.

TIP

This concept of growing faster than you can make and invest your profit is often called *the limit of sustainable growth*. Without delving too much into the mathematics, as your business grows your assets have to grow with it. You can either finance these assets by re-investing profits or you can finance them by taking out a loan. For example, if you can invest enough profit to increase your bank balance, debtors, equipment and so on by 10 per cent a year, your business can comfortably grow at 10 per cent a year.

Imagine that your business turns over $250,000 a year and you have around $50,000 in working capital. If you made a profit this year of $80,000 and you had personal drawings of $75,000, this result means you have put back only $5,000 into the business.

The $5,000 you have available to reinvest divided by $50,000 (the value of working capital) equals 10 per cent. This year's turnover of $250,000 plus 10 per cent equals $275,000, meaning this amount is the maximum you can grow your business in the next year without having to seek extra finance.

WARNING

The pace at which a business can comfortably grow *is* limited: To be very successful, too quickly, runs the risk of putting such a strain on your cashflow that, unless you can secure additional finance, your business may not survive.

WARNING

STAY AWAY FROM CASHFLOW GOBBLERS

Be canny about how you manage your working capital. In particular, don't pay for new assets outright unless you have to. For example, unless you have a very comfortable bank balance, don't even consider paying outright for equipment or motor vehicles that you can otherwise finance. Similarly, don't pay off loans in advance of your repayment schedule unless you can redraw those funds whenever you want.

Deciding what to include in your business plan

If you're creating a business plan for your own use only, the decision regarding what financial reports to include in your plan is simply based on whatever reports you find useful. So, if you rely on cashflow reports to help manage your bank balance, include these in your plan; if you find cashflow reports are overkill, skip 'em.

For more details about what financial reports to include in your business plan, skip ahead to Chapter 15.

Building Your First Budget

You may be feeling as if you've spent days or weeks assembling financial forecasts and surely, when complete, these figures form a budget. In some ways that's true, but the difference between a budget and a Profit & Loss Projection (or a Cashflow Projection for that matter) lies in the psychology of how you use the information.

An analogy using home finances may help clarify how budgets differ from projections. Imagine you're forever having problems managing your home finances, and you struggle to meet mortgage payments or repay credit card debts. So you sit down and look at the situation. You think about your income, you list your expenses and you try to figure out how to make ends meet. When you write everything down you can see how tight things are, and so you have to adjust your figures. Maybe you plan to earn a little more income by working some overtime; maybe you plan to reduce your spending by eating out less often or cutting back holidays. This process of balancing likely money in against likely money out is effectively your personal Profit & Loss Projection.

After you complete this process, the figures in this projection become your *budget*. Income budgets in turn become goals, and expense budgets become limits. Your job is to meet these goals and live within these limits. In this way, a budget is the tool that (hopefully) enables you to fulfil your plan.

In the context of your business, a *projection* looks to the future, usually extending at least 12 months ahead. As part of creating a projection, you experiment with different scenarios (what if sales decrease or expenses rise?) until you arrive at a Profit & Loss Projection that fits with your business plan and that you think you can achieve.

From this projection, you create your budget, which then sets the sales goals and expense limits that you intend to live or die by. If you're in an organization with several employees, responsibility for meeting this budget is usually shared. For example, the sales manager is responsible for meeting the sales budget, while the marketing manager is responsible for staying within the marketing budget.

I talk about budgets in this chapter because they are an essential part of your financial management toolkit. Interestingly, most business plans tend to skip budgets, and stick to Profit & Loss Projections instead. However, remember that the decision of what to include in your business plan is entirely yours, and if you decide to include budgets, that's absolutely fine.

Allocating budgets in detail

Sometimes you need to split budget figures into more detail in order to ensure the figures are achieved. For example, your Profit & Loss or Cashflow Projection may have just a single figure for sales, but your budget may split this figure into individual sales budgets for each salesperson, region or division. Similarly, your Profit & Loss or Cashflow Projection may have just a single figure for marketing, but your budget splits this figure into content marketing, sponsorships, media campaigns and so on.

TIP

One of the trickier aspects of budget management can be managing the psychology of sales budgets. On the one hand, if you make sales budgets too low, your sales team may become complacent. On the other hand, if you make sales budgets too high and you don't achieve these sales, you may find that you have overspent on business expenses and your business is unprofitable. A slightly sneaky solution is to keep two sets of sales budgets: One for sales staff and another for yourself or your finance manager. The lower set of sales budgets are what you use in order to set your expense budgets for the year, and provide a good, conservative base for financial management. The higher set of budgets is what you provide to your sales team, and which hopefully acts as a motivator.

Comparing budgets against actuals

The essence of a budget is control. For example, imagine you have a set budget for travel expenses for the year. If you compare your actual spending against your budget as the year progresses, you can take action ahead of time if it seems as if you're likely to exceed this budget.

TIP

The best way to monitor budgets is by entering monthly budgets into your accounting software and then, every month (come hail, rain or shine), comparing your budgets against actual results.

YOU CAN ALWAYS CUT MORE

For many years, I worked as a consultant to a family company in a sector of the manufacturing industry that was in decline. Money was tight, and I admired the way the family were tough on spending and kept expenses lean. Then disaster hit, in a triple whammy of plummeting exchange rates, an insurance claim gone wrong and a major customer who went into liquidation. Suddenly the company needed to cut expenses by 25 per cent almost overnight in order to keep trading and prevent the family members from losing their homes.

I didn't know how expenses could be cut any more, but necessity is the mother of invention. The second warehouse was closed, staff were cut, vehicles traded in, leased equipment returned and marketing budgets slashed. The result? Sales did decline (you usually can't maintain sales on a skeleton staff with little marketing) but the reduction in expenses more than compensated. The company survived.

This lesson taught me that a business, especially one that has been established for a while, almost always has areas in which it can save money. The intent and commitment just has to be there. For this reason, setting a budget and then sticking to it makes complete sense. A budget provides an imperative and a discipline that no business with clear goals can really afford to be without.

Creating Balance Sheet Projections

One of the reports that most business planning books suggest you include in the financial section of your plan is a Balance Sheet Projection. (Wondering what this is? A *Balance Sheet* is a report that provides a snapshot of your assets and liabilities at a single point in time. A *Balance Sheet Projection* is the same thing, but provides a forecast for some time in the future as to what you think your assets and liabilities will be.)

I'm hesitant about insisting on a Balance Sheet Projection as part of a business plan simply because this report requires a high level of accounting expertise. Unless you're using business planning software, a Balance Sheet Projection will probably require that you get help from your accountant, which could be an additional expense you can ill afford.

However, I'd be very slack if I didn't explain how this report works so that you can decide for yourself.

Figure 13-2 shows a simple Balance Sheet Projection that corresponds to the Cashflow Projection earlier in this chapter (refer to Figure 13-1). I don't really have scope in this book to cover how to construct a Balance Sheet from scratch, but the key concept of a Balance Sheet — and, indeed, of bookkeeping theory — is that Total Assets always equal the combined sum of Total Liabilities and Total Equity. Therefore, if the balance of an asset account changes, the balance of a liability or equity account must also change.

To construct a Balance Sheet Projection, you start with your Balance Sheet as it is right now. If your business hasn't started yet, chances are your Balance Sheet is a series of nil balances; if you've been trading for a while, use your accounting software to generate this report. You can see how this works in Figure 13-2, where the first column shows the actual Balance Sheet as at December 31.

Can you see how the Cashflow Projection in Figure 13-1 starts from January and runs through to June? For this reason, the second column in Figure 13-2 shows the Balance Sheet Projection at this same point, six months into the future.

I calculated the figures for this Balance Sheet Projection by looking at the balances for key accounts (bank accounts, debtors, inventory, equipment and loans) on the Cashflow Projection, and entering these balances in the second column of my Balance Sheet Projection. After a bit of muttering and cussing, not to mention a solid hour of brain-scratching, I got my projection to balance. An hour isn't very long, I admit, but I do have a degree in accounting *and* I've done many Cashflow Projections in my time *and* this is a very simple example. (A real-life Balance Sheet is normally much more complicated.)

You may think I'm not sounding very positive, but I like to think I'm a realist. In summary, if you're wondering whether to include a Balance Sheet Projection as part of your business plan, my answer is 'yes' if you have a method by which you can create this report quickly and easily (maybe you have a financial expert in-house or you're using business planning software). Otherwise, your time is probably better spent focusing on other tasks.

	A	B	C	D
1	**Balance Sheet Projection**			
2		**Dec-31**	**Jun-30**	**Difference**
3	**Current Assets**			
4	Business Transaction Account	$1,000	-$20,705	-$21,705
5	Accounts Receivable	$25,000	$48,200	$23,200
6	Inventory	$25,000	$30,172	$5,172
7		**$51,000**	**$57,667**	**$6,667**
8	**Non-Current Assets**			
9	Tools and Equipment	$32,000	$133,000	**$101,000**
10	Furniture	$5,600	$5,600	$0
11		**$37,600**	**$138,600**	**$101,000**
12				
13	**TOTAL ASSETS**	**$88,600**	**$196,267**	**$107,667**
14				
15	**Current Liabilities**			
16	Accounts Payable	$22,500	$22,500	$0
17	Employee Deductions Owing	$3,245	$3,245	$0
18		**$25,745**	**$25,745**	**$0**
19	**Non-Current Liabilities**			
20	Bank Loans	$25,000	$95,000	**$70,000**
21				
22	**TOTAL LIABILITIES**	**$50,745**	**$120,745**	**$70,000**
23				
24	Current Year Profits	$0	$37,667	$37,667
25	Retained Earnings	$12,000	$12,000	$0
26	**TOTAL EQUITY**	**$12,000**	**$49,667**	**$37,667**
27				
28	**ASSETS LESS LIABILITIES**	**$37,855**	**$75,522**	**$37,667**

FIGURE 13-2:
A Balance Sheet
Projection.

5

Joining the Dots and Writing a Plan

IN THIS CHAPTER

» Balancing risk management against creativity and innovation

» Looking at how a risk matrix works

» Thinking about everything that could possibly go wrong

» Putting plans in place to limit the damage

» Discussing risk in your business plan

Chapter **14**

Managing — and Taking Advantage of — Risk

Few businesses in this world don't carry some level of risk. Indeed, if your hope is to make above-average profits with your new venture, then almost implicit in this hope is a certain level of risk. (After all, if a business idea were super profitable and risk-free, chances are someone else would already have spotted the opportunity before you.)

This tension between being prepared to take risks while minimizing potential fallout makes for an interesting balancing act. On the one hand, you want to let your creativity take flight; on the other, you don't want to end up bankrupt.

In this chapter, with this duality in mind, I talk about managing risk without stifling creativity and how to assemble a risk management matrix. I cover how to identify potential risks, and include some practical risk mitigation advice, outlining everything from registering trademarks to protecting intellectual property, insuring yourself against litigation or using company structures to limit liability.

I also discuss how best to talk about risk in your business plan without terrifying potential investors half to death — easier said than done, but possible nonetheless.

Balancing Innovation and Risk-taking

What is your natural reaction to the concept of innovation and risk-taking? Perhaps you prefer to take the ostrich approach, sticking your head in the sand and maintaining a 'business as usual approach'. Or maybe you're more like a meerkat, always popping up and scanning the horizon for potential risks, and taking appropriate action. How do you find the right balance for you — encouraging innovation, both in yourself and in your employees, without taking risks at a level that you're uncomfortable with?

Innovation doesn't necessarily equate to grand ideas and multimillion-dollar investments, but can be as simple as dedicating time for creative thinking. For example, you might allocate one day a month for a planning day, running brainstorming sessions or 'innovation meetings'. If you're a solo business, I'd encourage you to involve trusted friends or business advisers in these sessions, so you can benefit from the spark of ideas from another person. If you have employees, allocating creative thinking time in this way sends the signal that you value innovation, and that you're prepared to let employees take time out from the treadmill of daily tasks.

A corporate example of innovation is 3M, which encourages employees to spend 15 per cent of their work time on projects of their own choosing. In doing so, the company encourages risk-taking by giving employees the freedom to experiment and develop new ideas without fear of failure. Not many small businesses could afford 15 per cent of staff labor to be spent in this way but, nonetheless, this way of operating is an interesting idea.

Another direct source of innovation can be your customers. Actively seeking feedback and insights from customers about their needs and pain points can provide amazing insights for new products, services or improvements. And, by involving customers in generating ideas, you arguably reduce risk, because you're aligning yourself with customer demand.

REMEMBER

Innovating and experimenting doesn't need to mean risking your life's savings. Small, quick experiments are often just as valuable as large, ambitious projects, and failure can be a learning opportunity. By testing ideas on a small scale and adapting quickly to customer response, you can discover what works and what doesn't without significant risk.

Assembling a Risk Matrix

A simple tool that can help you manage risk is a *risk matrix*. Designed specifically with a human's ostrich qualities in mind, a risk matrix provides a logical framework for balancing the likelihood of specific risks against the potential impact if that risk were to eventuate. This matrix may simply be an internal document, which you maintain for your own peace of mind; it can also form an important part of your business plan, and demonstrate to investors that you're a person who thinks ahead.

A risk matrix typically has five columns:

>> **Risk description:** A succinct description of the nature of the risk — for example, rising interest rates, an accident happening in the workplace, the loss of a major client, a change in government policy, or a project running overdue. See the following section for more help in identifying potential risks for your business.

>> **Likelihood of risk arising (almost certain, likely, possible, unlikely, or rare):** How likely is this risk to occur?

>> **The impact or consequences for your business if this risk were to eventuate:** Would the impact be critical, major, moderate, minor, or insignificant?

>> **An assessment of the risk level (low, medium, high, or extreme):** This assessment is a combination of the two preceding factors. So, for example, if something could have a critical impact on your business and the likelihood is possible, this presents a high risk; if something is unlikely and its impact minor, this presents a low risk. Figure 14-1 shows a summary of how you make this assessment.

>> **How you intend to minimize or mitigate this risk:** In this column of the matrix, you can also include controls already in place, if relevant.

Other columns you sometimes see on a risk matrix include the person responsible for managing the risk, and the ease of implementing the suggested risk management techniques.

		Medium risk	High risk	High risk	Extreme risk	Extreme risk
	Almost certain					
		Medium risk	Medium risk	High risk	High risk	Extreme risk
	Likely					
LIKELIHOOD		Low risk	Medium risk	Medium risk	High risk	High risk
	Possible					
		Low risk	Low risk	Medium risk	Medium risk	High risk
	Unlikely					
		Low risk	Low risk	Low risk	Medium risk	Medium risk
	Rare					
		Insignificant	**Minor**	**Moderate**	**Major**	**Critical**
				CONSEQUENCE		

FIGURE 14-1:
Assessing risk levels by considering both the likelihood of a risk as well as its potential impact.

Identifying Different Kinds of Risks

The role of a risk management matrix (refer to the preceding section) is not to catastrophize. Rather, a risk matrix helps you to think generatively about the many different situations, events or scenarios your business could encounter, and how you might best plan for these.

Unsurprisingly, business people tend to be optimistic, and thinking of all the things that could go wrong doesn't come naturally. However, becoming aware of possible risks is not necessarily a negative process; you can often identify really simple ways of managing or mitigating that risk without spending a heap of time or money.

Thinking about financial risks

When I talk about *financial risk*, I'm talking about the risk of a business being forced to close either because it's trading unprofitably or because it can't pay its debts when they fall due. (Interestingly enough, as I explain in Chapter 13, a business can be profitable yet still unable to pay its debts, particularly if it grows too fast.)

Any business carries financial risk, but some types of businesses are certainly riskier than others. On a positive note, if you can cultivate your financial management skills, plan conservatively *and* grow your business at a sustainable rate, you can usually mitigate negative results.

Table 14-1 shows an extract from a risk matrix that focuses on possible financial risks for a business. (Refer to 'Assembling a Risk Matrix', earlier in this chapter, for details of what a risk matrix is all about.)

TABLE 14-1   **Example Risk Matrix Assessing Financial Risks**

Risk	Likelihood (almost certain, likely, possible, unlikely, rare)	Consequences (critical, major, moderate, minor, insignificant)	Risk Assessment (low, medium, high, extreme)	Management or Mitigation of Risk
Interest rate increase of up to 2 per cent	Possible	Moderate	Medium	Ensure budget has a buffer so that this increase would be affordable
Interest rate increase of 3 per cent or more	Unlikely	Major	Medium	Decrease loan exposure within the next 24 months; look at alternative sources of finance
A major customer defaults on amounts owing	Possible	Major	High	Place limits so that no one customer can represent more than 20 per cent of outstanding receivables; consider bad debt insurance; implement rigorous collection procedures
Increase in cost of supplies by more than 5 per cent	Likely	Critical	Extreme	Prioritize sourcing alternative suppliers; prioritize looking at ways to increase profit margins; look at ways of decreasing wastage
Online banking fraud by staff member	Unlikely	Major	Medium	Ensure dual approval for all transactions; ensure multi-factor authentication
Cashflow constraints mean business can't maintain adequate stock levels or pay debts when they fall due	Possible	Major	High	Secure external assistance for cashflow reporting; ensure accounts updated weekly; implement budgets

While Table 14-1 may provide you with a few ideas, every business is different. Here are a few questions that may act as prompts for you to consider possible financial risks your business could face:

WARNING

>> Is your business very dependent on one or two large customers? What would happen if one of these customers ceased trading with you?

>> What influence would a 5 per cent change in exchange rates have on your business? Or 10 per cent? Or even 20 per cent?

>> How vulnerable are you to fluctuations in costs? What difference would a 5 per cent increase in your cost of sales or expenses have on your net profit?

>> What would happen if your sales were less than forecasted by 10 per cent or even 20 per cent?

>> If your business is trading unprofitably, how long can this be sustained for?

>> If your largest customer defaulted on the amount they owe you, how would this affect your viability?

>> Is your finance guaranteed? What would happen if the bank foreclosed on your loan, or an investor pulled out?

While asking yourself the preceding questions may not be the cheeriest way to spend an afternoon, I do suggest some risk mitigation measures later in this chapter. Skip ahead to 'Managing financial risk' for a pick-me-up.

Looking at legal and safety risks

The terms 'legal risk' and 'safety risks' cover many different things, but here are some prompts that may help you identify risks relevant to your business:

WARNING

>> Do you have adequate protection for your intellectual property? By *intellectual property* (otherwise known as IP), I'm talking everything from your company name, website name and logo, to your designs, method of manufacture or recipes, or customer list. Looking after your IP is an important part of the business-planning process.

>> On the flipside, are you confident that the resources or materials you're using in your business aren't infringing on the intellectual property or copyright of others?

>> Are you completely across all the terms of your client and supplier contracts? If a contract were breached, what might be the cost of a legal dispute or financial penalty?

>> Do you have good employment practices and policies in place? Would you be vulnerable to a claim for back wages, or unfair dismissal? Not paying

employees properly for overtime, minimum wage violations, or not providing required breaks can result in legal claims.

>> Are you confident you're complying with all tax requirements?

>> Do you have all the licenses and permits required?

>> Could any of your business activities cause risk or injury to another person? How, and why?

>> Do you have any risk of product liability from defective or harmful products?

For ideas about managing legal and safety risks, skip ahead to 'Using legal structures to limit liability', 'Protecting IP and trade secrets' and 'Ensuring employee and customer safety', later in this chapter.

Considering other kinds of risks

What other kinds of risks can you think of? Rack your brain to think of every possible eventuality. The following list of questions may act as a helpful prompt:

>> Is your business highly dependent on one person or key employee? What would happen if they left?

>> Could a change in government, such as a change in government policy or legislation, affect your business?

>> Is your property exposed to natural disasters, such as fire or flood? What would happen in such an eventuality?

>> Are your skills at risk of being out of date?

>> What would a breach of cybersecurity (hacking, leaking of data, ransom demands) represent for your business?

>> Could any personal risks impact your business, such as health issues, a divorce, or conflict between business partners?

>> Is your business vulnerable to a new competitor starting up in the same market niche or location?

>> If your business isn't operating online, how vulnerable is it to online competitors?

Hah! Cheery stuff. If you end up feeling a bit anxious as a result of this whole process, I counsel you to return to the grid in Figure 14-1. Remember that risk ratings are a combination of likelihood and impact. If a risk is unlikely and will present minor impact, you don't need to lose sleep over it.

BEWARE THE RISK OF A LEASE THAT ENDS

WARNING

If your business is very dependent on its location, don't forget to formulate a 'Plan B' for the eventuality that your lease may not be renewed when it comes to an end.

I know of a couple of businesses that have had either a great location in a central shopping strip, or a quirky location that's perfect for their needs (such as a converted theatre or the old post office). However, when the lease ended, the landlord didn't renew the lease (or increased the rent to a level the business would have become unprofitable). For these businesses, relocating and reinventing the business has been a real struggle. (Particularly in one scenario when the landlord started up exactly the same kind of business in the location they had forced the tenant to vacate.)

You can't completely guard against this kind of situation, but you can always try to lessen the risk by negotiating for longer lease terms and keeping on really good terms with your landlord.

Bringing Out Your Inner Meerkat

As I mention at the beginning of this chapter, for every risk in a business, you can usually find a way to counteract that risk. In other words, instead of sticking your head in the sand like an ostrich, you can cultivate your meerkat tendencies instead. Stay alert, think ahead, and figure out ways to avoid those natural predators.

Managing financial risks

When it comes to mitigating financial risk, I take for granted that you have the basics in place — including efficient bookkeeping systems, up-to-date financial reports, budgets, and cashflow management if needed. Other ways of minimizing financial risk include:

REMEMBER

>> If your financial skills are weak, ensure you employ professional assistance for bookkeeping, budgeting, and tax advice.

>> Protect yourself from bad debts by implementing procedures for thorough credit checks, setting realistic credit limits, chasing for money as soon as it's due, and refusing customer credit if allowing it would leave you too exposed.

>> Manage cashflow fluctuations by implementing good forecasting systems, leasing rather than purchasing new equipment, securing short-term finance in advance, or obtaining additional investment.

>> Stay on top of stock levels by investing in excellent inventory management software, closely monitoring stock turnover ratios, and being brutal about inventory divestment if products aren't selling.

>> Keep separate bank accounts for all taxes, and transfer an estimate for tax owing into these accounts at the end of every fortnight or month, rather than waiting until the tax bill is due.

>> Implement strong financial controls, including multi-factor authentication on bank accounts and, if relevant, stringent cash management procedures.

>> Avoid relying on a single source of income by diversifying the number of products or services you offer.

>> Maintain adequate cash reserves to allow for unexpected expenses or downturns in business.

>> Avoid excessive debt and ensure you can comfortably service company loans and consider refinancing if necessary.

Using legal structures to limit liability

You're probably already aware of the three most common structures for a small business: Sole trader, partnership or private company. (Other less common structures include co-operatives, limited partnerships, and trusts.)

A *sole trader* structure means that it's just you who controls and owns the business, and that you're entitled to receive all of the profits. A *partnership* is when two or more people go into business and share profits in agreed proportions. With both of these structures, the business and the owners are one and the same thing in the eyes of the law.

In contrast, a *company structure* is a separate legal entity in its own right. The office-holders who run the company are called *directors*; the investors who own the company are called *shareholders*; the people who work for the company are the *employees*. What this means is that if you set up a simple company (even just with $2 of capital) and you're the only person earning a living from the company, you're simultaneously the sole director, the sole shareholder and the sole employee.

Each of these business structures has pros and cons, but a company structure has one key advantage when compared to other structures: *The liability of the directors is limited to a maximum of the net assets of the company.* Sounds very technical, but imagine a company has been trading at a loss and now has $30,000 in assets and $100,000 owing to creditors. If this company were to go bust, the director (or directors) may not be personally liable to pay the creditors, despite the fact that the company doesn't have enough funds to pay all of its creditors. Similarly, if this company were sued by a customer and the company were found to be at fault, the directors may not be personally liable.

Sounds good? I need to qualify this explanation of limited liability on three counts:

>> If your company seeks to take out a loan, many lenders require a personal guarantee from directors, overriding the limited liability offered by a company structure.

>> If your company is sued and you as a director are found to have been negligent (maybe you didn't follow health and safety regulations, or you knowingly used faulty components), you may be personally liable.

>> If your company keeps trading when you know you can't meet your financial obligations (described variously as *wrongful trading*, *fraudulent conveyance*, or *trading while knowingly insolvent*, depending in what country you're in), directors may become personally liable for company debts, and could even face fines or criminal charges.

Despite these three qualifiers, a company structure may well provide you with an extra layer of protection and help to protect your personal assets. If you don't already have a company structure, you should probably discuss this idea with your accountant.

Protecting IP and trade secrets

Earlier in this chapter in the section 'Looking at legal and safety risks', I talk about the risk of somebody infringing upon your intellectual property. Ways to mitigate this particular risk include trademarks, patents, and registered designs:

>> A *trademark* is a word, name, symbol, or device that indicates the source of a product and distinguishes this product from others. Usually, you register a trademark under a specific *class* (usually using an international system of classification known as the *Nice Classification System*). For example, Lonely Planet is a trademarked term, and is registered under four classes: Software and publications, luggage and backpacks, travel agency services, and restaurant services.

Registering a business name doesn't mean you have ownership of that name. Even if you have registered as a company (which in most parts of the world affords a slightly higher level of protection than registering a trading name as a sole trader or partnership), the only sure way to protect your business name is to register a trademark.

>> A *patent* offers protection for new and brilliant inventions, and can protect the rights for any device, substance, method or process. When you register a patent, you acquire exclusive rights to commercially exploit this invention for the life of the patent.

>> A *registered design* gives you the exclusive rights to commercially use or sell a specific design, so long as this design is new and distinctive. This design refers to the shape, configuration, pattern or ornamentation that gives a product a unique appearance.

In addition, any confidential business information that provides your business with a competitive edge can be considered a *trade secret*. Typically, this kind of information includes things such as customer lists, supplier pricing structures, and manufacturing processes. This information can even include 'negative knowledge': services or products that you've tried but didn't work out.

The most likely people to divulge your trade secrets (whether intentionally or inadvertently) are your employees or ex-employees. You can seek to guard against this risk by asking employees to sign confidentiality agreements, protecting confidential files carefully, or possibly implementing future non-competition provisions in employment contracts.

Ensuring employee and customer safety

If your business involves any activities in which the life of your employees or customers could be endangered, whether this be a tree-lopping business, a reptile park, a whitewater rafting guiding service or a building contractor, then ensuring employee and customer safety becomes paramount.

Going back to the risk matrix at the beginning of this chapter, if the likelihood of serious injury is possible or likely, the risk level for your business immediately rockets to high or extreme. In other words, managing this risk becomes essential to the future of your business.

In this context, I can't be too specific about risk minimization strategies, because the question of safety will be so fundamental to your business. Suffice to say that you will need to spend time and resources thinking about worst-case scenarios, and guarding against these eventualities with everything you can think of — whether this be through checklists, safety audits, specialist training, or additional safety equipment.

REMEMBER

One of the overarching principles of minimizing risk in the workplace, almost regardless of the risk level, is to integrate safety practices and policies into every aspect of your business. Safety needs to be a habit for everyone, and employees need to be involved in identifying risks and dangers in their workplace.

For high-risk workplaces, health and safety needs to be on the agenda of every staff meeting, and discussions carefully documented. In lower risk environments, minimizing risk is still important and a focus for all employees — for example, it may include simple measures such as setting limits on lifting weights, ensuring clear operating instructions next to any machinery, having first-aid kits available, ensuring staff members have first-aid qualifications, and being alert for anything that may cause a slip, trip or a fall.

Signing up for insurance

Business insurance falls into three broad categories:

>> **Assets and revenue insurance:** Typical policies include insurance for building and contents, burglary, cybersecurity insurance, deterioration of stock, electronic equipment failure, employee dishonesty, goods in transit, interruption of business, machine breakdown, and many different kinds of motor vehicle insurance. You almost certainly don't need all these policies, but you'll likely require motor vehicle insurance of some kind, and probably contents insurance as well.

>> **Liability insurance:** As soon as you interact with the public in any way, you need public liability insurance (also sometimes known as general liability insurance). You may also require directors' insurance, professional indemnity (sometimes known as errors and omissions insurance), or product liability insurance.

>> **People insurance:** In almost all situations, you're obliged by law to have insurance that covers your employees in the event of an accident in the workplace. You may also want to take out income-protection insurance to cover yourself in the event of long-term sickness or disability.

TIP

Business insurance can be very costly, but one way that you may be able to economize is to increase your *excess*. An excess is the amount that you need to pay, and that the insurance company will not cover, in the eventuality that you make a claim.

Talking About Risk in Your Business Plan

I mention throughout this chapter that risk management is more important for some businesses than others. Clearly, if your business involves a high level of risk in any respect, it's best to disclose this in your business plan, and articulate to those reading your plan how you intend to mitigate or manage this risk.

The risk matrix in Figure 14-1 is a standard format that most investors will be familiar with. However, you do want to tread the line carefully between disclosing risk and avoiding scaring investors half to death, and so for this reason I recommend a somewhat measured approach! In particular, I suggest you insert a column called 'Controls already in place' to reassure external readers what actions you've already taken, or what precautions you already have in place.

IN THIS CHAPTER

» Exploring the different formats of a business plan, from one page to 50.

» Creating a narrative that tells the story of what you are, and where you're heading

» Demonstrating the viability of your idea with financial projections

» Getting AI (or business planning apps) to do the heavy lifting

Chapter **15**

Perfecting the Final Pitch

People have a fundamental need to listen to stories — whether these stories be a yarn told around the fireside, a blockbuster novel, a TikTok video, or a heartfelt story about a journey as yet unfinished.

For this reason, the best business plans are ones that tell a story. This might be a story about you, about your business, or perhaps about how your idea has the potential to change lives.

If you've been working on your plan over the course of many weeks, you may have ended up with a ragtag assembly of handwritten notes, Word files, financial projections and reports. In this chapter, I look at how you fit these pieces together to assemble not just a sensible justification for your business, but also a story that can inspire yourself and others.

Exploring Different Formats

Who is going to read your plan? Are you writing a business plan for your own eyes only, aiming to provide structure for your business model? Or are you writing this plan hoping to persuade a loans manager or investor to lend to, or invest in, your business?

The best way to present your plan depends on the intended audience. In the first part of this chapter, I look at what's involved in creating a pitch deck, a quick one-page plan, or a full business plan.

Preparing for your Shark Tank moment

Have you ever watched *Shark Tank*, the TV show where entrepreneurs pitch their idea in three minutes to a group of hard-nosed investors? (If you haven't, I suggest you take a few minutes to watch some shorts on YouTube.) *Shark Tank* participants are required to deliver a pitch in just a few minutes, using both public speaking skills and something called a *pitch deck*.

A pitch deck is a slideshow, typically using 10 to 20 slides, that aims to tell the story of an opportunity or business idea. Strong visual elements are key to a good pitch deck, delivering maximum impact with minimal text.

You won't find a right or wrong way to create a pitch deck, but the common convention is to start by explaining the problem that your business model will solve. The slideshow then proceeds to explain the proposed solution, followed by slides that touch on market size, business models, your team, and the competition. (The preceding chapters in this book enable you to do the foundational work for creating slides addressing these topics.) Finally, a pitch deck concludes with the 'ask' of how much investment you're seeking. (See 'Popping the question', later in this chapter, for more about this topic.)

In short, a pitch deck skips the high level of detail typically found in a business plan, and instead is designed to tell a story that captivates the interest of potential investors, and so pave the way for future conversations.

TIP

If you're not pitching to investors, you probably don't need a pitch deck. Nonetheless, an hour or two spent online looking at pitch decks that others have created for business ventures similar to yours may well be productive in sparking a more entrepreneurial mindset, or for generating more ideas in how you can sell your business.

Keeping things to a single page

Different from a pitch deck, and a world apart from a full business plan, is a one-page business plan. A one-page plan isn't a slide show, and nor is it a pitch; rather, it is a summary of your business idea. Typically, a one-page plan details the problem your product or service will solve and why this represents a good opportunity, followed by short descriptions of your industry, target market, marketing plan, financial model and how much funding you're looking for. A one-page plan also sets out what it is that your business will do differently from others. (For more on this, check out Chapter 2.)

One-page plans can be handy if you're time poor and still sketching out your business idea; the discipline of distilling everything into a single page is excellent for bringing clarity to your thinking. However, a one-page plan doesn't replace a full business plan, and incurs the risk that you skate over necessary detail, such as the analysis of competitors and industry trends, or the creation of detailed financial projections.

REMEMBER

In short, if you're still developing your business idea and seeking a format that summarizes your initial thoughts, a one-page plan may serve you well. However, as I talk about in the previous section, if you're thinking of using a one-page plan to pitch to an investor, you're probably best with a pitch deck instead. Finally, if you're hoping that a one-page plan will be more efficient than a full plan, do be aware that there is no such thing as a free lunch — this absence of detail may cost you dearly!

Structuring a full plan

Assuming you don't want to create a pitch deck or a quick one-page summary (refer to the preceding two sections for details), how do you go about assembling a full business plan? A format that works well (and which mirrors how I've organized the chapters in this book) is as follows:

>> **A cover page and table of contents:** Your final business plan will probably end up being between 15 and 20 pages long, so a table of contents helps you and others find what's what. If you plan to share this plan with others outside of your company, you may also choose to include a non-disclosure agreement at the front.

>> **An Executive Summary:** See 'Crafting an eloquent summary', later in this chapter, for details of what this should include.

>> **Your point of difference and strategic advantage:** In the ideal world, you cover these topics in your Executive Summary. For more on these topics, refer to Chapters 2 and 3.

>> **Where you see you and your business in the future:** I devote a whole chapter to the topic of separating yourself from your business and 'thinking big' in Chapter 4. However, for the purpose of your plan, you can distil the vision you have for growth into a sentence of two. This may form part of your Executive Summary, or could be part of your ask for funding.

>> **A summary of industry and economic trends, opportunities or threats:** I cover these topics in Chapter 5. Both the PESTEL analysis and the SWOT analysis I cover in that chapter are frameworks that most investors will be familiar with, and are an excellent way to provide a succinct summary to those reading your plan.

>> **A competitor analysis:** Chapters 3 and 6 talk about competitor analysis and competitive strategy. Providing a summary of this analysis in your business plan demonstrates to outside readers that you've done your homework.

>> **A marketing plan:** Chapter 6 provides a complete summary of how to construct a marketing plan. You don't include the whole marketing plan in your business plan, but you should include a summary of your target market, sales targets, marketing strategies, customer service plan and marketing activities.

>> **A people plan:** See 'Selling yourself and your team', later in this chapter, for details.

>> **A summary of operations, if appropriate:** See 'Providing an overview of operations', later in this chapter, for details.

>> **A risk-management plan, if appropriate:** Are you setting up business as a tree-lopper, circus acrobat, security consultant, or cryptocurrency trader? As I explain in Chapter 14, the more risk in your business, the more important it is to include a risk-management strategy in your plan, with a risk matrix being the most commonly accepted model for presenting this information.

>> **Financial reports:** See 'Showing Where the Money's At', later in this chapter, for details.

>> **The ask:** Ah, the gentle art of asking for money. I cover this delicate topic later in this chapter, in 'Popping the question'.

>> **An appendix:** Super-detailed information such as resumes of the management team, product photos, legal agreements or market research is often best provided as an online link. If providing info in this way isn't practical, including an appendix at the end of your plan can work just as well.

Don't feel obliged to stick to this suggested structure. In particular, if you've chosen to use business planning software (see 'Using AI for What It's Good At', later in this chapter), you'll almost certainly end up with a structure that's slightly different. The important thing is that you cover these topics in a way that makes sense both to you and to your likely readers.

Building a Cohesive Narrative

A business plan has many different sections, and one of the challenges can be finding a common thread that weaves its way from the first page to the last. Examples of what this thread could be include the following:

>> An imperative to act on an opportunity very quickly

>> A problem/solution narrative, such as the problem you're solving and why you're best placed to deliver

>> A significant profit potential, if only investment can be secured

While writing your plan, try to weave this thread through as a connecting message that binds the different sections of your plan together. In addition, keep returning to the question of what you want readers to feel. How can you best convey a feeling of inspiration or perhaps even excitement, and make others confident in your ability to deliver?

Telling a story that changes minds

As I've alluded to a few times so far in this chapter, the best business plans are ones that tell a story.

One approach is to tell the story of how your business product or service will, or has already, affected the lives of others. So, if you're starting a business consulting about permaculture, spend time talking about the transformation permaculture practice can have on the land and its ecology; if you're providing a service to people with disability, share how you improve the lives of those you work with; if you're setting up a manufacturing business in a regional town, describe the impact on community that new jobs can deliver.

An alternative approach, especially if you feel your business doesn't lend itself to inspirational stories, might be to tell your *own* story. Perhaps you're a single parent with three kids, and your business represents a ticket to financial independence; perhaps you left school at 14 but have taught yourself the skills necessary to start your own venture; perhaps you have already achieved some extraordinary things in your life, but this business represents a pivotal moment for you.

REMEMBER

Stories don't have to be on a grand scale to capture the imaginations of others, but can be relatively simple, especially if you can manage to convey your own love and excitement for what it is that you do.

Crafting an eloquent summary

Most business plans start with what's called an *Executive Summary*, a couple of pages that encapsulate everything that's about to follow. Seemingly straightforward, this summary can be agonizingly tricky to write, as you aim to provide enough detail to inspire the reader while remaining brilliantly concise.

TIP

You may even find it easiest to delay writing your Executive Summary until after you've worked on the rest of your plan, so that you can gain more clarity as to how the different elements fit together.

Here are some pointers for what makes for a strong Executive Summary:

>> **The context:** A description of your business and its products or services, or of your business idea.

>> **What drives you:** More traditionally referred to as a mission statement, here's where you get to say something a bit more aspirational about why you're in business and what you hope to achieve.

>> **The problem you want to solve:** If your business isn't trading yet, and you're selling a new idea or concept, leap straight into describing the problem you're trying to solve, and why this presents an opportunity. You want to convince readers that your idea is unique and valuable, and has the potential to succeed.

>> **What's different about you, and your strategic advantage:** Even if you're proposing to start a business that others have done before you (anything from gardening to physio, from consulting to events management), you still want to explain what you're going to do better than others. (For more about identifying strategic advantage and differentiating yourself from competitors, refer to Chapter 2.)

>> **A compelling story:** If possible, try to tell a story that will inspire readers to keep reading. This could be a story about how you had the idea to start this business, or a narrative about yourself and any special skills or talents that you have. Alternatively, this story could be about the scope of the opportunity.

>> **Your industry, the competition, and where the opportunities lie:** Talk about your particular industry, what the trends are, and where you see the opportunities. (Chapters 3 and 5 help you with compiling this info.)

>> **You and your crew:** Describe the structure of your business, who the owners are, who the employees are and, if possible, what makes your team a cut above.

>> **High-level financials:** I'm not talking detailed projections here, but rather two or three sentences that include the value of projected sales, gross profit and net profit for next 12 months, as well as the rate of expected growth.

>> **The ask:** If part of the purpose of this business plan is to persuade an investor or lender to give you money, include how much it is you're looking for and how you intend to use this investment. I suggest you provide more detail about this request later in the plan (see 'Popping the question', later in this chapter) but the benefit of summarizing the ask at the outset is that it sets the context, allowing the reader to focus on what you intend to achieve with the funding.

TIP

If you're in doubt about what to omit and what to include in your Executive Summary, keep in mind that nobody reading your plan from start to finish should stumble across a crucial piece of information deep inside the plan itself.

Presenting the context

In Chapter 5, I talk about minimizing risk and maximizing profitability by staying ahead of trends, and I explain how to draw up a PESTEL analysis to summarize industry trends, and a SWOT analysis to identify your strengths, weaknesses, opportunities and threats.

Both of these frameworks (PESTEL and SWOT analysis) will be recognized by those familiar with business plans, and your business plan will benefit from their inclusion. However, I suggest you take the time to return to the work you did, and reflect on whether you need to edit your PESTEL and SWOT analysis to fit more closely in the overall context of your plan.

Specifically, take time to check the following:

>> If your plan includes a risk matrix (covered in Chapter 14), does this matrix address the risks presented by negative industry trends identified in your PESTEL analysis? Similarly, does your risk matrix address the risks presented by the weaknesses identified in your SWOT analysis?

>> If your PESTEL analysis identified positive industry trends, does your business model and/or marketing plan capitalize on these?

>> Is the competitive or strategic advantage that you articulate in your Executive Summary reflected in the opportunities and strengths of your SWOT analysis?

>> Do the skills that you describe your team as having match with the strengths you identify in your SWOT analysis?

>> Is your SWOT analysis framed to highlight the overriding opportunity that your business plan identifies?

At risk of stating the obvious, the idea is to demonstrate to readers of your plan that not only have you considered the outside world and how it may impact your business, but also that your response to these trends is integral to your business strategy.

Selling yourself and your team

In Chapter 4, I stress the importance of thinking of your business as being separate from you. I explain that in order to leverage your business idea, you need to involve others. This slightly more entrepreneurial way of thinking is what makes the people part of your plan so important.

For the purposes of your plan, a concise description of the key people in your business, along with who is responsible for doing what, will usually suffice. If you're only just getting started — maybe you don't have any employees yet — include details of people in your network who are assisting you, such as your accountant, business mentor, or family and friends. Include a short description of each person's role, relevant work experience and qualifications, as well as the unique skills that each person contributes. (I don't normally suggest you include résumés or CVs in a business plan, but if you feel such documents would be relevant, stick them at the end of your plan as an appendix.)

REMEMBER

Ensure that your description of people's skills resonates with the SWOT analysis in your plan. For example, if your SWOT analysis identifies a lack of social media skills as an issue, address how you'll manage this in your people plan. Or, if your SWOT analysis identifies technical know-how as a particular strength, remember to include these skills when describing your team.

Providing an overview of operations

I don't dwell much on operations elsewhere in this book, but if you're a manufacturer or wholesaler, I suggest you include a brief summary of operations management at some point in your plan. For manufacturers, this summary typically describes the process of manufacture, where and how your product is manufactured, and what mechanisms you have in place for order fulfilment and delivery. For wholesalers, this summary describes automations, order fulfilment systems and delivery logistics.

What you include in this part of a plan is very specific to your business. Maybe key to your business strategy is the decision whether to manufacture in-house or to outsource production; maybe you have a particular manufacturing process; maybe long lead times require meticulous systems for managing inventory.

REMEMBER

As part of your description of operations for your business, return to the question of strategic advantage (a topic explored in Chapters 2 and 3). Is an aspect of operations integral to your strategic advantage, such as a highly competitive or innovative way of manufacturing or distributing products? If so, take the time to describe how your unique location, skill set, software systems or distribution networks influence operations, and how they serve to provide your business with the potential for a higher rate of return than your competitors.

Translating your plan into clear goals

As you progress through your plan, you inevitably end up with a whole heap of goals, whether these are sales, financial, customer-based, product-based or even simply personal. Some of these goals may reflect that you still have extra distance to go with the planning process, or some may reflect the necessity to keep reviewing your plan every six months or so.

As you pull the elements of your plan together, start listing your goals, and the necessary actions you need to take, remembering that the ideal goal is a SMART one: **S**pecific, **M**easurable, **A**chievable, **R**ealistic and **T**ime-bound. For example, if your marketing plan aims to reach a new customer demographic — for example, men aged 40 to 65 — list the actions by which you intend to reach this goal. Or, if your SWOT analysis identified that you haven't yet trademarked your logo and business name, translate this weakness into a plan of action, specifying the date by which you propose to initiate a trademark application.

TIP

A table sorted by date that lists goals and/or milestones, detailing what needs to happen by when, can be an excellent addition to a business plan, demonstrating a certain pragmatism and organizational ability.

Showing Where the Money's At

In working on the financial part of your plan, you may well have ended up with a wide selection of documents — everything from product costings to price comparisons, from historical sales reports to budgets for the years ahead. Which reports should you include in your final plan, and in what sequence should you present these?

The next couple of sections explain what you might include in this section of your plan, and also how to broach that most delicate of requests — namely, how much money you're looking for, and why.

Deciding what financial reports to include

What financial reports should you include in your plan? This very much depends on the stage your business is at, and the complexity of its finances.

For businesses that haven't started trading yet, I suggest the following:

>> **A summary of start-up expenses.** If some of these expenses have already been paid for, include this detail. I talk about start-up expenses in Chapter 7.

>> **Sales and gross profit projections for the next 12 months.** Chapters 8 and 9 explain how to assemble these reports.

>> **A Profit & Loss Projection for the next 12 months.** Chapters 10 and 11 explain what to do here.

>> **Break-even analysis:** In Chapter 12, I explain how you can calculate break-even analysis in several different ways.

For businesses that are already trading, financial reports should include:

>> **A Profit & Loss report for the last 12 months.** If the figures for the past 12 months are unusual for any reason, include some notes as to why.

>> **A Balance Sheet for the date that your Profit & Loss report goes up to.** So, if your Profit & Loss report goes for the 12 months from April to March, generate a Balance Sheet for March 31.

>> **A Profit & Loss Projection for the next 12 months.** If your business is growing quickly, extend this projection and include figures for the next 24 to 36 months as well. (For subsequent years, you can summarize projections to include one column per quarter, rather than one column per month.)

For businesses that are already trading, but where the rate of growth is putting pressure on cashflow, you should include all of the preceding financial reports as well as the following:

>> **A Cashflow Projection report for the next 12 months.** I explain how to create Cashflow Projections in Chapter 13. This report can be technical and time-consuming to create, even with the aid of business planning software.

>> **A Balance Sheet Projection for the end of the Cashflow Projection period (optional).** So, if your Cashflow Projection goes from April one year to March the next, your Balance Sheet Projection will forecast account balances for 31 March. Include this report if you're using an app that can create it for you. Otherwise, you may be best not to worry, because creating Balance Sheet Projections from scratch is out of reach for most ordinary mortals.

When you create financial projections, you have to make many assumptions along the way. Maybe you've assumed that you're going to hire a new employee in three months' time, that you're going to shift premises, or that a new sales contract is going to come through. Even if the plan is for your eyes only, list these assumptions below the report.

As you pull together the different elements of your plan, pay attention to consistency. For example, if your marketing plan shows significant growth, is this growth reflected in your people plan, and in your Profit & Loss projection? Similarly, if your SWOT analysis shows a weakness in working with social media, and social media is foundational to your marketing plan, does your budget allow for paying for social media advice?

Selling scalability

For many businesses, perhaps even the majority of businesses, the amount of profit you make is dependent on scale. When a business model is highly *scalable*, you have the potential to increase revenue significantly without a proportionate increase in expenses, often leveraging automations or technology to do so. For example, software applications are a highly scalable business: Once developed, software can usually be sold to an unlimited number of customers with minimal additional costs or physical infrastructure.

For investors, scalability is everything. If you know that doubling your revenue will quadruple your profit, take the time to include Profit & Loss Projections that prove this to be the case. These projections may be the clincher for securing additional investment.

Use AI apps such as ChatGPT to explore the scalability of your business model. Upload your existing financial reports (taking care to remove any identifying or personal information first, of course) and from there ask questions such as 'If income were to increase by 50 per cent and expenses increased by only 20 per cent, what would my profit be?'

Popping the question

Earlier in this chapter, in the section 'Crafting an eloquent summary', I suggest that you include any requests for finance in your Executive Summary. This request might go something like, 'We are seeking a business loan for $50,000 to allow us to expand into new premises. The funds will be spent on fit-out, rent in advance and marketing.'

This summary sets the context for anybody reading the plan, and the financials section of your plan then fleshes out this request in more detail. How best to frame this request depends on whether you're pitching to an investor, or to a bank.

Seeking a loan from a bank

In general, banks are interested in strong profitability, what collateral you can offer against the loan, your ability to service repayments, the stability of your business, the accuracy of your financial reports, and your personal credit rating. They'll also want to know exactly what you intend to use the finance for.

TIP

Use an online loan calculator tool to figure out the interest you should expect to pay on the loan amount you're requesting, as well as the likely repayment schedule. Don't forget to include the anticipated loan interest as an expense in your Profit & Loss Projection, and also include the full value of proposed loan repayments in your Cashflow Projection. (Alternatively, if your plan doesn't include a Cashflow Projection, show the full value of the loan repayment in the Profit & Loss Projection.)

If you require this loan for working capital, perhaps because your business is growing or you have particular times of the year when cash is particularly tight, a Cashflow Projection is ideal for corroborating your need for additional finance.

Pitching to investors

Typically, investors are on the hunt for a clever business idea that offers the potential to yield above-average returns. In contrast to banks, investors are less interested in past profitability and stability, and are more interested in future profitability and the potential for rapid growth. They may also be interested in leveraging their own expertise to facilitate this growth.

Similar to asking a bank for a loan, be explicit about how much funding you're seeking, and how you intend to use these funds. However, in addition, include a description of the *impact* this funding will have, including before and after Profit & Loss Projections demonstrating this likely impact. As I mention in 'Selling scalability', earlier in this chapter, demonstrating scalability, if you can, is key.

Any investment in somebody else's business represents a risk, and investors are generally more willing to take risks if they see the potential for high returns. As part of your ask, include the potential ROI (return on investment) for the investor, and clarify whether you're asking for a loan or selling a stake in your business. If asking for a loan, what interest rate are you proposing to pay, and what is the proposed term of the loan? If selling a stake in your business, what percentage of equity are you offering, what will be the likely rate of return, and how do you propose profits will be distributed?

REMEMBER

Regardless of whether you're asking for a loan or selling equity, make sure you outline potential exit strategies also. How will the investor get their money out, and when?

Using AI for What It's Good At

Creating business plans is one of the things that AI does pretty well. By AI, I'm not really talking about ChatGPT or an equivalent (although these apps can undoubtedly help), but rather a business planning software app that uses AI as part of its functionality. For example, apps such as LivePlan, Bizplan, Enloop and PlanGuru use AI to generate suggested text, tidy up expression and assemble financial forecasts. In doing so, these apps can greatly streamline the process of creating a business plan.

You may wonder why I'm recommending you subscribe to a business planning app — after all, if you do so, where does this book fit into the scheme of things? What this book provides, and which planning apps do not to the same extent, is a clear sense of priorities, a strong theoretical foundation, and an emphasis on the things many business owners struggle with.

What a business planning app provides that this book doesn't are design tools to make your plan look good, assistance with polishing your English, and templates to make preparing financial projections easy.

REMEMBER

If you're using a business planning app, endeavor to apply the colors or fonts from your brand into the pre-existing templates supplied. If high-end design is key to your brand and you're pitching to an investor, you may be wise to use the app to get your plan to a certain point only, and then employ a graphic designer to create the final presentation.

Getting the most out of planning apps

Here are some tips for getting the most value out of any one of the many business plan apps available:

» Try to get clarity around your business idea or business model before completing the different steps of the templates provided. An app isn't going to help you much unless you've done the hard thinking and analysis in advance.

» Apps such as LivePlan include a 'pitch deck' template, helping you create a concise 'sell' for your business idea. Even if you're not looking for a lender or potential investor, writing a pitch can be great practice for framing your thinking and preparing marketing materials.

» I sometimes like to use the app to generate financial forecasts and, once the first draft is complete, export these to Excel. From here, I can customize the forecasts further, taking time to understand the assumptions behind any calculations. (Apps can make financial reports so easy to generate that you risk not understanding the reasoning that lies behind them.)

TIP

» AI is part and parcel of most planning apps, but you can still garner that extra edge by pasting text into ChatGPT (or an equivalent AI app) and asking for edits. For example, you might use an app such as LivePlan to help you generate your executive summary but, once you've done so, you could paste the text of this summary into ChatGPT and ask it to review what you've written.

WARNING

Even the most brilliant business planning app won't be able to do all the legwork that's necessary, such as researching competitors, local conditions or new market opportunities. Indeed, do be careful if using any of the industry-specific data or template text supplied, because a lot of this information is country-specific and may not apply to you.

Letting your personality shine through

AI, along with the apps that use AI, is amazing at making your English seem polished and fluent. The downside, especially if you're working with suggested text prompts, is that you can lose the clarity and immediacy that your own voice naturally provides.

For example, what do you reckon of this sentence?

Relying on an evolving paradigm of dynamic synergies, our core competency lies in leveraging disruptive innovation to strategically align scalable solutions, thereby optimizing our holistic approach to stakeholder engagement and ensuring a robust ROI through seamless integration of cutting-edge technologies.

Mind-numbing? Here's how I could say the same thing, but using more accessible language.

We complement one another. Rick's inventiveness helps him adapt our product to all sizes of venues, and Alex is brilliant at bringing teams together. These skills, combined with the latest technology, are what make our business healthy and profitable.

REMEMBER

You want people reading your business plan to be excited by your idea and filled with confidence by how you intend to execute it. If you can, avoid business jargon, keep things simple, and let your personality shine through.

TIP

One last thing! Business planning apps usually default to US spelling (you know, 'summarize' not 'summarise', or 'labor' rather than 'labour'). All well and good if you're in North America, but less so if you're in the United Kingdom, New Zealand or Australia. Check if you can change the language settings in the app itself; if this isn't possible, take the time to double-check your spelling is correct for your market.

6

The Part of Tens

IN THIS CHAPTER

» **Returning to the question of what makes you different**

» **Looking at competitors one more time**

» **Making sure the elements of your plan align with one another**

» **Revisiting your target market**

» **Letting your dreams take flight**

Chapter **16**

Ten Questions to Ask before You're Done

I n this chapter, I assume that you've finished the first draft of your business plan. If this is true, congratulations on being part of the small percentage of humans who gets this far.

Before you present your plan to the outside world, I suggest you spend one last chunk of time making sure the plan is as good as it can be. As I explain in Chapter 15, a business plan is a narrative that serves to connect a collection of research, figures and fragments of information, creating a cohesive story that makes sense.

In this chapter, I share ten questions to ask yourself about your plan. I not only include practicalities such as checking the numbers and ensuring different sections of your plan align with one another, but also talk about checking in with your feelings, and looking after the initial dreams that got you to this point.

Does Your Difference Leap off the Page?

With your business plan complete, how succinctly can you express what you do, and what makes you different? Try this:

1. **Ready? Lay your hands on a recording device.**

   The voice memo app or something similar on your smartphone will do the job.

2. **Set? Find a timepiece.**

   Does anybody still have a watch? I know I don't. But I do have a great big red clock in my kitchen with the noisiest most infuriating tick in the world.

3. **Go! Click Record and talk aloud, describing your business and what's so special about it.**

   Don't talk for more than 30 seconds and if you stuff up your speech the first time, try again straightaway.

How did you go? When you listen to yourself, do you feel impressed by your succinct expression and communication style? Hopefully! But if not, take heart. First, head back to Chapter 2 to read about identifying strategic advantage for your business. Then continue to Chapter 3 where I explain how to craft the elevator speech from hell.

TIP

After working on your 30-second summary, read through the Executive Summary of your business plan one more time. If you weren't able to articulate the essence of your business immediately, chances are the introduction to your plan may be a little weak. Read through these pages and rework if necessary.

How Thorough is Your Competitor Analysis?

One thing I've observed when looking at business plans, particularly plans for new businesses, is how many people gloss over competitor analysis. I find this a real worry, because understanding competitors is so essential to doing well in business.

I think I've figured out the psychology of this head-in-the-sand behavior. When businesses are new, the 'dream' is still relatively intact. Spending too much time looking at competitors can make you feel like this dream is getting crushed, and engender anxiety about going head-to-head with established and well-financed competitors.

However, although competition is always a little scary, it can be inspirational too. By analyzing your competitors in depth, you may find ideas that you want to imitate, ways you can adapt your pricing to increase profits, or new market niches that you hadn't been aware of.

So remember, if you haven't analyzed competitors properly, your plan isn't complete. (If you're wondering what form a 'proper analysis' takes, skip back to Chapter 3.)

How Robust are the Numbers?

Any business venture walks a fine balance between profitability and risk. In general, the higher the rate of return, the higher the likely risk.

TIP

One way for you to assess the financial risk of your plan is to experiment with the numbers. For established businesses, try decreasing sales projections by 10 per cent and increasing expenses by 10 per cent, and recalculating net profits. For new businesses in unknown markets, you may want to be more radical, recalculating net profit if sales are only a third or a half of projections. (I talk about using AI to help with such calculations in Chapter 11.)

Now, reflect on what risk these worst-case scenarios represent, and how resilient your business model really is. Would a 30 per cent drop in projected sales mean that you can't make your mortgage payments, or does it simply mean your side hustle won't become your main squeeze?

Next, try to quantify your resilience in more detail by calculating your break-even point. I explain the different ways to calculate break-even in Chapter 12, but if you haven't already done these calculations, now's the time.

Do Different Elements Align?

With the first draft of your plan complete, take time to check that the different elements align, and are consistent with one another. For instance, if your marketing strategy suggests rapid growth, your operational plan should account for the resources needed to scale. Or if your SWOT analysis identifies financial management as a weakness, then your people plan needs to include resources to mitigate this vulnerability.

If your plan has included specific goals, check your Profit & Loss Projections align accordingly. For example, if your plan expresses the intent to open a retail outlet by the end of the year, the Profit & Loss should show a corresponding increase in Rental Expense from that month onwards.

In addition, if any goals articulated in your plan involve a time commitment from you, pause to consider whether the time required is realistic. For example, maybe one of your goals is to gain three new subscribers per week. If the person signing up these subscribers is you, do you have enough capacity to deliver on this target? If you don't personally have time, have you budgeted enough in Wages Expense?

Do You Play to Your Strengths?

Does the people part of the plan — the section where you describe who does what — play to your natural strengths?

One of the skills of growing a business is for you to focus on the things you're good at and then delegate the rest. (If your business is a service business, I don't necessarily mean that you focus on providing the service itself, which you're probably naturally good at and inspired your business in the first place. Rather, I'm talking about focusing on the parts of business management that come most naturally to you.)

Make a list of the functions of your business, such as administration, finance, marketing, people management, and production. Which of these functions appeal to you, and which of these functions correspond to your natural abilities?

Bring objectivity to the process by reflecting on what others recognize in you as your skills. Additionally, brainstorm how you might secure support for the business functions that aren't your areas of strength. You might consider hiring a virtual assistant, delegating bookkeeping to a contractor, working with a marketing consultant, or looking for a business partner. (Chapter 4 talks more about the people part of your business plan.)

WARNING

One of the reasons many entrepreneurs fail in business is that they try to do everything themselves. Avoid this trap, if you can.

Have You Made Any Assumptions You Can't Justify?

Almost any business plan includes some assumptions. Maybe you've assumed that sales will grow at a certain rate, that you're going to adopt a new line of products, that your lease will be renewed, or that you're going to upgrade your equipment. Or, if you're planning for a new business, maybe you've made assumptions about the size of the market, what price points customers are going to find acceptable, or the rate of repeat business.

For every assumption that you make in your plan, try first to spell out the assumption and second to provide the rationale. Here are some examples:

>> A plan assumes certain product costs and provides detailed costing sheets in the appendix to justify these.

>> A plan shows sales growth of 5 per cent per year and explains this by graphing last year's sales and showing this as a trend.

>> A plan shows sales growth of 20 per cent but includes a significant increase in online marketing in the budget.

>> A plan shows an increase in subscription income and justifies this by including an industry report that indicates this trend.

REMEMBER

Industry-specific analysis is like gold for a business plan. If you can get hold of a good industry report, especially one analyzing long-term trends, refer to this report in your plan and possibly include this report in the appendix. (Chapter 5 has lots of hints about where to find relevant industry research.)

Is Your Target Market Spot On?

With the first draft of your business plan complete, I suggest you take the time to revisit your target market.

Are you 100 per cent confident of who your target market is? Is this group of customers large enough to support your business? Do you truly understand your potential customers' needs and preferences, or is more market research required?

TIP

The trick when defining target markets is to find a balance between specificity and ambition. For example, perhaps you're a writer and you've designed an online course to teach others how to get their crime novel published. You may be tempted to define your target market as being anyone in the English-speaking world who is interested in writing crime, including countries all around the globe. Yet defining your target market so broadly may be overly ambitious: Breaking into any new market is hard, let alone one where you have no existing customers or connections. Instead, you're probably better to define your target market more conservatively, building on your existing networks of students.

On the flipside, having too narrow a target market may restrict the scope of your business idea, particularly if you're limiting your business to a small geographical area, and may set an unnecessary cap on its potential.

What's Your Plan for Getting Out?

Do you have a plan for selling your business? You may be bemused by this question, especially if you haven't actually started your business yet and you're still at the planning stage. However, if you're able to conceive of a future for your business that's independent of you and that you can sell to someone else, you've made the leap in thinking from being a businessperson to being an entrepreneur.

For more on creating a business that stands separate from yourself, see Chapter 4.

How Do You Feel?

With the first draft of your business plan complete, allow yourself time to reflect on how you feel. Do you still feel inspired? Or has the process of planning made you feel more anxious than anything?

If your gut is telling you that something isn't quite right, take time to tune into this emotion. Even if you've already invested precious savings getting this far, you may be best to pull the pin on your business idea now, rather than later. Try to imagine yourself in two years' time, or even ten. Where do you see yourself, and how does your business in its current form fit into this picture?

On the other hand, maybe you're still fired up about the idea of starting your own business, but feel that the whole kit and caboodle of financial projections, competitor analysis, industry research and so on has dampened your initial spark. In this case, take time to return to the bigger questions. Are you yet to explore some different avenues? Do you have any other crazy ideas that just won't go away? How can you insert new ambition into your plan and make it feel exciting once more?

What Do Others Think?

Once you reckon you've done as much as you can on your business plan, start sharing your plan with others. Show the financial section of your plan to your accountant, share your plan with family or friends, or, if you have employees, ask them to look through the plan and provide feedback.

Next, seek professional feedback from a business advisor or mentor. If you can't afford a consultant, that's fine. Many government-run business advisory centers offer free business advice, and the good thing about a written plan is that you have something concrete to offer as a starting point.

REMEMBER

Your business plan isn't a literary work — and not just because your plan doesn't include mystery murders, engaging dialogue and risqué sex scenes (more's the pity). The main reason is because, unlike a novel, your business plan is never finished. Be open to feedback and comments, and be prepared to let your plan continually evolve.

IN THIS CHAPTER

» **Staying on the right side of the law**

» **Taking the pressure off cashflow woes**

» **Ascertaining why others are succeeding when you're not**

» **Getting help to turn things around**

» **Selling your idea, rather than your business**

Chapter **17**

Ten Suggestions for a Plan that's Not Shaping Up

N ew business ideas are as much about experimentation, risk and human folly as they are about prosperity and profit.

In what is hopefully a fitting end to this book, this chapter considers what to do if you aren't trading profitably, or your business plan has only served to highlight problems with your business model. When should you persevere with your business, and when ought you pull the pin? What might you retrieve from the ashes of your ideas?

Ensure You're Still Legal

What should you do, if regardless of your planning efforts, your business is trading at a loss and you can't pay your bills on time? Regardless of your personal assets and business structure, you may be subject to civil or criminal penalties if you deliberately mislead creditors. Misleading creditors includes the act of continuing to trade despite knowing that you may be unable to pay any debts incurred.

If you have a company structure, you may be wondering whether I'm correct about these possible penalties. Indeed, in Chapter 14, I explain how in most jurisdictions, a company structure theoretically acts to limit liability, and thereby protects the personal assets of directors. So, for example, if your company goes into liquidation, you don't stand to lose personal assets such as your home or personal savings.

WARNING

The protection offered by a company structure depends on many factors, including whether you have previously provided personal guarantees to banks, suppliers or landlords. In addition, and of significance, this protection does not stand should you continue trading while knowing that your company is *insolvent*. Defining the term 'insolvent' can be tricky, but a simple definition of being insolvent is not being able to pay your debts as they fall due.

I raise the topic of solvency because this exposure of your personal assets, along with potential civil and criminal liability, is of immediate concern if your business is struggling to pay its bills on time. If finances are tight and you're continuing to purchase goods on credit, I suggest you seek professional advice in order to help assess your solvency. A tool that may be useful here is a Cashflow Projection report (a subject I explain in Chapter 13).

It may be that you can take advantage of *safe harbor provisions,* which are legal structures enabling you to continue trading while working on a recovery plan, or it may be that you need to take immediate steps to cease trading.

Find Ways to Take the Pressure Off

Perhaps your business is struggling because it took a while to find its feet, and during the interim period, the business sustained financial losses that continue to place pressure on cashflow. If you're confident you now have your business model working and you reckon all you need is a bit of a breathing space, your first priority is to create a Cashflow Projection report (refer to Chapter 13 for details), so you can quantify your potential financial shortfall, and ascertain how long it might take to trade out of this situation.

With this Cashflow Projection as your reference point, consider the following:

>> Can you generate working capital by collecting overdue debts and tightening up credit collection policies?

>> Can you sell off old stock, even if you do so at cost or a small loss, to free up working capital?

>> How might you reduce fixed expenses, such as insurances, rental expenses, monthly subscriptions, or professional services? (If you think such expenses are as lean as can be, seek a second opinion to verify your own.)

>> Do you own any assets, such as buildings, tools or vehicles, which you could sell at reasonable value? Would it make sense to liquidate these assets and, if necessary, lease them instead?

>> Do you have any debts? Could you look at rolling all your loans and credit cards into a single loan and refinancing at a lower interest rate?

If you can't find a way to ease your cashflow situation, you do need to check that you are not guilty of trading while insolvent. Refer to the previous section in this chapter for more details.

REMEMBER

Experiment with Margins

Does the problem with your business relate to profitability, rather than customer demand? Are you spending all hours of the day and night working, but not receiving enough return on your time to make your business worth it?

In this situation, return to Chapters 8 to 11 and experiment with pricing models and strategies. Review your pricing against that of competitors, and see whether you can sustain higher pricing, consider whether you can adjust pricing to charge premium services to certain customers, or experiment with sales volumes to see what impact an increase in sales might have.

Next, turn your mind to cost of sales and expenses. Can you buy products any more cheaply? How could you trim your expenses? If you manufacture items for resale, can you make the process more efficient?

You can use AI apps such as ChatGPT to do some of these pricing and budgeting calculations for you. Simply send your financial reports into a spreadsheet, and then copy these results into the app, stripped of any personal details. Next, ask 'what if?' questions. For example, ask 'how much would my net profit be if sales

REMEMBER

increased by 5 per cent but expenses stayed the same?' or 'how could I reduce expenses by 10 per cent?'

Return to Competitor Analysis

When creating your business plan, you hopefully did some kind of competitor analysis early on, looking at who your competitors were, and trying to assess who was doing well, and why. (I talk about competitor analysis in detail in Chapter 3.)

If your business isn't working out as you planned, it may be time to step outside of the day-to-day operations and return to the research phase. Cast your net widely to look for businesses similar to your own but which, to the outside eye at least, are doing well. These businesses may not be direct competitors — perhaps they're operating in different states or even countries — but chances are they will be experiencing many of the same opportunities and challenges as yourself.

You may even be able to find benchmarks for your industry (a topic I talk about in Chapter 10) so that you can compare your own financial performance against that of others in a more analytical fashion.

Involve Your Team

If your business plan isn't looking too promising — whether this plan is about a proposed expansion, a new idea, or continuing to do what you already do — and you have employees, I suggest you take the time to ask for input.

Of course, you want to be selective about how you ask for this input, because you don't want to disclose confidential information or scare off employees with pre-carious financial scenarios. However, employees often offer amazing insights for how you might save money, reach new customers, find more efficient ways of processing orders, and much more besides. The other benefit is that by involving employees in your planning, you'll end up with a more engaged team who feel invested in helping you to make the business work.

Your team isn't just employees, of course, but may also include family, colleagues, or your accountant.

Actively Seek Expert Advice

I've observed that running a business is one of those things where people overestimate their own ability and knowledge. The adage that 'you don't know what you don't know' is so true, and many of us assume that with a combination of hard work, common sense, online resources and capital, we can do well in business and figure out things as we go along.

While you may be lucky enough for this attitude to work, if your business plan isn't on track, you're best to go on the hunt for expert advice. You may be surprised by how much you can learn, how willing people are to offer their insights, and the difference these insights can make.

TIP

Advisory centers or a business-savvy accountant are a good start for advising whether the structure of your plan makes sense, the financials hang together, and if your pricing models look sustainable. However, for a deeper level of expertise, see who you can talk to within your industry. Look for consultants who specialize in your sector, or find somebody who had a successful business similar to your own but has since retired. Perhaps look for somebody working in the same field but who is operating outside of your region and is, therefore, willing to share advice. Or, if a member organization exists for your industry, consider signing up and participating in networking groups, conferences, and other member services.

Find a Business Partner

If your plan demonstrates that your business model is strong but your capacity or resources are limited, consider seeking a partner who can buy into your business. Not only does a business partner potentially contribute capital, but in the ideal world may have a skill set that complements your own.

This partnership approach makes particular sense if your business idea is time sensitive and you need additional resources in order to capitalize on a particular opportunity.

Know When to Call it a Day

Back in Chapter 1, I talk about something called the *anchor bias*, which is the human weakness that causes us to cling too much to the initial information we receive during a decision-making process. This bias sometimes means that business owners are reluctant to let go of their initial concept, despite evidence to the contrary, because of information they received early on that corroborated their idea.

The risk here, of course, is that people continue to throw good money after bad, stranded in a business that imposes significant costs in terms of time, money, health, and relationships.

What are the warning signs that your business model isn't working? Ask yourself the following:

WARNING

>> **Is your business experiencing consistent losses over a sustained period of time?** Of course, not every business with consistent losses is a dud (think, for example, of how Amazon made a loss for the first nine years of trading). However, consistent losses combined with no significant increase in revenue over a sustained period is clearly a red flag.

>> **Is your industry experiencing declining demand?** I talk about industry analysis in Chapter 5. If your industry is experiencing widespread decline, a swift exit is likely your best strategy.

>> **Can you pay your debts as they fall due?** If you can't, return to 'Ensure You're Still Legal', earlier in this chapter, to read more.

>> **Are you over the whole deal?** No matter the financial results, your business isn't doing what it should if you're miserable.

>> **Have attempts to adjust your business model made little difference?** If you've pivoted so often that you're almost a ballerina, but profits remain elusive, the essential premise of your business may be a dud.

I've stayed too long in two of the businesses that I've owned, and regret the opportunities wasted in each instance. I realize now that change, even when hard, brings its own energy and opportunities, and that by staying too long in a particular situation, I missed out on what this change had to offer.

Try to Sell Your Idea

Sometimes, you may not be in a position to leverage your business idea, regardless of its potential. For example, maybe you've designed a new product, but lack the capital to develop this product from its prototype. Or perhaps you have a cracking idea for a new service, but don't have access to the customer base to roll out this service on a suitable scale.

TRUE STORY

If you have some kind of strategic advantage that another company can leverage to greater success, *and* you can protect or trademark this advantage in some way, you may be able to sell your business for way more than if it were valued by traditional methods. I remember a colleague who started a boutique travel agency, developing a niche market for sports tours by registering a series of clever domain names. Despite four years of never making a cent's profit, this agency sold their business for a substantial sum to one of their large competitors, which was able to instantly leverage this intellectual property to generate the kind of profits the boutique agency never could.

Take the Lessons with You

If your business plan has helped you to do what's right for you, no matter whether this be a mega-expansion or the decision not to continue, then the plan has done what it was designed to do.

If you decide not to continue with your business venture, be gentle on yourself and remember that there is no such thing as failure — just as any invention usually requires many prototypes before it succeeds, so do business ideas.

Ask yourself, what's next? After all, now you understand what business planning is all about, maybe it's time to start thinking about the next idea . . .

Index

About the Author

Veechi Curtis is passionate about creating businesses that contribute to our society and help their owners achieve financial independence.

Born in Scotland, Veechi attended university in Australia where she completed both her undergraduate degree and her MBA. She has been a small business consultant for more than 20 years, training and mentoring hundreds of businesses over this time. She has written for many publications and has also been a columnist for *The Sydney Morning Herald*.

Running a business in theory is very different from running a business in practice. In *Creating a Business Plan For Dummies*, Veechi draws from the experience of running her own businesses, as well as being a mentor for dozens of start-ups. Veechi is also the author of *Small Business For Dummies*, 6th Edition, *MYOB Software For Dummies*, 8th Edition and *Bookkeeping For Dummies*, 3rd Edition.

Veechi lives in the Blue Mountains of NSW, where she is the Executive Director of Varuna, the National Writers' House.

Author's Acknowledgements

Thank you to my very silly and wonderful family, who provide me with all the inspiration I could ever need.

Publisher's Acknowledgements

Some of the people who helped bring this book to market include the following:

Acquisitions, Editorial and Media Development

Copy Editor: Charlotte Duff

Project Editor: Tamilmani Varadharaj

Acquisitions Editor: Lucy Raymond

Editorial Manager: Ingrid Bond

Production

Graphics: Straive

Proofreader: Susan Hobbs

Indexer: Estalita Slivoskey

The author and publisher would like to thank the following copyright holders, organizations and individuals for their permission to reproduce copyright material in this book.

- **Cover image:** © rh2010/Adobe Stock Photos.
- **Table 10-1:** © Maus Software, LLC. Maus Software.
- Microsoft Excel screenshots used with permission from Microsoft.

Every effort has been made to trace the ownership of copyright material. Information that will enable the publisher to rectify any error or omission in subsequent editions will be welcome. In such cases, please contact the Permissions Section of John Wiley & Sons Australia, Ltd.

Printed and bound by CPI Group (UK) Ltd, Croydon, CR0 4YY

10/01/2025

14623878-0001